INDIA AND WAR

INDIA AND WAR

By

M. N. ROY & OTHER

GYAN

ISBN : 978-81-212-1594-7(HB)

First Published, 1942

Published, 2018

Published by

Gyan Publishing House
5, Ansari Road
Daryaganj, New Delhi-110002
Phone: 011-47034999, 9811692060
www.gyanbooks.com
E-mail: books@gyanbooks.com

Printed at: G. Print Process, Delhi.

PREFACE

This volume is meant to be history presented in raw materials, so to say. The history of India's relation to the war is still to be written. For the moment, nothing much more could be done say. to described. he materials in a more or less Conference and co-ordinated form. The documents contained in this volume are meant to trace primarily the attitude of the Radical Democratic Party towards the war. But incidentally, the relation of India as a whole with the war has been volumely described. This volume is published on the occasion of the Conference of the Radical Democratic Party. On the same occasion, several other books are also being published. They all deal with India's relation to the war and the repercussion of the international events of the last three years on the political and economic life of India. Therefore, this should be read together with other volumes. All of them together describe and otherwise deal with the determine the of the different aspects of the oliticallife of India. which are bound to determine the future of the country. This volume can therefore be said to be a chapter of the history of India in the making.

Dehra Dun,
December 23, 1942.

M. N. ROY

INDIA AND WAR

TABLE OF CONTENTS

PART III

INTRODUCTION

Great Britian declared war against Germany on September 3, 1939. In reply to requests from left-wing Congressmen to call a conference for discussing the situation and requests what India should do, I issued a statement to the press on September 6. In that statement, I wrote:

"All freedom-loving people will encouraging the British Government on the decision, even though much belated, to put an end to Hitlerism, which it has been encouraging all the time. Had the decision been taken earlier, the freedom of many European countries would have been saved."

The Working Committee of the Congress met at Wardha on September 14. On the eve of its meeting, I addressed a letter to the Congress President. In the letter, I wrote:

"Holding fast to the principle that war is not the civilised method for settling controversial international issues, and firm in its determination not to allow the Indian people to be dragged into other people's quarrels, the Congress cannot but sympathise with the victims of Fascist aggression and be willing to co-operate in freeing the world from that standing menace. Such an attitude would be in complete harmony with the object of the Congress, which is to secure the liberation of the Indian people. Nor would it in any way amount to co-operation with Imperialism if the opportunity is availed for asserting India's right of self-determination. The guiding principle of the Congress attitude at this juncture has been correctly formulated by Pandit Jawahar Lal Nehru. In a press interview at Chungking, Panditji said that India must have democracy if she is to fight for democracy. The question, however, is: How is this principle to be put into practice as the condition for the Congress agreeing to co-operate in freeing the world from the menace of Fascism.

"The first step towards national Legislatures; and the establishment of democratic freedom will be made upon the introduction of the following measures: 1. Adult franchise for the Central as well as Provincial Legislatures; 2. Abolition of the Upper Chambers; 3. Full right of citizenship for the States peoples whose representatives to the Federal Legislature to be elected also by adult franchise; 4. Constitutional guarantee for the freedom of press, speech and association; 5. Enlargement of the functions of local self-government to the extent of amended the police and creation of local militias.

"Pending the making by a Constituent Assembly of the Constitution of the Democratic State of Free India, the present constitution is to be forthwith amended by the newly elected Central Legislature, and endorsed by the Provincial Legislative Assemblies, on the above lines."

On September 14, the Congress Working Committee issued the lengthy statement requesting the British Government to declare its war aims. Commenting on that document, I wrote:

"As far as the British Government is concerned, it has most authoritatively declared that the object of the present war is to end Hitlerism. The Congress has declared its sympathy with this object. Undoubtedly, it is an object worth sympathy and active support. But our leaders have chosen not to take that straightforward attitude against the wise advice of Gandhiji. It might not be altogether out of place to ask the British Government how it proposes to deal with the Indian problem in case of India joining in the fight against Hitlerism. But the scope of the question put in the Working Committee's statement is so wide as to include not only relevant issues, but to appear positively utopian......Imperialism is invited to commit suicide as the condition for its deserving Congress support in the war against Fascism. It is really difficult to understand why the Working Committee found it necessary to indulge in utopian speculations, when it was called upon to perform a very definite task, namely, to formulate terms on which it is *admittedly* prepared to favour India's participation in the war so long as it is a war against Fascism. Throughout the statement, co-operation *is* offered. It is also said time and again that co-operation cannot be unconditional, although Gandhiji was of a different opinion. That being the case, the statement cannot be said to be altogether free from 'spirit of bargaining'. Why should it be? Indeed, it is not a matter of bargaining. The Congress is in a position to dictate terms, and its leaders should have done that. Instead they failed to take the initiative, which is left to the other side. This may be considered to be good manners, but it is bad leadership.

"Why all this beating about the bush? Why not mention the terms acceptable, and ask the other party either to take it or leave it? Eventually, it will come to that. Only, the initiative will be from the other side; the Congress will be asked to take or leave whatever is offered. That will not be a very dignified position, *unless our leaders have made up their mind to decide in favour of resistance*, in case the offer from the other side will fall short of what they consider to be "the largest possible extent."

"That possibility, however, can scarcely be contemplated, given the decisive opinion of Gandhiji that the country is not ready for a large-scale struggle. One may or may not agree with that opinion; but the point is that it will determine the final attitude of our leaders. The attitude being thus predetermined, the statement of the Working Committee is only a statement device.

"Wholesale resistance being excluded for the time being, our offer to co-operate in the fight against Fascism, being voluntarily given, the immediate objective is to capture the largest possible measure of political power, which will enable us to conquer freedom and establish democrary, irrespective of what others may desire. The object must be formulated in concrete terms. We recommend for their consideration the measures suggested in the letter addressed to the Congress President on the eve of the last meeting of the Working Committee.

"Let there be no more suspension and indecision. Let the minimum demands of the nation be formulated. If we want to advance on the road to democracy and freedom, while helping the destruction of Fascism, let us avail of this opportune moment to occupy strategic positions which will guarantee our ultimate victory."*

It should be noted that the Radicals were at that time members of the Congress. Many of us were members of Congress Committees up to the A. I. C. C. We also held offices in the Congress organisation throughout the country. Although from the very first moment, the Radicals adopted an attitude towards the war fundamentally different from that of the Congress leaders, as Congressmen they had to adjust their views to the official policy of the Congress, and try to influence the policy step by step. The method adopted was to raise concrete issues and compel

**Editorial in 'Independent India', September 24, 1939.*

the Congress leaders to tackle them positively instead of pursuing a shirking policy of shirking responsibility.

Immediately after the meeting of the Congress Working Committee, leading Radical Congressmen met to discuss the line of action practical under the given situation. In a statement of policy, issued after the meeting, my letter to the Congress President was endorsed. The following are extracts from the Statement of Radical Policy:

"No resolution of the Congress commits it irrevocably to resistance to India's participation in any war. Therefore, when the war came, and India as a part of the British Empire was automatically involved in it, there was only one thing for the Congress leadership to do. It was to formulate the terms of co-operation......

"It is more dignified to go with the eyes open than to be led by the nose. The central fact of the situation is that the leaders of the Congrees have declared their readiness to support Britian in the present war, if India will be allowed to do so as a free nation. Apart from the obvious illusion on the part of those who formulate such a demand, it is pertinent to ask them to formulate it in concrete terms. Assuming that Britian will accept the demand, for the moment she cannot be expected to do more than make a declaration to that effect. Will that satisfy our leaders? Presumably not. On the other hand, again assuming that Britian will readily grant that, no radical change in the political status of India could take place from to-day to tomorrow. But India is already involved in the war. As regards the support for the war, that will not wait until our leaders have made up their mind. As a part of the British Empire, India is obliged to give that. Therefore, in order to avoid the indignity of the failure or reluctance to act according to the Congress resolutions, our leaders should forthwith formulate the conditions of support according to those resolutions. The Working Committee's statement does not contain any such demands. The only thing it appears to suggest is that Imperialism should commit suicide. That is utopian. Barring a wholesale resistance, which the present leadership of the Congress cannot certainly have in view, given Gandhiji's decisive opinion that the country is not prepared for it, what can be attempted under the given conditions is pre-determind. There must be an interim arrangement. The pseudo-ethical disdain for the spirit of bargaining may be an expression of ill-conceived indealism, but it certainly has no place in political strategy. Just now we cannot have all we want. We do not possess the requisite certainly! power. We cannot have it for the asking. Therefore, let us try to secure the utmost possible, so as to occupy some positions of vantage wherefrom we shall be able to fight for all we want. This state of mind is inherent in the present policy of the Congress. Why then do not our leaders act in a straightforward way? That would be more dignified as well as practical."

The All-India Congress Committee met at Wardha on October 9 to endorse the statement of the Working Committee. In an appeal to the members of the A. I. C. C., I wrote:

"Itself engaged in the struggle for freedom and democracy, the Indian National Congress welcomed the decision of the British Government to fight Hitlerism which it had encouraged persistently over a number of years. The end of Hitlerism is an object which can count upon the fullest sympathy and active support of the Indian National Congress, which has always been opposed to Fascism and vehemently condemned its successive acts of aggression."

Having analysed the European situation created by military moves on the part of the U. S S. R., I drew the conclusion "that the present European war has become situation I unnecessary. Although the British Government contributed nothing to it, the object of attained Hitlerism has been attained to a very large extent. Therefore, the question of India's participation in the war for international considerations has disappeared. The problem must be approached exclusively from the point of view of the exigencies of the national situation.

"The question is: Can India remain aloof if leading European countries are involved in a first class military conflict? Politically, she will be involved against her will. As a part of the British Empire, she will be in war automatically, unless she outgrows that status of dependency not by any grace of Imperialism, but by her own might. Economically also, she will be involved, neither with any grief, nor with any reluctance.

"Under the given situation, the Congress policy should be a direct approach to the British people with the appeal to prevail upon their

Government to put an end to this useless war. The British Government should be made to understand that the Congress will not be a party to a war which has ceased to have any international justification. Most probably the war in Europe will stop before long. Therefore, let us not be stampeded into any commitment. If the Congress Ministries could protect our elementary civil liberties, we should go ahead with our own tasks of organisation and political preparation, completely indifferent to the senseless military operations in Europe. The question of active resistance does not arise. There cannot be any objection to legitimate commercial and industrial activities which may be helpful to military purposes. The war can affect India injuriously, for the time being, only in two ways: firstly, through the restriction of the freedom of press, speech and other civil liberties; and secondly, through increased economic burdens upon the masses resulting from profiteering. Let the Congress Ministries prove their mettle by protecting popular welfare on both these scores. Measures for fixing prices should be introduced and effectively administered. Congress Ministries should refuse to adminser Ordinances restricting the elementary democratic rights of the people. Thus, it will be for Imperialism to decide whether it wishes to precipitate a conflict. On its part, the Congress should be prepared for all emergencies."

The change in our policy from voluntary support, given under conditions, which would make it most effective, to indifference, was determined by the change in the war situation. We welcomed the British declaration of war against Fascist Germany. But the war did not actually break out, nor there appeared to be any indication that military operations against Nazi Germany would be undertaken by the Western Powers. As a matter of fact, there were thick rumours about an early peace. The danger was that the war would develop into a crusade against the U. S. S. R., which, for the great services it rendered to the anti-aggression cause, became the object of the most malicious propaganda in all the countries, including India. As a war against the U. S. S. R., waged either by all the European Powers or by Nazi Germany alone, backed up by the Western Powers, would immensely strengthen Fascism, instead of destroying it, we came to the conclusion that a desperate effort should be made to avert that possible catastrophe. Hitler had received a serious setback in his design of aggression eastwards. On the other hand, the Western Powers did not show any intention of undertaking serious become operations. The war had evidently become a useless and senseless affair. Therefore, we believed that it could end, decided the first stage of the process of checking Fascist aggression.

On October 17, the Viceroy issued a statement in answer to the Congress request for a clear declaration of Britain's and aims. The Central Executive Committee of the League of Radical Congressmen was in session. It discussed the Viceroy's declaration and decided to address a letter to the Congress President making concrete suggestions regarding the policy to be adopted at this juncture Meanwhile, the following was said in a short statement issued to the press :

The Viceroy's declaration and Mr. Chamberlain's latest speech manifest a deplorable change in the British Government's war and peace aims. The Chamber- had expressed sympathy with the object of ending Hitlerism and was prepared to render help for the attainment of that object on certain conditions regarding India's own status being fulfilled. Britain's ostensible war aims having been dropped, the Congress must withdraw the previous offer and conduct energetically India's struggle for freedom, completely indifferent to other peoples' quarrels. While the Western Powers contributed nothing in that respect, the Soviet Union has decisively checked Nazi aggression. As far as the Congress is concerned, the plausible object of the war has been largely attained. The Congress should appeal for an early termination of the armed conflict, which is bound to cause incalculable injuries to all peoples concerned."

In the letter to the Congress President, dated October 19, I wrote: "True to its ideals of freedom and democracy, the Congress always condemned the violence and the aggressiveness of the Fascist Powers. No freedom-loving Indian could ever approve of the British foreign policy during the last years, which aided and abetted the destruction of freedom of weak and small nations. When finally the British Government abandoned the policy of connivance with Fascism, the Congress naturally expressed its sympathy for the object and offered its readiness to help the attainment of the laudable object of freeing Europe and the world from the greatest menace of our time.

"India was concerned with the conflict in Europe because it was precipitated ostensibly with the noble object of destroying the Fascist menace. Now the war and peace aims of the British Government, as declared by the Viceroy, and previously by the British Prime Minister, are such as will involve Europe in a large-scale and protracted war, which will be a great calamity in every respect. The war and peace aims of the British Government seem to be to restore the unstable status created by the vindictive, ill-conceived and inequitous Treaty of Versailles... Having itself, over a period of years, connived at the practical repudiation of the Versailles Treaty, the British Government to-day wants to plunge Europe into another orgy of death and destruction for restoring that broken down *status quo*.

"Although the British Government contributed little to the attainment of its object professed originally, Fascism as an international force, and German Nazism, in particular, have suffered a heavy defeat at the hands of the Soviet Union.

The Nazis have been compelled to abandon their long cherished plan of expansion eastwards at the cost of the East-European peoples and finally of the Soviet Union. The Hitler regime could command the support of a considerable section of the German people on account of diplomatic triumphs and the glory of successful military feats. Thanks to the recent actions of the Soviet Union, it has been deprived of any credit on both the fronts. The inevitable consequence will be a serious weakening of the moral and emotional foundations of the Nazi regime, which can be expected to be overthrown in due course of time by the action of the German people, provided that it will not be reinforced by those very Powers which have been, by an accident, involved in a war with it. However, the plausible object of checking Hitlerism having been attained to a large extent, the war in Europe has become completely useless and cannot be of any concern for India.

"In this situation, the immediate thing for the Congress to do is to throw its influence on the side of peace. A fervent appeal should be forthwith made to the peoples of Europe, and particularly of England and France, to demand immediate termination of armed hostilities and such a peaceful solution of the outstanding problems as would spare Europe the cataclysm of a large-scale war. The Nazi aggressiveness, which precipitated the present armed conflict, has been checked. The guarantee against any revival of the danger will be found in the recognition of the most salient fact of the present European situation; that guarantee can be afforded only by the Soviet Union. The latter would willingly co-operate in any honest effort to keep Nazism at bay, and to help the German people to set their house in order. The guarantee action on the part of the Congress will be the most valuable contribution to the solution of the European crisis, and consequently will win for India the credit of giving the tormented world a courageous lead

"The appeal for an early termination of the war is sure to find a widespread response. Nevertheless, even in the "democratic" countries, democracy may not be able to assert its sovereignty. In that case, India shall have no other alternative but to leave Europe to its fate and turn her attention exclusively to her immediate task of winning freedom. The Congress should take up an attitude of neutrality. As a part of the British Empire, India has been involved in the war. But that alone does not guarantee willing cooperation of the Indian people. Let the British Government carry on its war, if our counsel will not prevail.

"When the Congress will be obliged to fall back on the alternative policy, we shall have to proceed with great caution and circumspection. While declaring its neutrality, the Congress should not withdraw its representives in office. The Congress Ministries in the given situation should be actuated by an entirely different motive. The primary task of the Congress Ministries should be to protect civil liberties, particularly the freedom of press, platform and movement."

The Congress Working Committee also met to consider the Viceroy's declaration. But unfortunately, the positive policy suggested by us was not accepted. Its reaction was entirely different. It still pursued the policy of sitting on the fence as far as the international situation was concerned, but at the same time resolved to withdraw Congressmen from office. The resolution declared:—

"The Viceroy's statement is an unequivocal reiteration of the old imperialist policy. The Committee must therefore regard the Viceroy's statement as in every way unfortunate. In the circumstances, it cannot possibly give any support to Great Britain, for it would amount to an endorsement of the imperialist policy which the Congress has always sought to end. As a first step in this direction, the Committee calls upon the Congress Ministries to tender their resignation.

"The Committee warns Congressmen against any hasty action in the shape of civil disobedience, political strike and the like. The Committee will watch the situation and the activites of the British Government in India, and will not hesitate to guide the country and take farther steps whenever the necessity arises."

It is evident that our policy was not just to support any war. We supported it unhesitatingly when it was declared against Nazi Germany. But as soon as the original object was pushed to the back-ground and the war threatened to become an anti-Soviet war, we could not possibly continue our policy of unreserved support. But at the same time, we were of the opinion that the Congress Working Committee resolution shirked an international responsibility and failed to grasp the possibilities of the Indian situation. Particularly, we considered the resignation of

Congress Ministries to be a grave mistake. Therefore, on October 24, I issued the following statement in this connection:—

"There is no sense in the resignation of the Ministries except as the beginning of a campaign of civil disobedience. Experience should occasion grave doubts in the efficacy of that form of struggle. The best result possible will be another Delhi Pact and another Round Table Conference. I apprehend ruinous consequences if prestige and emotionalism would be allowed to overwhelm realistic political considerations. The occasion requires the highest skill in political strategy. The tone of finality in the Working Committee resolution may be apparent Therefore, I hope that the far-reaching implications of the resolution will be dispassionately considered before implementing it. It is time to realise the futility of cheap martyrdom. It is unnecessary to risk repression for another round in the vicious circle. That will not bring the country anywhere near freedom. The fight for real freedom is not so easy. It requires foresight, cold calculation, patience, determination and self-confidence. The leadership is put to the supreme test."

While changing our war attitude from active

support to neutrality, we still were opposed to any war resistance. We disapproved of the Working Committee resolution to withdraw Congressmen from office, because that heralded war resistance. On November 5, I wrote:—

"Themselves having been of the opinon that the country is not prepared for a fight, it is the height of irresponsibility on the part of the leaders of the Congress to have prectipitated the present crisis. The only thing that can be said in their defence is that they did not want the crisis. That defence is even more damaging. What sort of a leadership is that which can be so easily driven to a position it wanted to avoid ?

"Supposing that all the Congress Ministries will resign, there arises the question: What next ? Unless the decision to withdraw from office has been taken with the sneaking expectation that presently the Congress Ministries will be called back, the next step is predetermined. If the present policy is pursued with the expectation that before long the Congress Ministries will be called back, why then all this fuss ? For once the leaders of the Congress tried to be cleverer than their conscience-keeper and acted against his advice. The result is that they have made a mess of things. Had they rightaway adopted the policy of unconditional co-operation recommended by Gandhiji, they would not find themselves in the present dilemma. Not having the courage to take a realistic view of the situation, they prefer to appear more courageous in a romantic way. The reality of the situation is that India is a part of the British Empire and therefore cannot stay out of the war except by severing that relation. The Congress leaders issued a dignified call for Imperialism to liquidate itself. They received a snubbing which naturally pricked their vanity and sent them in search of face-saving devices. The most imposing device is Satyagraha, which, under the present conditions of the country, will be political *harakiri*."*

By that time, the war entered its "phony stage". Apart from the dangerous possibilities in Europe, it was completely out of the picture as far as India was concerned. Consequently, the controversy about India's relation to the war practically ceased for the time being. Having withdrawn Congressmen from office, the Congress Working Committee kept the anti-imperialist struggle in suspense and invented an organised

**Editorial in Independent India's, Nov. 6, 1939.*

offensive for destroying democracy inside the Congress On the pretext of preparing for the "coming struggle", elected Congress Committees were superceded by so-called Satyagraha Committees and the Congress "Independence Pledge" was so radically changed as to make it devoid of any political content.

Soon after the war was declared in September 1939, leading Radical Congressmen met and discussed at length and in detail all the implications and possibilities of the international situation. The theoretical foundation of the Radical war policy was laid down in the Thesis adopted on that occasion. In that fundamental document, alternative developments of the international situation were visualised. During the first months of the war, the development tended to be in the dangerous direction apprehended in the Thesis. During that period, the Radical policy, therefore, was a reaction to that immediate situation. England having during that period failed to wage war against Nazi Germany, a general conclusion of armed hostilities at that point would have fortified the position of the anti-fascist forces. On the one hand, France might not have fallen and, on the other hand, the Soviet

Union would have had the time for perhapsg for the eventual show-down. If that respite was available, perhaps the war against Fascism, when it eventually did break out, might have been much shorter. The Radical policy during the period of "phony war" was carefully calculated on the basis of all these considerations.

But before long, the war actually broke out. Hitler again precipitated the situation. The reluctance of the Western Powers to take any initiative, even when the Nazi army was heavily engaged on the East, was interpreted by Hitler as a sign of their weakness. He, therefore, went over to the offensive. Having swept Norway and the Netherlands with lighting speed, he attacked France, the fall of which had already been prepared by traitors and the Fascist Fifth Column. The international situation became crystal clear. The issues at stake were evident. Having sat on the fence during the period of uncertainty, the Congress at last, just at that juncture, clearly began its move towards war resistance. The new line was sketched in the Working Committee resolution which was to be endorsed by the Ramgarh Session of the Congress. That resolution declared:

"The Congress considers the declaration by the British Government of India as a belligerent country, without any reference to the people of India, and exploitation of India's resources in this war, as an affront to them, which no self-respecting and freedom-loving people can accept or tolerate The recent pronouncements made on behalf of the British Government in regard to India demonstrate that Great Britian is carrying on the war fundamentally for imperialist ends and for the preservation and strengthening of her Empire, which is based on the exploitation of the people of India as well as of other Asiatic and African countries. Under these circumstances, it is clear that the Congress cannot in any way, directly or indirectly, be party to the war. The Congress, therefore, strongly disapproves of Indian troops being made to fight for Great Britain and of the drain from India of men and material for the purposes of the war. Congressmen and those under Congress influence cannot help in the prosecution of the war with men, money or material.

"The Congress withdrew the Ministries in order to dissociate India from the war. This preliminary step must naturally be followed by civil disobedience, to which the Congress will unhesitatingly resort as soon as the Congress organisation is considered fit enough for the purpose, or in case circumstances so shape themselves as to precipitate a crisis."

That was clearly the initation of the policy of non-cooperation, which was logically bound to lead to active war resistance. The threat was clear enough, and to back it up, preparations for the "coming struggle" began with all earnestness.

Fascist hordes overran Norway and Denmark hardly a month after the above resolution was passed. The Congress was not disturbed by that alarming development. On the contrary, soon afterwards, on April 18, the Working Committee confirmed the threat of civil disobedience contained in the Ramgarh Resolution.

Hitler's war machine rolled on mercilessly. The Low Countries were gone. Even then, the Congress held on to the theory of imperialist war and went ahead with the preparations for resisting India's participation in it. Then France fell, and Britain was threatened with an invasion by the triumphant hordes of Hitler. How did the Congress react to those nerve-wrecking events? It met on June 17 and deliberated for nearly a week, finally to adopt a resolution which declared :—

"The Working Committee has been deeply moved by the tragic events that have taken place in Europe in startling succession, and in particular by the misfortune that has befallen the people of France. These events have already had far-reaching consequences, and they are likely to be followed by other happenings, which will lead to novel situations and complex pro- blems."

But even then, the Congress maintained the opinion that "the war in Europe resulting from a desire for imperialist domination over other peoples and countries and a suicidal race in armaments, has led to human sorrows and miseries on a scale hitherto unknown, and came to the following conclusion:

"The critical situation that faces the world today requires vigilant attention and action whenever needed for this purpose. The Working Committee will meet at frequent intervals and all members must keep in readiness to obey urgent summons."

It is quite clear what was expected. The resolution was obviously based on the expectation that Great Britain would fall under a Fascist invasion before long. But in any case, the most remarkable thing was that, when the drama of the war was unfolding so very rapidly, the Congress leaders did not have a word to say against those who precipitated the conflict, and still clung to the theory that the war was caused by the imperialist designs of Britain. The designs presumably were against Nazi Germany. Consequently, the conclusion of the Congress theory about the cause of the war was obvious. It was that Nazi Germany, having been a victim of British imperialist designs, deserved sympathy. Before long, that logical conclusion determined political events in India.

During the fateful summer months of 1940, the Congress Working Committee remained practically in permanent session. The All-India Congress Committee also met twice. Believing that Britian was done for, the Congress leaders felt that they could dictate terms. The demand for a National Government was put forth. There was nothing wrong in that. But what was remarkable was their complete indifference for the dreadful fact of the whole of Europe coming under the iron heels of triumphant Fascism. To witness the downfall of British Imperialism might have been a natural and concern desire on the part of Congressmen. But they should have shown some concern for the British people who were then in the danger of coming under the domination of triumphant Fascism.

France fell two weeks before the anniversary of the Great Revolution. The Congress Working Committee met on July 7. I wrote to the Congress President, suggesting that an All-India demonstration should be organised on the day of the anniversary of the French Revolution to express India's sympathy for the French people in distress. I was simply dumb-founded to receive the President's reply saying that no useful purpose would be served by the Congress holding such a demonstration at that moment. He went even farther and remarked that the moment for such a demonstation was inopportune. Presumably, the Congress leaders did not favour the demonstration which, at that juncture, was bound to be an anti-fascist demonstration, and a demonstration of the Indian people's will to participate in the war in order to destroy the force which was annihilating the freedom of one European country after another.

Finally, the A. I. C. C. met in the historic

session at Poona. It was to formulate the demand for a National Government, which was to be presented to the Viceroy by the Mahatma. It was maintained that the National Government was to be formed so that India could participate in the war more effectively. I submitted the following resolution to the meeting of the A. I. C. C. at Poona.

"Seriously alarmed by the recent events in Europe, and having regard for the fact that the Congress has always condemned the acts of Fascist aggression, this meeting of the All-India Congress Committee declares that the fight for Indian freedom cannot be isolated from the larger fight for the defence of human liberty and modern civilisation against the fierce onslaught of Fascism. The All-India Congress Committee believes that active participation in that larger fight will enable the fighters for Indian freedom to attain their goal in the near future. To grant or withhold India's right of self-determination is not the prerogative of the British Government The right belongs to the people of India and must be conquered by all available means. Therefore, India's participation in the struggle for world freedom need not be conditional upon any declaration on the part of the British Government.

"Moreover, under the given relation of forces, India's situation, in the war cannot be prevented. Neither from the point of view of the international situation, nor in the interest of Indian freedom, is it necessary to do that. Nor is it possible to do that in view of the fact that the great bulk of the Indian people stand to be benefitted immediately, more or less, as a result of India's participation in the war. If the situation was favourable, India could make her contribution to the solution of the international problem by striking a decisive blow for her own freedom. Unfortunately, that is not yet the case. The task of the moment is to preserve the popular forces and prepare them for decisive action on a more favourable occasion, which may come before long.

"Therefore, the All-India Congress Committee resolves that the people of India should actively participate in the struggle against Fascism in every way available to them. That will not be helping imperialism, because the co-operation of India will strengthen the position of the genuinely anti-fascist elements in England

and enable the masses of the British people to prevent the liquidation of the struggle against Fascism under the influence of the more reactionary forces who still wield considerable power in the British ruling circles."

At the Poona session of the All-India Congress Committee, the Congress leaders spoke as the "potential and immediate rulers of the country." Taking note of the fact that Britain was in great difficulty in Europe, they were confident of ousting the British from power in this country. Although they spoke of "helping the British", the real mind of the Congress leaders was expressed by Vallabhbhai Patel, who declared that the war would not last more than another two or three months, and if Britain conceded their demand, that would be good; but even if Britain did not, the Congress would be free to choose its own course, and would do so.

In reply to the Poona Resolution offering to "help the British", came the offer made by the Viceroy on behalf of the British Government on August 8, 1940. The offer was to invite representative Indians forthwith to join the Viceroy's Executive Council without insisting on the condition that the major political parties should come to an agreement as regards provincial matters.

The Congress President refused to see the Viceroy to discuss the offer, so sure were the Congress leaders that the days of British power were counted. The Working Committee met on August 22 and emphatically denounced the offer. Although the refusal even to consider my resolution submitted to the A. I. C. C. meeting at Poona revealed that the Congress leaders had no intention of participating in the fight against Fascism, and they were only waiting for an invasion of Britain, I still took them on their words, and issued a statement advising the acceptance of the Viceroy's offer. I wrote:

"The Viceroy's declaration once for all proves that the Congress leaders have all along been chasing a chimera by demanding from the Brttish Government the recognition of Indian independence. It is now clear that the British Government can never be expected to recognise Indian independence before it will be an accomplished fact, and that no real power will ever be voluntarily transferred so as to liquidate Imperialism.

"Unless its policy is forthwith recast radically,

the Congress is bound to meet political and organisational disaster in consequence either of some rash action or of forced passivity. The question is how to avoid that.

"Having anticipated that the Congress policy was heading towards this crisis, I all along advocated an alternative course. A false sense of prestige and the craving for cheap heroics prevented the bulk of vocal Congressmen as well as the leaders from taking a realistic view of the situation and from trying to do what could be done instead of indulging in wishful thinking and day-dreams.

"To begin with, the futile policy of negation, inaugurated by the utopian September Declaration of the Congress Working Committee must be scrapped. The mistakes committed in pursuance thereof must be forthwith rectified. The Congress leaders are admittedly ready to accept office even at the Centre. A few months ago, they could do so, perhaps with some advantage. But haggling for more, they hava lost the strategic position.

"The greatest blunder, however, was to abandon the strategic positions in the provinces. Tha t can still be rectified, and the strategic positionsutilised for promoting the Indian people's struggle for their own freepom, and for organising their contribution to the fight against Fascism.

"The fight against Fascism must be the immediate object of all fighters for freedom and democracy. Any policy which will not accept this as the point of departure will be wrong. Fascism is the instrument forged to bolster up a system which has decayed throughout the world. With its destruction, the system itself will collapse. A free India will then take her rightful place in a world of free men engaged in the task of building a higher civilisation.

"Therefore, India should participate in the fight irrespective of Imperialist Britain's policy towards us. The fighters for Indian freedom should co-operate with British Democracy, as distinct from British Imperialism, for the common cause. Provincial Governments, controlled by popular representatives, can be the medium of that co-operation.

"Fascism being a growth on the decayed structure of capitalist society, it is to be found, in one form or other, wherever capitalism is not yet overthrown. To check incipient Fascism at home is the primary condition for protecting any country against the danger of Fascist invasion. If the anti-imperialist complex prevents India from doing so, she will jump from the frying pan into the fire, though with the heroic gesture of defying imperialist dictation.

"India has been making her contribution to the war. Under the given situation, it consists of supplying war materials and recruits for the army. The one is bound to be unlimited, because it is a good business proposition; the other is guaranteed by the existence of a numberless army of rural unemployed. But the danger of Fascism is not in remote Europe. It is to be found also near at hand. Therefore, a popular movement is necessary to combat it before it is too late. That purpose will not be served by the present method of organising India's war effort through the War Committee and Civic Guards.

"Entirely different methods must be adopted for making the masses conscious of the danger of Fascism lurking in their midst, and to mobilise them in resistance to that danger. That can be done by Provincial Governments controlled by elected representatives of the people.

"India's contribution to the world-wide struggle against Fascism can be most effectively organised through the medium of People's Councils composed of duly elected representatives of the local population. Those organs of democratic will and mass action can rise under the protection of popular Provincial Governments. They will be acting as the organs of anti-fascist propaganda and vigilance against the incipient forces of Fascism. The danger of internal peace being disturbed by popular discontent will be there if the moneyed people will be allowed to pass on the burden of contributing to the war funds to the shoulders oi the starving masses. Under the protection of popular Provincial Governments, the People's Councils cannot only guarantee against that danger, but also defend the masses against all forms of war profiteering.

"Having helped the rise of those organs of democratic will and popular power in course of the fight against Fascism, elected members of the Provincial Legislatures will eventually meet in a joint sesion to enunciate the fundamental principles of the Constitution of Free India, and call upon the People's Councils to elect deputies to a National Asembly which will meet to ratify those principles. Thus India will work out her own freedom while contributing voluntarily her share to the world struggle against Fascism."

But the Congress leaders could no longer retrace their steps. Wishful thinking and the belief that, defeated by victorious Fascism, the British Government would be compelled to accept the terms dictated by them, had egged the Congress leaders on to go too far. On August 22, the Working Committee resolved to take the step which had been predetermined by its policy adopted in the very beginning of the war. On September 17, the A. I. C. C. met in Bombay and endorsed the Working Committee resolution. The Mahatma had two long interviews with the Viceroy. He wanted the freedom to preach against Indians giving any aid for the prosecution of the war. The Mahatma refused to be satisfied with the concession made to the conscientious objectors in England. The negotiations finally broke down, and on October 13, the Working Committee resolved to launch a campaign of civil disobedience for asserting the right of preaching against India's participation in the war. After his interview with the Viceroy, the Mahatma declared : "Indians are not interested in the war. They make no distinction between Nazism and the double autocracy that rules India."

The end of the period of the "phony war in Europe caused two divergent developments in India regarding her attitude towards the war. The Congress attitude progressively stiffened and ultimately culminated in the movement of war resistance, as it was bound to by its internal logic. The Radicals were faced with the primary necessity of assisting the defeat of Fascism at all cost, disregarding all other considerations. It was not necessary for them to make opportunistic adjustments from time to time. All along they were guided by the theoretical analysis of the causes and possible consequences of the war made in the very beginning. Consequently, as soon as the fight against Fascism actually broke out, the Radical policy developed consistently on the lines of unreserved support to the war, and in the latter stages, it is marked mainly by efforts to make this support more and more effective and decisive.

The book is a collection of documents depicting the whole history of our efforts to enable India to make the greatest contribution to the destruction of the most ruthless enemy of human freedom, and thus pave the way to her own freedom.

Dehradun,
December 1, 1942.

M. N. ROY.

PART ONE

INDIA AND WAR

THESIS ADOPTED BY THE RADICALS IN THE MIDDLE OF OCTOBER, 1939

I

Analysis of the International Situation and its Perspectives

The nature of the present war is to be determined in the light of (1) the social and political character of the forces involved, directly and indirectly; (2) its alternative lines of development; (3) its possible outcomes; (4) the attitude of the U. S. S. R.

The fundamental fact of the situation is that the present international conflict takes place on the background of irreconcilable social and political conflicts inside the various nations involved in it. There is a relation between these two conflicts, and the development of the military conflict on the international front is bound to be determined by the anxiety of the ruling classes, in the countries directly or indirectly involved in the international conflict, to hold their own in the civil conflicts at home. The more deep-seated social conflict is not limited by national boundaries. It takes place on an international scale, cutting across the antagonisms and rivalries between national States. This fundamental fact determined international relations during the recent years. The outstanding feature of those relations was to smooth over antagonisms between national States, and a persistent effort to avoid a large-scale armed conflict at the cost not only of a series of small and weak nations, but even of the prestige of powerful imperialist States.

In view of that background of international relations, it is not permissible to start from the mechanical assumption that the present conflict is the outcome of the rivalry between two groups of imperialist States for the domination of Europe or of the world. The present conflict has been precipitated by an accident which, for the time being, has disturbed the plan underlying international relations during the last years. That immediate cause of the present conflict must be taken into due consideration, in order to have a proper perspective of possible developments.

The nature of a conflict is determined by the forces involved in it. The forces can be characterised by different standards. The problem can be approached from different points of view.

The popular point of view that it is a fight between Democracy and Fascism can be immediately rejected. The political situation in England and France is apparently different from that in Germany. In the former countries, civil liberties may not as yet have been so completely destroyed as in the latter. But the British and French Governments to-day are not democratic Governments even as they were before the last war. In both the countries, of late, Fascism has been gaining ground, for all practical purposes, if not as yet formally. Immediately upon entering the war, declared ostensibly with the purpose of ending Hitlerism, the French Government suppressed the Communist Party. The organisation of the People's Front in 1934 checked the advent of Fascism in France. The initiative in that respect was taken by the Communist Party which since then stood at the forefront of the anti-Fascist democratic forces. In view of this recent history, the significance of the suppression of the

Communist Party, immediately after it had voted credits for the war to be waged against Fascism, is evident. In Italy and Germany also, the victory of Fascism was celebrated by the suppression of the Communist Parties; other democratic forces met the same fate subsequently.

This highly significant event has not taken place in England. But that does not necessarily prove that the British Government is more democratic than the French, or the Fascist tendency is less pronounced in England than in France. The British Communist Party has not been suppressed, simply because it is a negligible factor. The weakness of the British Communist Party, in its turn, reflects the weakness of the revolutionary forces in England. The absence in England of the peculiarly Fascist features of the suspension of civil liberties and suppression of popular movements is to be explained by that weakness. Democracy is still tolerated in England, because there it is not a force but a mere formality. Why discard the democratic facade so long as it can camouflage totalitarianism in operation ?

Apart from the fundamental consideration that an imperialist State cannot be really democratic, the fact is that even parliamentary democracy has been practically abolished in England ever since the formation of the "National Government". Parliamentary opposition is still allowed simply because it is completely impotent to check or even influence the policy of the overwhelming conservative majority. Besides, on every crucial occasion, the opposition readily falls in line with the Government. A totalitarian regime has been established in England, although the crass acts of violence and barbarity, associated with that political phenomenon, have not yet been committed. The violence on the part of the rulers is always proportional to the potentiality of the opposition. In England, the anti-Fascist forces being weak, Fascism creeps in gradually and peacefully.

That being the position, in England as well as in France, there is no reason to accept the point of view that the present conflict is a war between Democracy and Fascism.

Another point of view is that it is a conflict between two systems of Imperialism. This view is based on a simplification of matters. It does not take into account the complex under-currents of the international situation and ignores the specific features of the economic structure of the two systems. It is a superficial view: Imperialism is the last stage of Capitalism; Fascism is the most brutal form of bourgeois dictatorship; ergo, Fascism and Imperialism are identical. From this simple, formalist syllogism, it is deduced that the present war is a war between imperialist States, and therefore is not to be distinguished in any way from previous wars.

But the relation of forces is not so simple as all that. Fascism, indeed, is a phase of Capitalism. It is the last ditch of Capitalism, so to say. It is also true that, in contemporary Europe, the terms Capitalism and Imperialism can be interchangeably used, all the leading capitalist countries there having attained, to a greater or lesser degree, the stage of Imperialism. But from that, it does not necessarily follow that Fascism is identical with Imperialism in the strict sense of the term. Owing to their expansionist tendencies, the Fascist States have been called imperialist States. But territorial expansion is not the characteristic feature of modern Imperialism. The United States of America is a typical, first-class, modern imperialist country; yet, to conquer colonies politically has not been, as a rule, its policy.

Surplus capital for export is the economic foundation of modern Imperialism. That was the case with Germany before the war but that is not the case with post-war Germany. Germany recovered from the severe economic crisis immediately after the war as a dependency of American capital. Between 1924 and 1928, the period of the reconstruction of the German industrial system, a vast bulk of foreign capital, mostly American, was invested in Germany. When industrial reconstruction and expansion led to the accumulation of capital, German foreign policy manifested neo-imperialist tendencies. But at the same time, Germany remained under the obligation of paying the interests of borrowed foreign capital, which was large enough to absorb practically the entire new capital accumulated in her industries. In those days, Germany represented a peculiar, unprecedented, unforeseen, type of economy. It was imperialist and colonial at the same time. Eventually, Germany came out of that peculiar position by simply repudiating not only her obligations under the Versailles Treaty, but also commercial obligations voluntarily incurred. That was not a gesture of a triumphant imperialist Power. It was an act which gave a staggering blow to capitalist ethics as well as to capitalist economics. It was a large-scale repudiation of the right of private property—the rock-bottom of capitalist economy. A system that arose thus, violating the ethical and economic principles of Capitalism, could not be *normally* capitalist, and therefore did not contain the germ of modern Imperialism. Fascist expansionism may be analogous to Roman Imperialism, but certainly not to British Imperialism.

Even after repudiating her financial obligations abroad, Germany had little capital to export. Neo-militarism, inaugurated with a feverish speed after the advent of the Nazis, promoted a new expansion of heavy industries absorbing all the newly accumulated capital which might have been exported. Thus, the rapid growth of military power and the manifestation of extravagant expansionism coincided with a financial weakening of Germany. Growing as a formidable Fascist Power, she became negligible as an imperialist rival. Excessive expenditure on account of the army, navy and air-forces has left in Germany so little exportable capital that of late she has not been able to pay for the raw-materials, indispensable for her war industries, to be imported from abroad. Autarchy is the peculiar principle of Fascist economy. Self-containedness and expansionism are mutually exclusive. Autarchy is the economics of Capitalism in an insoluble crisis. Modern Imperialism is the outcome of capitalist prosperity. Therefore, Fascist economy provides no foundation for modern imperialist expansion.

Such being the specific features of the economic structure of Nazi Germany, she cannot be a serious rival of British Imperialism. Instead of any rivalry, there has been a systematic cooperation between England and Germany ever since the signing of the Locarno Pact in 1924. The outstanding imperialist rivalry in post-war Europe was the rivalry between France and England. The Versailles Treaty established French diplomatic supremacy and military hegemony over the European Continent. France emerged out of the war not only as a formidable military Power, but also as a great industrialist country with tremendous imperialist potentialities. England was naturally alarmed, and quietly set about the task of upsetting the balance of power. Germany was the obvious ally in that venture. But there was a counter-attraction for her. When she was outcasted and humiliated by entire Europe, the Soviet Union was the only friend and ally of the German Republic. The Rappallo Treaty of 1922 was an evil omen for England. She must hurry up, if she was not to lose the only possible ally in her struggle against French supremacy in Europe. The Locarno Pact was the counter-move. During the last years, Mr. Nevile Chamberlain has been carrying on the policy of pampering the German ruling class, a policy inaugurated by his brother in 1924. It was under the patronage of Sir Austen Chamberlain that Germany was reintroduced in the respectable diplomatic parlours of Europe. France came to be haunted by the fear of a possible Anglo-German alliance against her. With that fear, she was persuaded by British diplomacy to relieve Germany from the most onerous and humiliating clauses of the Versailles Treaty.

The initial stages of the economic recovery of Germany had taken place with financial aid from America. With a financial hold on Germany, the United States could eventually dominate the whole of Continental Europe. A new rival entered the arena. England was alarmed. Her alarm was all the greater because of the possibility of a Franco-American alliance. By introducing Germany in the League of Nations, and having her recognised as a Great Power, British diplomacy headed off the danger of an alliance between the Soviet Union and the German Republic. The next step was to encourage Germany to repudiate the American financial bondage. Assured of the sympathy and support of British diplomacy, Germany, which by 1929 had ceased to be a Republic except in name, revolted against her financial obligations to America as well as to France. The spearhead of that revolt was the National-Socialist movement headed by Hitler. That movement was patronised and financed by big German industrialists in close touch with the City of London. The Nazis triumphed in Germany, on the one hand, as an open challenge to the French military hegemony of Europe and, on the other hand, as the bulwark against the spread of Bolshevism. In both these respects, they were welcome to British diplomacy.

That being the diplomatic background of the present relation of forces in Europe, it is an altogether unfounded theory that Europe is experiencing another imperialist war brought about by the antagonism between the imperialist interests of

England and the imperialist ambitions of Nazi Germany.

It is well known how, ever since the invasion of Abyssinia, England refused to raise a finger to resist repeated Fascist aggressions. In every single occasion of those successive acts of aggression—Abyssinia, Spain, Austria, Czechoslovakia,—England could call a halt if she wanted. Terribly alarmed by the growing military power of Germany, and also by the expansionist policy of Italy, France would have readily joined England in any action against Fascist aggression. Then, the Soviet Union was always there, ready to throw in her weight on the side of democracy and freedom. Yet, it was British diplomacy which did not allow any concerted anti-Fascist action.

That curious policy of a "democratic" Power aiding and abetting the predatory acts of Fascism puzzled the naive, accustomed to take people on their words, and was interpreted by others as the sign of the senility of British Imperialism. Both were equally wrong, incapable of seeing beneath the surface of things.

The Nazi victories have not harmed England in any way. On the contrary, she has been the real gainer. Nazi military aggressions and diplomatic penetration in Eastern and South-Eastern Europe have destroyed the French hegemony of Europe. That was very welcome to England, who had all along been working with that purpose. So, the rise of the Nazi Power has eliminated from the complex of the alignment of forces in Europe the only factor of imperialist rivalry—that between England and France, the latter having been reduced to the status of a second-rate Power, completely subservient to British diplomacy. On the other hand, Fascism, instead of being a new rival to British Imperialism, has served as an instrument in its hand.

Territorial acquisitions are of little practical value, unless they can offer profitable investment for capital exported from the conquering country. Nazi Germany having little capital to export, new territories cannot be transformed into valuable economic assets, unless the capital comes from some other quarter. And in that case, the real profit of territorial expansion does not belong to the conquering State, which has to be satisfied with the empty glory of military victory; the real benefit accrues to the third party which has the surplus capital to invest.

British financial interest in Nazi expansionism

is an open secret. Even when negotiations were going on in Moscow for the formation of an Anglo-French-Soviet anti-aggression pact, news leaked out of a gigantic financial deal between the London bankers and Nazi Germany. The huge armament works of Skoda were largely owned by French financiers. After the conquest of Czechoslovakia, the Germans seized the factory. Naturally, the shares of that enterprise became practically worthless. They were presently bought over for a song by London bankers. The only thing that the Nazis have gained from the conquest of Czechoslovakia is the privilege of acting as the gunmen for protecting British financial interest. They must be paid for the services rendered. The payment is made partly by further financial aid (in the form of profitable investments) and partly in kind—toleration of the conquest of yet other fruitful fields of capital investment.

The predatory system of German Nazism is not a rival of, but a subsidiary to, British Imperialism. Without financial aid from a third party, the Nazi Empire would collapse like the Roman Empire. The prop is provided by British bankers. Thus, whatever antagonism between the two countries may be apparent, that is only superficial, and cannot be the cause of a serious military conflict.

The analogy of the last war does not evidently apply to the present conflict. It is not the culmination of a pre-meditated plan of one imperialist Power to weaken another. Nor is it the bloody consequence of a scramble for colonies or of a rivalry for world domination. The Nazi demand for colonies is only a bargaining counter, and serves the propagandist purpose of strengthening the Hitler regime by encouraging chauvinism on the part of a certain section of the German people. The alternative demand is expansion eastward—to the extent of annexing the Ukraine as far as the Black Sea. Events of the last years have proved that Britain was not particularly opposed to the alternative demand. So, the Nazi demand for colonies was never taken seriously. As regards rivalry for world domination, Nazi Germany never really entered the list. The "ideological outposts" in practically all the countries of the world were mere propaganda centres, kept up rather for impressing the home population with the idea that Fascism was a far-flung world force. Without any economic foundation, the propaganda for world domination is only a matter of words meant to deceive the people at home to be emotionally attached to an unpopular regime.

Events leading up to the last war were entirely different. At the end of the century, Germany was a full-fledged imperialist State, openly bidding for a "place in the sun." The world had already been divided between older imperialist Powers. In order to live as an imperialist Power, Germany had to challenge their monopoly, and deliberately prepare for a war with the object of weakening the other imperialist Powers. The Bismarckian plan of eastward push was checked by the British Lion, forgetting his suspicion of the Russian Bear, and the inclusion of the Tzarist Absolutism in an Entente Cordiale with the western democratic Powers. The next German scheme of imperialist expansion was to reach Asia overland by means of the projected Berlin-Baghdad Railway. England again came on the way of German ambition. Russia was encouraged to preach Pan-Slavism in the Balkans as the counter-blast to Pan-Germanism. Thus, step by step, all expansionist efforts of the new German Imperialism were frustrated by the older rivals.

As a matter of fact, the last imperialist war started already in the beginning of the century, when an armed conflict was imminent owing to the German Kaiser's dramatic appearance in Morocco, his visit to Constantinople and his telegram to the president of the Boer Republic, when this was engaged in a war with Britain. If a general conflagration did not break out on any one of those occasions, ever since then, skirmishes and local wars were continuously waged, either side trying to occupy strategic positions before the inevitable final struggle. These facts prove that, in the case of the last war, the rival groups of Powers deliberately prepared for it, and the eventual clash was the anticipated climax of that process of preparation. That was a typical imperialist war.

Imperialist wars are waged with the purpose of some imperialist Power or Powers profiting at the cost of others. When the result of a large-scale general war threatens to be such as to be ruinous to the imperialist system as a whole, imperialist wars no longer happen. In the contemporary period of world history, only a war between England and the United States of America will still be an imperialist war. A war between

France and England would also have that character, but it is not very probable to happen owing to the end of French hegemony over Europe. A war with Japan will also be an imperialist war, although, Japan's Financial subservience to both the Anglo-Saxon rivals, would greatly affect the character of that war. However, the point is that the present armed conflict in Europe, assuming that it will develop into a large-scale war, does not have the specific characteristics of an imperialist war, which is deliberately prepared by both the parties, and is expected to end in the defeat of one party, whichever party may be defeated, Imperialism as such remaining unweakened.

The character of a war is, after all, determined by the period of history in which it takes place. Wars, taking place in the period of the bourgeois revolution, were all national wars, waged with the purpose of either establishing or defending national States. The wars in the period of early imperialist expansion were colonial wars, waged for subjugating weaker peoples and annexing backward territories. When, in the period of general capitalist prosperity, several countries strive for imperialist expansion, imperialist wars are on the order of the day. Finally, Capitalism decays, and the world enters into the period of revolution. The wars in that period usually prepare the ground for impending revolutions; therefore, in that period, capitalist States do not deliberately prepare for an armed conflict among themselves. If they arm themselves to the teeth, that is *immediately* for giving an artificial stimulus to the stagnant industrial system, and ultimately with the purpose of defence against the maturing revolution. But when neighbouring countries are armed to the teeth and, in the midst of a perennial economic crisis, jingoist nationalism may serve as a safety-valve, armed conflicts of more or less serious nature may be precipitated by any chance event or by some unfortunate miscalculation. That sort of war, however, is not an imperialist war; it is an internecine conflict, bound to weaken both the parties involved and thus open the floodgates of revolution. Therefore, such a war is bound to be waged half-heartedly, both the parties striving for an early settlement.

The present war is a war of this nature. It is an internecine conflict precipitated by an accident or a miscalculation. While the probability of its continuing is not altogether excluded, and even if it is fought until one of the parties is defeated, it is not a typical imperialist war. If it continues, its result most probably will not be the strengthening of some imperialist Powers at the cost of others, but the mutual destruction, serious weaking, at any rate, of all the capitalist States involved. And that would only further the cause of their common enemy—revolution. The most outstanding antagonism of the present epoch is the antagonism between all the capitalist States on the one side, and the international forces of revolution. For their very existence, the former must reconcile whatever mutual antagonism they still may have, to face the common enemy. That is the real alignment of international forces to-day, and the character of all wars taking place in this epoch must of antagonism by it.

The new factor

Notwithstanding all the peculiar features of the present conflict, the present war could possibly have the same consequences as of a typically imperialist war, but for the existence of the Union of Socialist Soviet Republics. Theoretically, the last war also could usher in the era of revolutions. As a matter of fact, *historically*, it did have that significance. For that reason, the present war could not be a typically transition war. It is taking place in the era of wars and revolutions anticipated by Marx as the transition period from typically n to Socialism.

Revolutions did break out towards the end of the last war. For several years, Europe was haunted by the spectre of revolution. But ultimately, it could not triumph except in one country. Although that single turning is to be regarded as the turning point in world history, determining all future developments, the post-war years were marked by the defeat of several revolutionary outbreaks, and subsequently by the general suppression of the revolutionary movement throughout Europe. The defeat of the revolutions represented the outbreak of the class war on an international scale. That greater war has been going on all these intervening years, and Fascism is the weapon forged by Capitalism fighting for its life.

Theoretically, there was no reason for the revolutionary outbreaks in the post-war years to be defeated. Objective conditions had been created as predicted by Marx. Capitalist exploitation had broken up European society into two irreconcilably antagonistic classes. Mechanisation of production, contributing to the collective performance of labour, had laid down the economic foundation, and created the psychological atmosphere, for Socialist reconstruction. The working class was very numerous, constituting a majority in the industrially most advanced countries. It had developed powerful organisations. On the other hand, Capitalism was thrown into a severe crisis by the consequences of the war. Even the final condition for a triumphant revolution, namely, the break-down of the capitalist State. obtained in some of the countries. Yet, in one country after another—Germany, Austria, Hungary, the Baltic States, Bulgaria, and again Germany and Austria, and finally in Spain—the revolution was defeated. That most remarkable phenomenon of post-war Europe must be explained; otherwise, the Marxian theory of revolution would be open to grave doubt.

The explanation is provided by the proper appreciation of a factor which did not expressly enter into the calculation of Marx. Implicitly, it was there, to become evident, as the most decisive factor, in Lenin's exposition of the function of the State. That factor is the military power. In past revolutions, this factor did not play so very decisive a part. Those revolutions took place on national scales. External forces were not applied for suppressing them. On the other hand, thanks to the relatively backward state of armament, the military forces of the national States could be overwhelmed by mass upheavals even with the most primitive weapons. The revolutions in post-war Europe took place under entirely different conditions, in both the respects. The revolutionary outbreaks were not local affairs, they were to face the opposition not only of the national States concerned, but of the force of international counter-revolution. They were so many battles in the international class war. Almost in every case, they were suppressed, not by the forces of the particular national State concerned, but by military intervention from outside. Wherever the intervention actually did not take place, the threat was there. The revolution triumphed in Russia, because the intervention from outside could not be so very effective there, as in the case of smaller countries surrounded by capitalist States not yet threatened by revolution. Engaged elsewhere, the military forces of international capitalism could intervene in Russia only after the revolution had sufficiently consolidated its position.

The lesson of the experience is clear enough. Under the present alignment of international forces, the success of a revolution is not guaranteed even by the most favourable conditions in any single conntry. Simultaneous revolutionary outbreaks in a number of adjoining countries may be an ideal perspective, but the probability of that ever happening is almost nil. Every single revolutionary outbreak must be fought and won as a battle in the international class war. To be successful, the revolution should have its military power, strong enough to meet and overwhelm the military forces of international counter-revolution. This decisive factor was absent during the period of revolutions which followed immediately after the last war. To-day, the relation of forces has radically changed; the change has been brought about by the existence and growth of the Soviet Union.

The decisive guarantee for the success of revolutionary outbreaks, almost sure to take place in consequence of the weakening of the capitalist States involved in the present war, rules out the view that this conflict has been brought about premeditatedly with the purpose of one group of capitalist countries establishing their supremacy at the cost of others.

The view that the present conflict in Europe is not an imperialist war does not, however, imply it is an anti-Fascist war. This latter view is to be rejected on the strength of the self-same analysis of the relation of international forces as leads to the conclusion that it is not an imperialist war. Since the present conflict is not the outcome of a premeditated plan, it must have broken out owing to some accidental cause. That is not very difficult to discover. Until the very last moment, neither party really believed that it would come to an armed conflict. Previous experience had made the Nazis confident that, in the last moment, they would be allowed to have their way. All they had to do was to present the Western Powers, particularly England, with another "accomplished fact", the reality of which had previously had such a magical influence on British diplomacy. The Western Powers, on the other hand, did not expect Poland to take their guarantee very seriously. It was not believed that the Poles would act any differently from the Czechs. Danzig was already gone; once the Corridor and Upper Silesia were occupied by German troops, the moment would come for another Munich. The Nazi demand was the return of those territories, previously parts of Germany. The Western Powers were not opposed to the demand on principle. Only, they did not want Germany to settle the matter unilaterally. The German ultimatum to Poland was not an unprecedented thing. During the last two years, Europe had experienced several such diplomatic shocks. In the meeting held after the ultimatum was delivered to Poland, the British Government decided to mediate, and informed the German Government to that effect. Had the representative of the Polish Government reached Berlin, within the time specified in the ultimatum, he would have been advised by the Western Powers to do exactly as the President of Czochoslovakia had done previously. There would have been no resistance to German occupation of the Corridor and Upper Silesia and the world would have been spared the farce of an "anti-Fascist" war. But unfortunately for both the parties, the British

Government did everything short of "producing a Polish representative" before midnight in Berlin. German troops were mobilised on the Polish frontiers, ready to march, just as in the case of Austria and Czechoslovakia. As on previous occasions, diplomacy should have done its part before the time fixed for the troops to march. For once, diplomacy could not keep pace with impatient militarism. German troops marched into Poland before her protectors had sanctioned her violation. That was bad manners; the Nazis had been very useful, but they should not be allowed to become too much of a nuisance. They should be taught to behave. But the halt was called when it was too late. Meanwhile, the Poles had spoiled the delicate situation irreparably. Unexpectedly, they had taken into their head to resist German invasion. The fat was on the fire. The situation was out of hand. For the sake of prestige, England had to declare war, and France had no option but to follow suit. An accidental combination of circumstances provoked the armed conflict which nobody wanted.

There is yet another fact proving decisively that the Western Powers did not want a war with Nazi Germany on the issue of Poland. That fact was their sabotage of the Moscow negotiations for the formation of an Anglo-Franco-Soviet. anti-aggression pact. Whatever might have been the difficulties previously, the aggression. came to a deadlock upon the refusal of the Polish delegates to allow Soviet troops entering Poland in discharge of the responsibility of protecting her against German aggression. The semi-Fascist Polish Government might be more afraid of Russian aid than of Nazi aggression. Diplomacy might bungle and blunder. But military experts were present, and the point at issue was, after all, military. They could not make any possible mistake on the point that, if Poland required military assistance in case of a German attack, assistance could come only from the Soviet Union. When Poland refused to accept that only possible effective help, it was an act of great irresponsibility, if not of down right deception, to give her any guarantee against German aggression. Yet, that act of irresponsibiliy was committed, and the consequence was the unwanted war.

The fact of rejecting Soviet co-operaion, so very essential for the purpose of checking Nazi aggression, proves that the Western Powers did not want to precipitate a war on the Polish issue for ending Hitlerism. Had they ever had any such intention in general, they could have acted much more effectively on several previous occasions; and in that case, Hitlerism would not have the chance of growing so very powerful as it did with the aid and connivance of the Western Powers, particularly England.

Although the view that it is an anti-Fascist war is altogether groundless, its immediate consequence, nevertheless, may be the defeat of Fascism, provided that the mistake unwittingly committed will not be rectified as soon as possible, and armed hostilities suspended before long. If the war continues, and is waged by the Western Powers seriously, Germany most probably will be defeated sooner or later. In spite of the much advertised pact with Russia, Germany is completely isolated to-day. The Nazis are left in the lurch by their spiritual allies. They will have to fight single-handed. All the ill-informed and malicious talk about the unholy alliance of Fascism and Bolshevism must stop after the recent categorical declaration from Moscow that the Soviet Government does not propose to extend any military help to Nazi Germany. Smarting under the heavy defeat in the hand of the Russians, the Nazis cannot lay much stock on the non-aggression pact, and their hatred and fear for Bolshevism will compel them to keep a considerable army on the Eastern front which may still become the real front of the war. Therefore, if the Western Powers, particularly France, decide to undertake serious military operations, Germany will be at a disadvantage. Whatever has hitherto happened on the Western front, is no indication of the real relation of forces. When the bulk of the German Army was engaged in Poland, the French could have easily broken through the Western front, if they meant serious business. From the very beginning, the French forces have been concentrated on the weakest sector of German defence. It is evident that any serious operation has until now been avoided purposefully. Germany, on the other hand, is also temporising. The repeated peace offers of the Nazis indicate their weakness. Fragmentary news filtering through the rigid cordon of censorship reveal that the internal conditions of Germany are not at all favourable for a protracted war. Suppressed popular discontent is already breaking out into sporadic outbursts. For all these reasons, it is almost a foregone conclusion that Germany will be defeated if the formally declared war breaks out into a serious military conflict.

The result of a military defeat is also an almost foregone conclusion. The Nazi regime will be overthrown, and that can happen only in consequence of a popular upheaval. In other words, the immediate consequence of the war, should it become a serious affair, will be a revolution in Germany. Whatever may be the desire of the Western Powers in precipitating the present conflict, it may result in the end of Hitlerism. Events take place according to their own logic, and often upset all wishful human calculations. The perspective of the development of the international situation will not be determined by subjective factors which to-day are altogether helpless to stem the tide of predetermined events; it will be determined by the objective potentialities of the situation.

The almost certain immediate consequence of the war is not very likely to remain confined to Germany. Even if it did, that would certainly not be the attainment of the object with which imperialist wars are waged. This is done to weaken one imperialist power or a group of imperialist Powers for the benefit of other imperialist Powers. The object does not include overthrow of rival Imperialisms by a revolution. Yet, that precisely would be the almost inevitable result of this war, even if that undesirable dire consequence could be kept confined to Germany. The triumphant revolution in one country and the consequent rise of a Socialist State have been the nightmare of the capitalist world for these two decades. The repetition of the dreadful event in another important country like Germany would so seriously menace the entire capitalist system of Europe that the immediate consequence, if it were allowed to continue, should be as terrifying to some as welcome to others.

These possible developments were to be anticipated by those acquainted with the dynamics of the European international situation. Therefore, it would be positively insane for the directors of the capitalist States, whether Fascist or "democratic" to have deleberately precipitated a war ruinous for themselves.

The immediate consequence of a serious armed conflict being so very undesirable, not only for the defeated Nazis, but also for the would-be victors, strenuous efforts are sure to be made from both the sides to prevent that dangerous development. While carrying on an interminable wordy warfare and scrupulously avoiding any serious military encounter, all possible avenues for an early cessation of hostilities are being explored through secret diplomacy. At the same time, isolated terrorist acts are being committed on the high seas for cowing the opponent down to submission. Thus, the possibility of an early peace still remains, and it results from the fact that the present war is not a typical imperialist war.

The alternative perspective is the inauguration of the era of wars and revolutions. In that case, the internecine war among capitalist States will before long be converted into the international class war. The revolution in Germany, after the military defeat of the Nazi regime, may not immediately spread to other countries. But the experience of the years immediately following upon the last war will most probably be repeated. Other capitalist States will most certainly try to combat the dreadful phenomenon, in the first place, by trying to set up in the place of the overthrown Nazi regime a counter-revolutionary "democratic" Government, under their protection. The recent success of that strategy in Spain will encourage them to do so. But to-day, the revolution is no longer without military forces of its own. A revolutionary Government in Germany, rising upon the ruins of the Nazi regime, will immediately enter into an alliance with the Russian Soviet Union; as a matter of fact, that will not be a new alliance, but the continuation of the present non-aggression pact. Since the highly mechanised, professional, part of the present German Army will surely support the "democratic" Government which may replacet he Nazi regime in order to arrest the march of democracy to victory, the revolutionary democratic forces, embracing the overwhelming military of the nation, will be able to hold their own only with swift military aid from the Soviet Union. That action on the part of the Soviet Union, undertaken with the object of helping the establishment of democracy in Germany, will be condemned as an "invasion". The military forces of the capitalist States will be rushed to the support of the puppet Government likely to be set up in the place of the present Nazi regime. Germany will be the scene of decisive battles in the international class war. The consequences of that epoch-making event will be determined by the operation of many other factors even outside Europe. But ultimately it will depend on the might of the Red Army and the ability of the Soviet Union to defend the far-flung base of the revolution, while coming to the aid of the forces of democracy in revolt in other countries.

Only in the light of this analysis of the alignment of forces involved in the present European conflict, and also of the alternative lines of possible developments, is it possible to appreciate properly the far-reaching implications of the recent diplomatic and military moves on the part of the Soviet Union. It can be safely assumed that the Soviet policy has been determined by a similar analysis. It represents an approach to the fundamental problems of the contemporary international situation, identical with the above.

Having regard for recent events, in connection with Abyssinia, Spain, Austria, Czecho-Slovakia, the Soviet Government would be the last to believe that the Western Powers at last really wanted to check Nazi aggression just when it would threaten the Soviet Union itself. It was clear to the Soviet Government as well as to all intelligent observers of recent European events that the negotiations for an Anglo-Franco-Soviet anti-aggression pact was meant to be only a threat to the Nazis, so that they might be taught to behave themselves somewhat better. Democratic opinion in England and France had been exasperated by the policy of appeasement. Anti-Fascist spirit had been gaining ground. There was to be a general election in England soon. It was very doubtful whether the electorate would support the appeasement policy which appeared to be so humiliating to the man in the street. For improving its chances in the coming election, the Chamberlain Government had to make an anti-Nazi gesture.

Nevertheless, without any illusion about the real motive of the Western Powers, the Soviet Government readily agreed to be a party to the proposed anti-aggression pact. The Soviet desire was not to revive the bankrupt policy of collective security. The Soviet policy was determined by one consideration : whatever might be the motive of the Western Powers, any move, ostensible or sincere, against Hitlerism should be welcomed and supported. Once the initial step was taken, the Western Powers might be compelled to go much farther than they wished, indeed, possibly to the extent of the overthrow of the Nazi regime. Therefore, it was a very correct policy on the part of the Soviet Union to do everything thereby so that the fateful first step was taken. The projected anti-aggression pact might have served the purpose.

Realising that they might be driven to a real resistance to Nazi aggression, and thereby endanger the very existence of a very useful weapon for preserving capitalist domination, the Western Powers sabotaged the plan. But the first step had already been partially taken. It could not be retraced. Apart from other considerations, the anti-Fascist gesture was indispensable for the exigencies of British home politics. The guarantee was given to Poland knowing fully well that it could not be implemented. That irresponsible act, committed under the pressure of circumstances, nevertheless, encouraged Poland to decide upon resistence. With all their desire to the contrary, the Western Powers presently found themselves in a situation wherein the formal declaration of war upon Nazi Germany was unavoidable. The subjective question of prestige, after all, cannot be altogether excluded from human affairs.

Soviet statesmen and diplomats had anticipated

the alternative lines of development. They were ready to enter the abortive anti-aggression pact for two reasons: firstly for the consideration that it may lead up to the eventual overthrow of the Nazi regime in Germany; secondly, for a purely defensive purpose. If Germany was allowed to overrun Poland, she would presently reach the Soviet frontiers, and her cherished desire to push farther eastwards would certainly not be crossed by the Western Power.

This second, purely defensive, consideration persuaded the Soviet Government to enter into the negotiations for a non-aggression pact with Germany. Having anticipated, thanks to lessons learned from previous experiences, the breakdown of the negotiations with England and France, and German occupation of Poland, which was almost inevitable, the Soviet Government had kept a line of retreat open. As soon as the rejection of its offered military help to Poland rendered the appearance of the Nazi hordes on its frontiers imminent, the Soviet Government fell back upon the prepared line of defensive, and signed the non-aggression pact with Germany. Poland could not be saved; but the Nazi hordes could be kept at a sufficiently long distance from the Soviet frontiers. That was provided for in the pact.

The conclusion of the projected Anglo-Franco-Soviet pact would have committed the Soviet Government to be on the side of imperialist Powers in a possible war. Would that be permissible? The answer cannot be given mechanically, from a superficial view of the problem. The Soviet Policy can be correctly appraised only in view of the outcome of the possible war. If Nazi Germany is almost sure to be defeated, should the war continue under the present alignment of forces, the certainty of her defeat would have been much greater if she had to fight on two fronts. In that case, the overthrow of the Nazi regime would take place in no time. That alone would be an object worth fighting for, whether the Western Powers really desired it or not. There would be no analogy between that war and the previous war against Germany. On that occasion, the defeat of Germany only benefitted the rival group of imperialist Powers. This time, it would mean a revolution in Germany, and that would have its repercussions in other countries also. Moreover, the existence of the Soviet Union guaranteed the triumph of that revolution. That being the case, the Soviet Union was prepared to take sides in a war which objectively was not imperialist; it would be a war which was bound to be the prelude to a great revolution.

While it is true that essentially there is very little difference between Fascism and Imperialism, both being different stages of Capitalism, it is also true that, as the spearhead of the counter-revolution on the offensive, Fascism is more dangerous and, therefore, should be dealt with in the first place. Whatever contributes to its weakening or downfall, advances the cause of democracy and freedom. If by some blunder, or miscalculation, or accident, or under the pressure of circumstances, this or that imperialist Power unwillingly becomes instrumental for the attainment of that purpose, it is perfectly permissible to egg it on by every possible means. The attitude may vary from benevolent neutrality to active support to those involved in a war with Fascism. Any other policy in the given situation would be suicidal. Because, it would decrease the chances of the defeat of Fascism and even go to the extent of indirectly contributing to its victory. One need not shed any tears over the defeat of imperialist Powers. But those intelligently concerned with the cause of democracy and freedom must shrink before the most probable consequence of that defeat. If Germany comes triumphant out of the present conflict, entire Europe will go Fascist. Who dare maintain that it would make no difference for the immediate future of humanity? The evil effects of that misfortune will not remain confined to Europe. An openly Fascist England would certainly be a greater menace to Indian freedom.

The Russian policy, therefore, should serve as the object-lesson for all intelligent and determined fighters for freedom and democracy throughout the world.

While the original policy of Russia was not alliance with Imperialism, the alternative policy is not to support Nazi Germany. Any doubt about the Soviet motive in concluding the non-aggression pact with Germany, was cleared by acts which followed swiftly. Instead of supporting Germany, the Soviet Union has decisively checked Nazi aggression. It has disorganised Fascism as an international force. In other words, single-handed, without firing a shot, the Soviet Government has to a large extent attained the object for which it wanted to ally with the Western democracies, even when these latter refused to enter that alliance. Finally, the Soviet policy has, from the other direction, created an international situation which may yet result in the overthrow of the Nazi regime in Germany. Had the Soviet Union not signed the non-aggression pact with Germany, the international situation might have developed in a very dangerous direction. In that case, Germany most probably would not go beyond occupying the Corridor and Upper Silesia in addition to Danzig. The Munich Conference would have been re-enacted to "recognise the reality of an accomplished fact." The Munich Pact was the logical consequence of the Locarno Treaty. It practically created the united front of all the leading capitalist States, whether Fascist or democratic. Another conference of that nature would have been further consolidation of that united front which can be directed only against one common enemy, namely, the Soviet Union, and freedom and democracy at home. By taking the bold step of concluding the non-aggression pact with Germany, the Soviet Government, on the one hand, broke the Fascist Axis, and, on the other hand, disorganised, at least for the time being, the plan of a counter-revolutionary international united front, just when it was on the point of consumation.

The Soviet policy has put a stop to Nazi expansionism. It has dealt a heavy blow to Nazi prestige; and while doing all that, it has encouraged Nazi Germany to precipitate the war, so long scrupulously avoided, in which she will almost certainly be defeated. Briefly, Soviet policy has determined the downfall of Hitlerism which can now be prevented only by the Western Powers admitting that their belated anti-Nazi crusade was all a bluff. That would discredit their present Governments which would perhaps be driven out of office. So, whatever may be the immediate consequence of the present European conflict, the cause of democracy and freedom stands to gain by it, provided that its supporters are intelligent enough to take a realistic view of affairs and have the boldness to act with cold calculation. They even need not have any originality; with their revolutionary experience, and that of dealing with deceptive capitalist diplomacy, the Russians have shown the way.

While the immediate consequence of the present conflict is bound to be favourable for the cause of freedom and democracy, its supporters must be conscious of the danger ahead. The present international situation may develop directly towards that danger, or there may be an intervening period of preparation. Events will take the latter course if the present conflict can be ended soon. The policy of the Soviet Government seems to favour that course of development. Its definite refusal to give any military help has damped the enthusiasm of the Nazi militarists. What ever the politicians and propagandists may say or desire, in a state of war, the opinion of the Army leaders will prevail. They cannot have much illusion about a swift victory as in Poland, on the Western front. Therefore, they will most probably counsel moderation, and press for peace. Should the fire-eating Nazis insist upon the disastrous adventure, there might be a *coup d'etat* in Germany. By the nature of things, the new Government will gravitate back to the sphere of influence of the Western Powers, particularly England. Nevertheless, again by the nature of things, it is bound to be democratic by profession, and even by formal practice. That would certainly be an improvement upon the present state of affairs in Germany.

Of course, the other side of the picture is dark. The discordant factor of Nazi gansterism eliminated from the delicate international situation, the ground for an *Entente Cordiale* of all the capitalist States will be at last completely cleared. But on the other hand, the Soviet Union will emerge from this crisis very securely entrenched, its diplomatic prestige and military power greater than ever. There will be a breathing space for it to prepare for the imminent last stage of the international class war, and for the forces of revolution in other countries to mature and take up strategic positions from where they can strike most effectively in the next favourable opportunity.

The danger lies in the other, the direct, line of development of the present international crisis. In the beginning, the rulers of the Western countries evinced eagerness to treat the Soviet Union very carefully. It can be assumed that this attitude will be at least outwardly maintained so long as all the efforts for an early termination of hostilities are not exhausted. But the possibility of the war continuing and inevitably developing into a serious affair, is there, and grows greater every day. In that eventuality, the attitude of the Soviet Union will be the decisive factor. The point of view of the| Soviet Union is so very different, that it cannot be understood by the average hard-boiled capitalist statesman or diplomat. They are not able to see that the Soviet Union can never desire that Nazi Germany should come out victorious from a major military conflict. Therefore, they are haunted by the fear of some secret understanding between Germany and the Soviet Union. And at the back of all, there is the largest fear—of Bolshevism sweeping Europe. Therefore, on the pretext of the Soviet Government helping Germany, or "invading" this or that small neighbouring country, which may admirably serve as a base of operation of anti-Soviet forces, eventually war may be declared against Russia. As a matter of fact, prepra-tions with that purpose have already begun.

The consolidation of the Soviet Power all along the Western front from the Gulf of Finland down to the Black Sea could not be prevented. Germany is not in a position to do anything in that respect. The Western Powers cannot put their fingers there. Therefore, the Near East has become the centre of all sorts of diplomatic intrigues. Under pressure, Turkey has been compelled to break off the negotations for a closer alliance with the Soviet Union. British diplomacy has won an important battle on the Bosphorus—with bullets of gold. But against whom are those mysterious diplomatic battles being fought?

The ostensible anxiety is to protect the Balkan States against aggression. Lately, the danger has come from two quarters. Nazi Germany has been extending its influence down the Danube. But there it came up against the ambition of her spiritual ally. Italy, on her part, having found that the Danubian alliance sponsored by her could not successfully check Nazi expansionism, conquered Albania to serve as a new base of operation for penetrating the Balkans. Although the Balkan States came under the hegemony of the Western Powers in consequence of the Versailles Treaty, lately, they have been receiving little protection from that quarter. The German Army was to sweep across Poland down upon Rumania. That movement was effectively checkmated by the Soviet Union. That act on the part of this latter was welcome in the Balkan

States. Russia offered guarantee against aggression to Rumania and Bulgaria. The offer was to be extended to other Balkan States, if they were to enter into an anti-Fascist bloc.

Russian diplomatic moves were open, and were not directed against anybody. Yet, the old bogey of Pan-Slavism was revived as the pretext for diplomatic intrigues in the Near East. Evidently, Fascist Italy stands behind the intrigue, and the Western Powers are playing its game. Mussolini must be definitely detached from the German ally. As bribe he wants his ambition in the Balkans to be satisfied. It seems that the bargain has been closed.

If the Balkan States do not want to pro-tected and would rather be handed by their Western patrons over to the tender mercies of Mussolini, that is their look-out. But the Soviet Union has its own interests to defend. Just as it did not want the German Nazis to establish themselves on its frontier, just so it would not tolerate the Balkan States becoming vassals of Italian Fascism. Having saved Rumania from imminent German invasion, the Soviet Union cannot allow her to be used as a base of operation against itself. Therefore, it wanted to come to an understanding with Turkey, according to which the Straits would be closed to battle-ships in time of war. Great pressure was brought to bear upon Turkey to compel her not to come to an agreement with Russia on that point. Why this insistence to keep the Straits open to battle-ships belonging to belligerent nations. The Black Sea cannot be the scene of any naval operation, unless Russia is a party to the war. Therefore, the insistence could be motivated only with the intention of attacking Russia eventually from the South. None except Russia and Turkey can have any interest in the "freedom" of the Black Sea. The only exceptions are Rumania and Bulgaria, which have a short coast-line. The only plausible pretext for insisting upon keeping the Straits open is to help those Balkan countries in case of aggression. Since the Soviet Union is prepared to offer them the guarantee, they do not stand in need of that hypothetical help from some unknown quarter at a distance, which will most probably not arrive in the hour of need, as has been the bitter experience of Poland. In view of these considerations, the diplomatic intrigues, culminating in the suspension of the Russo-Turkish negotiations, and the hasty conclusion of the Anglo-Frano-Turkish pact, must be regarded as preparations for a possible war against Russia, in which case the attack must be delivered from the South.

The danger lies in that perspective. The strategy of the fighters for freedom and democracy throughout the world must be determined, having due regard for that danger. All along the long Western front, the Soviet Union is practically invulnerable to-day. On the Far East also, it is fairly well-protected. But the southern frontier is still open to attack. It will take still some time to secure it. Precisely for that reason, and in view of the dreadful perspective of the intervention of the Red Army in the imminent international class war in Europe, to involve the Soviet Union in a war along its still undefended frontier would be the cleverest strategy on the part of the present rulers of the world. Once the Soviet Union is so engaged, the quarrel with Nazi Germany will be composed. The long coveted granary of the Ukraine will be offered to the Nazis as the bribe for some concessions in Poland for saving the face of the Western Powers. Japan will naturally pounce upon the opportunity to grab the Eastern part of Siberia.

Immensely strong as it is even to-day, the Soviet Union cannot as yet fight the entire capitalist world on all the three fronts.

Only in the case of that dangerous development will India be directly involved in the war. She will be the base of supply for the military operations against Russia from the South. Even to-day, strenuous efforts are being made to create a psychological atmosphere wherein she could be stampeded to perform that shameful task. The revived bogey of Russian invasion is causing sleepless nights to Indian editors. Mechanically repeating inspired anti-Nazi propaganda, the Indian press carries on a persistent campaign for maligning the Soviet Union by misinterpreting its motives. The danger of the Soviet Union invading India or any of the Asiatic countries is altogether imaginary. It will never happen. But the danger of India becoming a willing partner in a war against the Soviet Union is there. To be alive to that danger, with the firm determination to head it off, is the international responsibility of the fighters for freedom and democracy in India. That is the only contribution that India can make to the creation of a new world order.

Conclusions

The present war is not an imperialist war. Nor is it an anti-Fascist war. Yet, if it continues, the immediate consequence will most probably be the end of Hitlerism, whether the British Government wants that or not. Therefore, it is not permissible for the fighters for democracy and freedom, not only in Europe, but throughout the world, including India, to be indifferent about the outcome of the conflict and its possible developments. Pacifism or dogmatic anti-war propaganda is altogether out of place in the present world situation. No sensible person can talk of freedom and democracy, and at the same time not admit that the fall of Hitlerism and the elimination of the Fascist menace in general will greatly contribute to the triumph of the cause of freedom and democracy. There should be no hesitation in utilising as instriument whoever may happen to serve the purpose. Are we, then, to support Imperialism? The question is altogether irrelevant. Here is an occasion wherein astute fighters for freedom and democracy can push Imperialism perhaps to the extent of destroying the bloodiest weapon of its own creation, and thus rendering itself vulnerable to the coming revolutionary onslaught.

Under the given situation, any movement for war resistance in the countries involved in a war against Hitlerism, even though by accident, will be postively harmful for the cause of democracy and freedom inasmuchas it will reduce the chances of the defeat of Nazi Germany. It would be an entirely different proposition if the resistance could be expected to rise to the level of a revolutionary upheaval. To-day, that possibility does not exist in any one of those countries. The revolutionary forces in those countries, assuming that they are sufficiently powerful, are no better situated to-day than were the revolutionary forces in Central Europe during the years immediately following upon the last war. Even a sufficiently serious outbreak will be easily suppressed. Because, the military forces of the international revolution cannot as yet be made easily available to those countries. That being the case, by far the greater probability is for any such outbreak to provoke the ruling class to discard all democratic pretences and put on the war-paint of Fascism. Not only will Hitlerism be helped indirectly to escape an almost certain defeat, but what is still worse is that Fascism will openly triumph even in the countries to-day engaged unwillingly in a war against Nazi Germany. Every intelligent fighter for freedom and democracy must recoil before such a possibility.

It is evident that, in the present situation, the slogan "Transform the imperialist war into a civil war" has no application. Indeed, the slogan had never anything more than a propagandist value. To-day, the slogan would be altogether misleading, because it is not an imperialist war. In the case of an imperialist war, the result of the conflict is of no concern for revolutionaries. But the result of the present conflict cannot be a matter of indifference. The defeat of one party will undoubtedly promote the cause of freedom and democracy. They need not be perturbed by the incidental victory of the other party, because it is bound to be a pyrrhic victory. Therefore, wherever they are, it is the duty of all the fighters for the cause to make every possible contribution to the defeat of Hitlerism. In this situation, there cannot be a uniform policy for the revolutionaries inside both the camps. The defeat of Hitlerism will be facilitated by internal troubles in Germany. There the perspective of civil war is not remote, and its success is guaranteed to a very large extent by the presence of the decisive factor of the military force of revolution within a striking distance. That is not the case in the countries on the other side. In the first place, internal troubles there will help the Nazi regime in Germany; secondly, civil war (war for national liberation in colonial countries) is not an immediate issue; thirdly, if it breaks out in the near future, the civil war will almost certainly end in a defeat of the forces of revolution. That again will mean triumphant march of Fascism in those countries.

In the countries involved in the war against Germany, directly or indirectly, willingly or obligatorily, the immediate object of the fighters for democracy and freedom is negative, so to say. The defeat of Hitlerism is not to be confounded with the triumph of the rulers of those countries. The concern of far-seeing revolutionaries in those countries is not to do anything which might hinder the defeat of Hitlerism. Therefore, active resistance to war, which, under the given conditions of those countries, cannot develop into a successful revolutionary outbreak, is not to be conclusion: because that will defeat the object of those organising such a resistance.

The analysis of the present international situation leads to one basic conclusion: Contrary to their carefully laid plan, the capitalist States of Europe have involved themselves into an internecine conflict. If it continues, the immediate result most probably will be the destruction of the most dangerous spearhead of international counter-revolution, namely, Fascism. That being the case, in the present juncture, the task of the fighters for human liberation is to do everything to facilitate the consummation of that event which will make of the present European war the prelude to the period of revolutions.

Analysis of the Indian Situation

India is still a part of 'the British Empire. That is the fundamental fact of the situation. No analysis will be correct unless it starts from the recognition of the fact. Any other point of departure will be a wrong approach to the actual problems of the situation, and the result will be necessarily misleading. The dislike for the fact and the desire for changing it do not alter the truth that meanwhile it remains a fact. That being the case, it is entirely meaningless and misleading to talk of India approaching international problems as an independent nation. India is still a subject nation, and while striving for freedom, she can act in the meantime necessarily within the limitations of her political subordination.

The present European war finds India in that position. The immediate problem for the fighters for freedom and democracy in India is to ascertain whether the opportunity afforded by the European conflict can be utilised for securing her freedom. The ultimate outcome of the struggle in India will be conditional upon the strength of the popular forces. Therefore, a realistic estimation of that strength should precede the undertaking of any action in the direction of a decisive struggle for freedom.

In the absence of conditions favourable for a decisive struggle for Indian freedom, to be undertaken immediately, taking advantage of the international situation, the fighters for freedom and democracy in India should work with a long perspective. In that case, they should adjust their political strategy to the analysis of the international situation given in the preceding chapter. The creation in Europe of such a situation as will be favourable for the ultimate triumph of the cause of freedom and democracy will improve the prospects of the struggle for Indian freedom. The revolution in Europe will contribute to the liberation of the Indian people inasmuchas it will seriously threaten the base of Imperialism which keeps India in subjugation. Since the defeat of Hitlerism will promote the cause of revolution in Europe, it will be beneficial also for India; therefore, failing to strike the final blow for Indian freedom immediately, the popular forces in this country should do their utmost to bring about that defeat. How that can be done is the alternative problem for the fighters for democracy and freedom in India.

A realistic appreciation of the strength of the popular forces in India, and of the possibility of its growth in the near future, does not permit any optimism regarding the prospect of striking the decisive blow for freedom, taking advantage of the European conflict.

The given conditions being not favourable for a decisive struggle for freedom in the immediate future, the idea of resisting India's participation in the war is impractical, if not worse. In order to attain the object, resistance must be effective. India cannot be kept out of the war so long as she remains a part of the British Empire. Therefore, to be effective, resistance must go to the extent of ending the imperialist domination of India. Those who are constrained, by regard for the rude realities, of the given situation, to hold the opinion that the popular forces are not strong enough to strike for freedom in the immediate future, therefore, cannot entertain the idea of resistance to India's participation in war.

Resistance for the sake of resistance is not a serious proposition. It may serve the purpose of compelling Imperialism to make some concessions for securing India's willing participation in the war. That sort of resistance is no resistance, but only a bargaining counter. That is neither anti-Imperialism, nor fight for freedom, but a deceptive method of striving for a compromise with Imperialism. Assuming that the resistance will be sufficiently strong, though it may fall short of being successful, the result will be even worse than a compromise with Imperialism. In that case, India will not attain freedom; the ill-advised resistance broken down, imperialist domination will be strengthened. But the repercussion on the international sitution may be very adverse. Hitlerism may be spared the military defeat which is almost sure to-day. In that case, Fascisation of England as well as of France will be an almost foregone conclusion. An openly Fascist England will not improve the conditions in India, who will lie prostrate after her contemplated resistance is broken down.

The strategy of the fighters for freedom in India, however, is to be determined in the first place by the realistic appreciation of the relation of forces in India.

The Princes, who control one-third of the country, as well as the dominating classes throughout the country, are enthusiastic supporters of India's participation in the war. Many of them have declared their readiness to stand by England in whatever she undertakes. By their own social character, these Indian allies of Imperialism are not taking to the war-path to end Hitlerism; nor do they care a straw for democracy. They are interested neither in the future of Poland, nor do they want to help England. They are enthusiastic supporters of India's participation in the war, because of their own interest; they will make profit out of the wholesale massacre.

The Muslim League, the Hindu Mahasabha, the Non-Brahman communal organisations and other minor political groups have disowned the desire to join any resistance. All taken together, they represent a considerable volume of Indian opinion. The danger inherent in the wrong and stupid approach to the communal and minority problems has become acute to-day. It was to be expected that the Muslims and other minority communities, haunted, rightly or wrongly, by the fear of the domination by the Hindu majority, in a critical moment, would be won over by Imperialism, if, in the meantime, their doubts and suspicions were not removed by a bold approach to the problem. Orthodox Hindus stood on the way to such an approach, questioning the sincerity of Muslim Nationalism and actuated by a false notion of democracy. In this critical moment, despite their aggressive nationalism, the orthodox Hindus are also found in the same boat, seeking imperialist protection against the bogey of Muslim invasion, and what is still worse, against the aggressiveness of the minorities belonging to the so-called martial races.

The point is that, in this critical moment, the British Government can count upon the support and co-operation of a considerable section of the Indian people, including those controlling the nation's economy. The relation of forces inside India is obviously not favourable for any struggle with the object of keeping her out of the war.

On a closer examination, the relation is still more unfavourable. India being not situated near the scene of armed hostilities, and not being otherwise directly involved in them, her participation in the war will be all profitable for herself. Not only will the merchants and manufacturers do a prosperous business; the price of agricultural products will rise. It cannot be altogether prevented that at least a small part of that benefit will trickle down to the peasantry. On the other hand, expansion of industry expected to be caused by the demand for military supplies, will not only benefit Indian Capitalism, but will create new employments for workers and cause wages to rise. Thus, making due allowance for war profiteering, and of increased wages being upset by higher prices of foodstuff, there will be a general economic gain, of course distributed unevenly to the different classes. That being the perspective of the immediate results of India's participation in the war, the chances of a general resistance cannot be very bright.

It will be practically impossible to prevent enlistment in the army. Given the wide-spread unemployment among the rural population, there will be a keen competition in the enlistment of, at the most, say, a million men. Another incentive for thousands offering themselves for enlistment is the fact that the salary of an ordinary soldier is higher than the wages of an average rural workman, and the conditions of life in the army are much better than those in the Indian village. Apart from the ordinary soldiers, military training for the educated youth is a very popular demand of Indian nationalism. If that chance is offered, thousands of young men would rally under the colours of British Imperialism. No matter whatever may be their ultimate object, for the moment, the British Government will have plenty of co-operation as regards military services.

That being the case, the possibility of resistance to India's participation in the war hypothetically exists only in so far as the section of the people organised in the Congress is concerned. In relation to the vast bulk of the population, which will be directly or indirectly benefitted by the war, that is not a very impressive force. By checking war profiteering, and by compelling the merchants and manufacturers to allow a part of their profit to go down to the masses, the Government will be able to detach the latter from the Congress. Without a mass support, no resistance can be eflective.

Then, under its present leadership, the Congress does not propose to put up an effective resistance even if it decides on that course. Resistance organised by the Congress, will take place within the principles of Gandhism. Therefore, it will never be allowed to go to the extent of being really dangerous to the Government. Congress resistance will be a bargaining counter. As on previous occasions, it will end in a compromise with the Government. The compromise will strengthen the Government instead of weakening it. Therefore, whatever resistance is possible under the given relation of forces, will not serve the purpose of a real resistance, but will have the contrary effect of consolidating Imperialism with the eventual co-operation of the Congress.

Finally, what are the chances of the oppositional groups inside the Congress and other revolutionary groups organising a resistance, not limited by the prejudices of the official Congress policy? The subjective factor, that is, the desire to resist, may be in operation in that case. But that will not change the relation of forces from today to to-morrow, will not create the objective conditions for an effective resistance. The crowd applauding Mr. Bose's call for direct action is a very uncertain quantity. Besides, Mr. Bose appeals only for Satyagraha. But very few of his admirers will even go to the extent of courting imprisonment. The Communist Party and the Kisan Sabha hold one or two cards which they may be prepared to throw in a hopeless game. They may be able to set in motion the peasantry in certain localities and workers in some industrial areas. But a country-wide general strike appears to be altogether out of the question; and the Kisan Sabha cannot possibly organise a no-rent campaign throughout the country. Moreover, it has also adopted Satyagraha as the method of its struggle, the scope of which must, therefore, be restricted by the limitations of that method. No rent campaign is a form of Satyagraha. Of course, it has greater potentialities, which cannot assert themselves within the limits of the Gandhist principles. If resistance, organised by the Kishan Sabha, develops in that direction, the result will be isolated peasant revolts to be suppressed easily.

Organisational position is the decisive factor. There does not exist as yet a political party with a mass basis. The Congress is not a political party in the proper sense of the term. It is still rather a movement,–very largely. It has the potentiality of developing into a revolutionary political party of the popular masses. It is in the process of development in that direction. Meanwhile, it is broken up into a primitively organised amorphous mass and a rigid machinery of leadership which does not approve of the objectively revolutionary urge of the movement. Consequently, the large membership of the Congress is not an organised force. Very largely, they are not even politically conscious. The overwhelming majority of them do not participate in any political activity. The masses forming the periphery of the primitive organisation of the Congress are still more backward in every respect. The leadership, on the other hand, does not represent the consciously revolutionary vanguard of the movement. It is composed of politically innocent humanitarians, utopian social reformers, wild-eyed romanticists, with a numerous contingent of opportunists and reformists. On the whole, it is guided more by the concern for reactionary interests than by any ideal of popular freedom. Whatever organisation there is, it has lately degenerated into an election machinery and agency of ministerialist propaganda.

Two years and more of ministerialism has spread reformist illusions far and wide, down to the ranks of the Congress. Whatever real fighting spirit there ever was, has been systematically discouraged during this time, and the masses have been exhorted by Congressmen high and low to expect salvation from the legislative achievements of the Ministers of the Imperialist State. The benefit of Congressmen accepting office, in the form of political education of the masses derived from their own experience, and of organisational consolidation on that foundation, has been reaped only partially, thanks to the tireless activity of the comparatively small bands of consciously revolutionary Congressmen working in the teeth of persistent opposition and obstruction, not only from the organisational machinery at the service of Ministerialism, but also from the misguided, romantic, pseudo-leftists.

Under these conditions, the Congress as a whole could not possibly be a fighting mass organisation. Even as a movement, it has been stagnant. Yet, it is the only weapon accessible to the popular masses for the moment. But before it can be serviceable for them, it must be freed from its rustiness and rehabilitated so as to become a properly organised political party. Meanwhile, no serious struggle is possible and any effort in that direction is bound to be a dangerous misadventure.

If the Congress is so weak organisationally, other political groups are practically negligible. The Muslim League has of late secured a mass following which is temporarily more combative. But organisationally the League remains only a coterie of leaders who are either convinced reactionaries or playing a mischievous role for spiting the Congress. In any case, there is little chance of freeing the Muslim masses from the League leadership so that they may be drawn into a revolutionary struggle in the immediate future.

The non-Muslim peasantry remains spellbound by the name of the Mahatma, and, through that semi-religious sentiment, under the moral domination of the Congress. Wherever the lessons of Congressmen accepting office could be driven home, the most elementary consciousness is just dawning among the peasantry. But still they can be moved to any action only in the name and authority of the Congress. Local Congress organisations, systematically promoting the political consciousness of the peasant masses and thus preparing them for planned revolutionary action, are, however, still exceptions to the rule of lower Congress Committees existing only in name. The work for building them up as local organs of mass struggle, spear-heads of a maturing popular upheaval, is done only by a comparatively few, scattered all over the vast country. Swimming against the powerful currents of popular inertia, fostered by the persistent propaganda of blind faith, hostility of those in control of the organisational machinery, and handicapped by the lack of means, the small, but growing, band of Radical Congressmen is making headway. Meanwhile, the organisational control of the Congress as a whole remains still in the hands of people who do not want it to grow as a formidable weapon for revolutionary struggle. No serious popular movement, on a sufficiently large scale, is possible except in the name of the Congress. And, by and large, the Congress still remains in the control of a leadership which does not want any such movement. That is the fundamental fact of the situation.

There remains the industrial working class which, to a large extent, stands outside the ambit of Congress control. But the larger part of the sector in that position is under reformist leadership, politically more anti-revolutionary than the Congress leadership. The smaller part under revolutionary leadership may be moved to action but in this vast country it is too insignificant to make any mark. Assuming that it can act as the determined, consciously revolutionary, vanguard of the popular movement, it can do nothing until the masses are mobilised in the struggle and have come under its influence. That is not the case. There is absolutely no reason to believe that a political strike by the workers of Bombay or Cawnpore will be the signal for a mass upheaval througout the country. If the vanguard makes the mistake of striking before the army is marshalled in proper position, it will only destroy itself in a vain struggle which may be very heroic. Besides, it is a matter of doubt what is the extent of political consciousness even of the advanced section of the working class. Readiness to strike for economic or other immediate issues is not necessarily the indication of that.

That is the estimate of the power and position of the popular forces at the present moment. Wishful thinking may mislead some to a different conclusion. But such false optimism is dangerous, and therefore must be discouraged.

Conclusions.

1. Under the given relation of forces, India's participation in the war cannot be prevented.

2. Neither from the point of view of the international situation nor for the interests of Indian freedom is it necessary to do that; nor is it possible to do so in view of the fact that the great bulk of the Indian people stand to be benefitted, immediately more or less by India's participation in war. If the possibility was there, India could make her contribution to the solution of the international problem by striking a decisive blow for

her own freedom. But the conditions necessary for that decisive struggle are woefully absent.

3. There is no desire for serious resistence on the part of any major political organisation.

4. The Congaess may be forced to make a show of resistence, but, in pursuance of the predetermined policy of its present leaders, it will come to some imperialism no with imperialism at the earliest available opportunity.

5. Being organisationally weak, and having discouraged the fighting spirit of the masses by spreading illusions about the possibilities of ministerialism, the Congress is not in a position to organise any effective resistence, even if it wanted to.

6. Satyagraha, even in the form of mass Civil Disobedience, is useless as a method of effective resistence. Just as on previous occasions, it is bound to end in a collapse or compromise which will strengthen imperialism.

7. The oppositional groups inside the Congress or other political parties do not possess the organised mass basis indispensable for one to assume the leadership of a popular movement.

8. Under these circumstances, resistence, either by the Congress officially or by any opposi-

tional group, will seriously jeopardise the future of India's struggle for freedom.

II

WORLD CRISIS

SPEECHES BY M. N. ROY

during the discussion on the international situation in the Radical Summer Camp for Political Study, Dehradun, May 24, 1940

There is a difference of opinion regarding the character of the war. In our last C. E. C. meeting, we had a very thorough discussion on this point and came to a generally agreed decision which is formulated in our publication "India and War." Later on, our characterisation of the war was questioned by others; as far as I know, there is some doubt in this respect even among our own comrades. Our publication "India and War" leaves no room for doubt. Yet, since there appears to be some doubt, we shall have to raise, and once again answer, the question: Is it an imperialist war?

The next point to be discussed is the general

characterisation of the international situation. Our fundamental thesis on this point is that everything taking place in the international field recently is preparation for the international class war. The result of our analysis of the international situation is this: The dominating and determining factor is the conflict between two systems, a rising system, represented by the Union of Socialist Soviet Republics, and a decaying system, represented by the Fascists as well as the so-called democratic Powers. But the relations have been so very confused, and so many apparently inexplicable events have taken place, especially since the conclusion of the non-aggression pact between the Soviet Union and Germany, that this thesis of ours seems to have become untenable.

Many people do not approach the international situation from our point of view. It is natural for them to have doubts regarding the relation between Germany and the Soviet Union, or between the Soviet Union and England, or between England and Germany. We could have neglected their opinion in our discussion, if there was no confusion even among our own comrades. We have always maintained that all capitalist

Powers, Fascist or so-called democratic alike, are united among themselves for a war against the Soviet Union. But today, they are divided into two camps; they are actually fighting. On the other hand, there is a strange relation between one of these groups and the Soviet Union. In this situation, how can we still maintain the thesis that the world is divided only into two camps—revolutionary and counter-revolutionary? That question seems to be bothering some of our comrades. I shall answer it.

Every event on the international scene can still be interpreted according to our thesis. Whatever has happened since our last C. E. C. meeting is not unexpected for us. The Soviet-German non-aggression pact was concluded before the publication of our thesis. We had said and written at length to explain the cause and the real significance of the pact. In a number of public speeches, I have shown that the Soviet Union alone pursues a consistent and effective anti-Fascist policy. I have nothing to add. New events have taken place since then; but it is not difficult to fit them into the scheme of the development of the international situation as we visualise it. Therefore, unless some comrade states the reason why our thesis had become untenable, I need not say anything more on that point now.

Another conclusion was that it is an epoch of wars and revolutions. The wars waged in this epoch are neither imperialist wars nor nationalist wars. They all are symptoms of acute crisis of a decayed system. They are convulsions of death. They are bound to lead up to a period of revolutionary upheavals. As a matter of fact, looked at from a broader point of view, the world entered into the period of wars and revolutions already with the last great war. Only in one country, revolution triumphed immediately. In a number of other countries, it was defeated. But since then, the crisis of the decayed capitalist system aggravated. The most outstanding expression of that aggravation is the rise of Fascism. The present armed conflict therefore is to be regarded as a new and more acute outburst of that crisis.

We also characterised the present war as an internecine war in the camp of counter-revolution. If we have learned our Marxism thoroughly, we should not at all be surprised. It will not at all be difficult to explain this phenomenon of a fierce struggle inside the camp which is united as against revolution. If there was no internal conflict, the camp of counter-revolution would be so very powerful that there would be no chance for a revolution to succeed. The chance of success results from the very fact that the international unity of counter-revolution is constantly being impaired by the contradictions within the camp itself.

Another point on which doubts have been expressed, is the Soviet foreign policy. When we met last to discuss the international situation, there was not yet so much doubt on this score. The Soviet-German non-aggreesion pact had been signed. The Polish war was nearly over. But since then, another event occurred, the so-called invasion of Finland which perplexed even many friends of the Soviet Union, and aroused doubts in the minds of many, perhaps even among ourselves. I had occasion to speak on this subject repeatedly. A very lengthy speech on the Soviet foreign policy appeared in the Congress Special of the 'Independent India'. Again, I must say that, on this point too, I have nothing more to add. I do not find any difficulty in explaining the Soviet foreign policy. It is perfectly consistent with the principles of the Soviet regime. It is determined at every step by the needs for the development of the world revolution.

Now we come to what is perhaps the most serious point. A superficial study of our publication "India and War" may make the impression that we were certain of the conflict in Europe not developing into a war as it has actually done, of the Fascist and other Powers coming to some understanding before long, and of the Anti-Soviet united front being established in the near future. Any such categorical statement about the possible perspective of a situation would be wrong. But I would advise you to read the book more carefully, and you will find that we have not produced such a non-Marxist document. Marxism does not permit any categorical statement. While examining a situation, we may say that this or that thing appears to be the most likely to happen, so very probably that it can be expected to take place almost certainly. But at the same time, we must keep in mind all the other possible and probable alternative lines of development. Our analysis of the internationl situation was strictly guided by this Marxist approach to problems. The immediate perspective visualised in our thesis may appear to have been mistaken, but who would dispute that in the long run the relation of international forces is bound to develop that way? Certinly no Marxist.

The main contention was that neither the Fascist Powers nor the other Powers wanted this war. The contention was based upon an examination of the facts of the situation. But at the same time, we also said that, when neighbouring countries armed themselves to the teeth and carried on jingoist propaganda against each other, there was always occasion for provocation, and any small frontier incident might lead to a war. We also proved, not as a matter of theory, but as a point of fact, that the Polish war did break out as an accident like that. We have been ridiculed for this contention. But anybody who maintains that the Marxist reading of history rules out all accident is no Marxist. Marxism does not preach predestination. There is a world of difference between historical determinism and heological predetermination. As long as we do not claim perfect knowledge, we cannot rule out accidents. We cannot predict all possible events, unless we know everything that exists in the world. No Marxist would claim omniscience.

Indeed, for us, this war was not exactly an

accident. But it was an accident for the belligerents. They were playing with fire; suddenly, the spark went off, and the war broke out. That being the case, it was quite reasonable to expect them to make all efforts to retrieve the step which none of them wanted to take. They had not wanted the war; it was very obvious why they did not want it. Both of them would be the losers, and the laughing third would be the forces of revolution. We should not believe that we are the only clever people in the world. To underestimate the intelligence of the enemy is dangerous. We did not do that. Therefore, we anticipated an early termination of hostilities. But an early termination need not necessarily mean within six months. Moreover, we did visualise the alternative possibility. On the basis of our thesis, it was also provided in the resolution what would be our line of action in case the war would go on and break out in all seriousness. So, it is clear that the present development of the international situation was anticipated by us. We have not been taken unawares. Only, we thought that an early settlement was more probable than the development of the conflict into a serious war. Even now we shall have to see how serious it will really be.

Another impression seems to be that we anticipated, in case of a serious war, a speedy defeat of Fascism and a victory of the other Powers. That again is not a correct impression. We only maintained that a victory of Fascism would be harmful for the cause of revolution, and therefore its defeat was desirable. But now here it is stated that the desirable was certainly going to happen. The impression results from our analysis of the relative strength of the two groups in the camp of counter-revolution. We were of the opinion that, in case of a real conflict, the Fascist powers were more likely to lose ultimately. I am still of that opinion. In spite of Holland, Belgium, Norway and Denmark, I am still of the opinion that the Fascist Powers are going to be defeated ultimately, if the other Powers will definitely throw in their whole weight and carry on this war, now that it has broken out, with the determination to win. Not that I feel that the world will be lost if England and France are defeated. But greater issues are at stake. However, I shall stop here, and wait for your questions to be answered at the end of the discussion. But I request you to deal only with facts.

Many have been puzzled by the Norwegian

campaign. I wonder what conclusion you have drawn from it. It also goes to substantiate our thesis. Norway was the last victim of the appeasement policy. She was sacrificed for avoiding a wholesale conflagration. If you have any doubts, I can only refer you to the facts mentioned during the recent debate in the House of Commons. From them it is clear that England could have prevented the German occupation of Norway, if she really wanted.

Those and many other points must be discussed before we come to the conclusion that our reading of the international situation was wrong, and should therefore be revised. I am of the opinion that our reading of the international situation was quite correct, and our thesis does not need any revision. Consequently, as regards our policy in India, in connection with the internationl situation, the general principles adopted in our last meeting of the C. E. C. are sound and hold good even to-day.

Now it has become a matter of practical politics. The international conflict has developed into a first class war, which we did not expect to be the most likely to happen. We thought that an early conclusion of peace was more likely. But the less likely, though not the unexpected, has happened. At that time, our plan of action was made according to the opinion that an early settlement was more likely to take place. Our plan of action to-day has to be readjusted slightly in that respect. But I would request you to bear in mind that, in the earlier part of our discussion, we are dealing only with the international situation. Its repercussion on the Indian situation should not be discussed now. We shall do that more fruitfully once we have made a proper appreciation of the international situation.

However, by way of initiating the debate, I might say a few words also in that connection. Although we thought an early settlement to be more likely, our resolution on "India and War" did not overlook the alternative perspective of a protracted war. Analysing the Indian situation, we came to the conclusion that, situated as we are to-day, we are not in a position to resist In dia's forcible participation in the war. We also came to the conclusion that, by far the larger part of the Indian population would be, more or less, benefitted by India's participation in the war. The business people are making profit; there is a great boom for India industries. Those amassing fortunes from war profiteering control the press and mould public opinion. Practically everybody today wants India's participation in the war. The Congressmen are not excepted. They are only bargaining.

All this goes to prove that our forecast was not wrong. It is a fact that India is not losing anything by her participation in the war, forcible or otherwise. Therefore, we came to the conclusion that India's participation in the war could not be prevented. We pointed out that, even if the Congress officially decided to resist war, it would not succeed, because the majority of the Indian population expected to be benefitted, more or less, at least for the moment. We also expressed the opinion that, on principle, war resistance is not a revolutionary policy. I am still of that opinion. War resistance can be an ideal only for those who believe that war as such is an evil. War resistance is a pacifist slogan, not a revolutionary act. Then, in India, our task is not to resist war, but to win our freedom. The pseudo-revolutionary cry of war resistance has actually succeeded in pushing our main task, namely the fight for freedom, to the background. We put it into its proper place. We said that our task is not to resist the war, but to win our freedom. The question of the moment was how to promote our fight for freedom under the conditions of war. Therefore, we dismissed the idea of war resistance and took up the problem of of how to prepare for taking advantage of the opportunity.

By analysing the forces, we discovered that India was not in a position to undertake any offensive. Therefore, our plan of action was to prepare those forces, so as not to dissipate them on an ineffective war resistance; to lie low under the storm and prepare the forces, so that, when in course of a year or two, the opportunity may come, we shall be ready to do what we cannot do to-day. Unfortunately, the opportunity may come before we are ready. In that case, it will go over our head. Suppose that the Germans occupy Paris, London is bombarded, the Governments of those countries totter, what can we possibly do in India? We need not have any love for France or England; but if entire Europe goes Fascist, what do we gain? Already Fascism is raising its head everywhere. We have more of it here in India than you can imagine. Fascist tendencies have been growing remarkably. Fascism is inherent in the nationalist ideology. I pointed out the danger already many years ago. But a Fascist movement as a political force cannot develop without State protection. In India, to be popular, Fascism must appear as nationalism. It can easily manage that. But the difficulty is that an imperialist State cannot patronise an Indian nationalist movement. That difficulty may disappear soon. A "National Government" established upon British Imperialism recognising Indian independence will be a Fascist regime. Otherwise, the recognition will never come simply for asking.

To-day, that is the alarming perspective of the Indian situation. But no use being desperate. We must think. Although the situation appears almost hopeless, what can be done to save it? We knew what was coming. We knew what preparations were necessary. We indicated the way; but those guiding our destinies, would not pay any heed to our advice. The opportunity is almost there, and we are not prepared. Even to-day, we know what should be done; but the swift march of events may find us helpless. Confronted with the spectre of Fascism instead of freedom, let us concentrate our discussion on the question; What now? What can be possibly done?

Concluding Speech by M. N. Roy

The immediate purpose of the present discussion is to make a correct estimate of the possibilities of the present international situation, in order to determine what should be the proper thing for us to do in this country. You will permit me a few introductory remarks about a subject dealt with recently in an editorial of the 'Independent India.' I mean, the tyranny of words. In that editorial, we pointed out that the political life of of our country is tyrannised by a number of words and set phrases. Sometimes, we allow ourselves to be tyrannised by words of our own making. In this discussion, that has happened. Some comrades have tried to find profound theoretical justification for their fascination for certain words. In that sense, the discussion may have been an enjoyable intellectual gymnastic. I would like to hear Safdar, for example, pound his theory of accidentalism, which must have intrigued you all. The proposition that every law expresses itself through an accident is not very easily understood. The matter of fact statement that the present war broke out in consequence of unexpected events has privoded a good deal of discussion, which sounded very philosophical. The concept of accident was the point at issue. Believing in historical determinism, we naturally agree regarding the philosophical concept of accident. But, for the moment, we are not engaged in philosophies. Our purpose is to clear a point of fact. Similarly, many other propositions have been made, for instance, about monopoly and its relation to the export capital, etc., which could be discussed for intellectual entertainment as well as for our practical guidance. But they also have no direct bearing upon the immediate causes and the possible consequences of the present international conflict. Therefore, let us turn to more practical propositions. We are restricted by time. And the German army is marching.

Nevertheless, a few more introductory remarks will be helpful for clearing the atmosphere. The name does not precede a thing. Names are given to certain ideas or things. We have been talking so much about the imperialist war. The last war has come to be known as an imperialist war. But it should be remembered that the name was given to it more than two years after it started. To-day, we use the term as if it had been incorporated in the English vocabulary ever since the language was created. The name has no function, unless it das some connection with the thing bearing it. It takes some time before all the characteristics of a new thing are known. Therefore, a name cannot be invented as a thing happens. In the beginning, all sorts of names were given to the last war. It was called the Great War, the world war, and finally, the imperialist war. All those terms have found place in language.

The present war is a new thing. Whoever disputes that proposition, simply ignores the most essential feature of the international situation. Even if we leave other considerations apart, the existence of the Soviet Union must be regarded as a decisive factor in the present international situation. That factor makes the relation of international forces to-day very much different from that obtaining in 1914. This fact must necessarily make the character of the present war different from the last war.

Our approach to the problems under discussion should be more practical, more pragmatic, than abstractly theoretical. To be fruitful, our study should of course take place on the background of certain theoretical principles deduced from previous experience. But confusion is created by raising prejudices and preconceived ideas to the dignity of theories. The last war was the greatest war known until then. It created such a terrific impression on us that we cannot think of a great armed conflict except as its repetition, perhaps on a larger scale. The last war was an imperialist war; the present war is equally fierce, destructive and bad; therefore, it is also an imperialist war. The term expresses disapproval. Therefore, it is so very popular with anti-imperialist fighters. But that is simplifying things. Emotions or preconceived nations are not reliable guides for a scientific study. There was a great war twenty years ago. It has come to be known as an imperialist war. The simplest way of characterising the present war is to compare it with the last war.

We did not prefer to simplify the matter. We wanted to have a close look at the thing, before we gave it a name. We were very cautious. Our definition is negative. We are of the opinion that the present war is not an imperialist war. That is to say, it is not of the same kind as the last war. A new child is born. It is not an ordinary child. We are gradually getting acquainted with this new monster; in course of time, a suitable name will be found to express the positive characteristics of the present war, which are still to be discovered in detail. All its characteristics may not be yet known. Our definition, therefore, is strictly scientific. we have not been dogmatic. We have compared this war with the wars of the past. We have found it to be a new type of war. Therefore, we have not affixed to it a familiar, but unsuitable, label. If that is not a scientific method, Comrade Pramanik must teach us. To recognise our ignorance, is inherent in the spirit of science. If there is a new phenomenon, we admit at first that we do not know it. Then, by and by, we find out its characteristics and name the thing accordingly. So did we exactly with this war. We found out certain features, and from them concluded that such and such would most probably be its results.

Such expressions as "I do not like that term," "if it is not an imperialist war, then it must be an anti-imperialist war", so on and so forth, used in course of the discussion, only show that we are being tyrannised by certain words which have become prejudices. Imperialist war is a fashionable term. Yesterday, I ridiculed the habit of using the term 'bourgeois' as an abuse. The term 'imperialist' is also used in the same unscientific sense. We do not like this war, therefore, we give it a bad name. A fashionable phrase is repeated parrot-like, and that is being done with a scientific pretension. The war is there. Its causes are known. Its consequences can also be imagined. We have described it, and thereby made a contribution to naming it eventually. The object of the present discussion is to find out whether our analysis is correct or not. It is more important to deal with the thing than with the name. Let us understand the thing; the suitable name will automatically suggest itself.

We are studying the international situation. The outstanding feature of the present international situation is a gigantic armed conflict. Hence, the necessity of correctly characterising the war. Two-hundred years ago, a war in Europe might have gone on for years, and we might not have bothered about it here in India. Today, we cannot take that attitude, because the war will have its repercussions in India. We may have to play a part in it. We must examine the scene to find our place in it. How do we fit into it? If it is an imperialist war, I would be entirely indifferent, and would not care to spend so much time in discussing it. Incidentally, it may be pointed out that none of those, who talk so much about it, know exactly what is an imperialist war. Nobody has ever defined it precisely. However, an imperialist war, as we understand it, is an armed conflict between two imperialist States or groups of such States, with the object of thriving at the cost of one or the other. If the present war was like that, its outcome would have no meaning for us. It would be a conflict between Anglo-French and German Imperialisms, and whatever may be the outcome, we would not be very much affected What difference does it make if English Imperialism is victorious? The fact that we are so very interested in this war, and so much concerned about its outcome, the fact that we believe that the outcome of this war is going to be a life-and-death question for us, as for the rest of the world, is enough reason for us to free ourselves from the tyranny of the fashionable phrase 'Imperialist War'. If Germany loses, England will be strengthened; we don't want that. The average nationalist looks at the situation that way. But it is not as simple as all that. People, who claim to be more than selfish nationalists, and pretend to be vitally interested in the affairs of the world, cannot take up such a prejudiced attitude.

But for the sake of argument, let us take up that attitude. I would ask you to look at the other side. If England loses, Nazi Germany will win. The worst form of reaction will be established in Europe, and before long dominate the whole world. What guarantee is there that India will become an oasis of freedom and a new order in the midst of the desert of a world reaction? Nationalist narrow-mindedness and the slavish attitude of spitefulness lurk behind all these theoretical prompensities, with which the present war is called an imperialist war. On the other hand, you cannot call this war an imperialist war, and remain indifferent. If it is an imperialist war, and as such bound to be harmful for the cause of freedom, it is your duty to oppose the war. There has been no objection to our rejection of the idea of war resistance. Therefore, all this hair-splitting about our characterisation of the war is simple squeamishness.

There cannot be any doubt and much less confusion about our thesis. This or that part of it cannot be picked out for criticism. It is a rigidly logical construction. You must either accept the whole, or reject the whole. It is possible that the entire thesis is wrong. In that case, prove it to be so, and let us reject it. There are certain premises based on indisputable facts and generally accepted principles. Logical conclusions are deduced from them. No criticism can have any force, unless it is shown that the premises are wrong. The case for any revision will be proved only by showing that. There is no question of theory. It is all a matter of facts. The last war as well as the present war have been described. The description makes it evident that there is a difference between the two. I cannot help that. Nobody has invented it. If the facts do not fit into a theory, we need not immediately jump to the conclusion that the theory has been falsified. There may be something wrong with your understanding of the theory. It is due to that misunderstanding that some of you have been quarrelling with facts, on the authority of what you believe to be the purest form of the theory.

The term 'imperialist war' is a derivation from the concept of imperialism. What is an imperialist war ? The last war was called an imperialist war, because it was a war between two groups of imperialist Powers. If any war waged simply for an expansionist purpose is an imperialist war, then, a war like the Boer War should also be called an imperialist war. With such a view, one would find imperialist wars waged even before the rise of modern imperialism. All the wars waged for the conquest of colonies since the Spanish invasion of America must then be called imperialist wars. But that can hardly be called a scientific view.

Apart from decisive theoretical considerations, an imperialist war in the strict sense is an inter-imperialist war. That standard should be applied for characterising the present war. The fundamental question, therefore, is: Are the two groups of States involved in this conflict imperialist in the same sense, assuming that Fascism is a form of imperialism ? This question again leads to the yet more fundamental question: What is imperialism ?

A definition is given in our thesis. I do not say that it is an exhaustive definition. It might be made more comprehensive. It is true that imperialism is more than the export of capital; there is a counter-part to it, namely, the conditions in the colonial countries. Nevertheless, it must be generally admitted that export of capital is the foundation of modern capitalism. That is its most characteristic feature. So, we shall have to find out whether this fundamental characteristic of modern imperialism is possessed equally by both the parties in the present conflict. Safdar has dealt with the theoretical aspect of the thing. But, after all, theory also does not precede facts. We observe the facts first, and then we construct a theory for the sake of the economy of thought. Whatever may be its internal structure, primarily imperialism expresses the expansionist urge of capitalism. Certain forces grow inside a highly developed country which create the expansionist urge. The characteristic feature of normal capitalism is expansion of production. Imperialism is the expansion of capitalism—on a larger scale and on a broader basis. So long as capitalist expansion takes place within national boundaries, it remains simple capitalism. When it operates on the international scale, capitalism becomes imperialism.

Expansionism as such is not new. It is very old. But in different periods, the urge to expand was brought about by different causes. Beginning from the great migrations of the pre-historic time, expansionism has assumed different forms in succeeding periods of history. Everyone of those forms was determined by causes of different natures. There were the old-world empires which represented also urge for expansion. But there is a great difference between that expansion and modern imperialist expansion. As scientists, we should have the objectivity and courage to recognise imperialism as an agency of civilisation. That would not be very far from the truth. The scientist should accord that distinction even to the Roman and other empires of the antiquity, as well as to the mediaeval empires. In a scientific analysis, terms should not be used for expressing approval or disapproval. They must indicate objective truths.

When we talk of the export of capital, one may think that a certain country possesses a heap of gold which is shipped to another country. It is not so simple as that. India has a large stock of gold, and she is free to export it. But that would not make her an imperialist country. As a matter of fact, she has of late been exporting gold. It is nonsense to say that it is a drain.

None could compel the possessors of the stock of gold to sell it, if they did not want to part with it. They have been selling gold, because it is profitable.

Export of gold is not export of capital. The export of capital takes place through the expansion of trade. Capitalist production expands in a country; more goods are produced than can be sold at home at a profit. The surplus production must be exported to other countries. Gradually, not only the surplus is disposed of, but there takes place an expansion of the production of commodities for export.. When a country exports manufactured commodities, to be exchanged with products containing more labour power, the export of capital begins. England sends to India two crores rupees worth of manufactured goods. They are sold. The raw material necessary for manufacturing an equal, or even a larger, amount of goods could be bought for less. The balance does not go back to England. It is invested in India for the purpose of developing the means of transportation, for instance, so that trade can reach more distant parts of the country, and new sources of raw matarial be opened and become more easily and cheaply available.

Export of capital means export of commodities. A country which has attained that expansionist state, in which it can export manufactured commodities, is in a position to export capital. When, for the investment of that capital, its owners acquire privileged positions in foreign countries, they become standard-bearers of imperialism. Their country, then, is called an imperialist country. Before the last war, Germany was such a country. England had attained that status much earlier, and consequently occupied most of the privileged positions. There was competition between the two, the older imperialist Power and the newcomer. That was not the ordinary capitalist competition. It was a competition for monopoly. Export of capital is conditiona upon the mono-expolist control of foreign markets. Powers exporting commodities acquire political rights in other countries, where their surplus export is invested as capital. Those rights allow them to control the market in those countries, so that they are given the most privileged position in every respect.

After the last war, Germany ceased to be such an imperialist State, because the exports could no longer be the medium for the investment of capital abroad on the basis of a monopoly market. The payment of war reparations absorbed all her exports. Indeed, German capital, exported before the war, had to be written off on account of reparations. The foundation of German imperialism was thus blasted. Because it produced that result the last war was an imperialist war. It aggrandised some imperialist Powers at the cost of other imperialist Powers.

Later on, Germany recovered her position and again attained a stage which looked like a new development towards imperialism. But in the meantime, there had appeared a new phenomenon in Germany. It was Fascism. That was not an accident. There must have been some reason for Fascism to grow in Germany and not in France, for example. As a matter of fact, Fascist tendencies did manifest themselves also in France as well as in England. But there, they did not develop as in Germany. The story of the growth of Fascism, under what circumstances it triumphed in Germany, is now well known. Fascism was forged as the weapon for the defence of capitalism in decay. The defeat in the last war not only destroyed German imperialism; the economic clauses of the Versailles

Treaty rendered it impossible for Germany to live even on the basis of normal capitalist production. A highly developed country cannot live in a perpetual crisis. Post-War Germany represented the danger of revolution, which actually broke out more than once, and, if successful, was sure to spread in other countries. Therefore, the victorious Powers assured the German ruling class support for defeating the revolution. But a disrupted economic system cannot be stabilised by suppressing the forces of revolution. And so long as the economic crisis continues, the forces of revolution remain in operation, threatening to break out again and again. Therefore, a standing instrument for combating the perennial danger of revolution becomes necessary in a situation created in Germany in consequence of the last war. Hence the rise and triumph of Fascism there. This has been more or less known all along; but lately, the cause of the rise of Fascism has been revealed from the most authoritative quarter.

One of the greatest German capitalists, Fritz Thyssen, has the other day informed the world that, ever since 1923, he together with his colleagues, financed and patronised the Fascist movement under Hitler. After the revolutionary crisis of 1923, Germany recovered her position; capitalist production could continue; but it was realised before long that economic expansion could not take place on the basis of normal capitalist relations. If that was possible, Fascism would not be necessary. The advent of Fascism showed that in Germany the conditions for normal expansion of production were no longer there. In other words, the foundation of imperialism was absent.

Those are matters of fact. Now, let us turn to consider the position theoretically. The fundamental principle of capitalist economy is laissez-faire: produce as much as you like; buy and sell wherever you like; no restriction of any kind; the laws of supply and demand are supposed to keep the balance. On the contrary, the fundamental principle of Fascist economy is autarchy—self-containedness. That necessarily means restriction of consumption which, in its turn, retards production. Thus, in a way, Fascism indeed is the anti-thesis of capitalism. Therefore, Fascist economy cannot be the foundation of imperialism. Imperialism is conditional upon expanding capitalist production. Of course, Germany is still a capitalist country. But Fascism is capitalism in the throes of death. Both England and Germany are capitalist countries; but they represent two distinct phases of capitalism. That being the case, it is wrong to characterise Fascist Germany as an imperialist State in the strict sense of the term. It is a Fascist State. If there is no distinction, why use a different name? Consequently, the present war is not an imperialist war, if that term means a war between two imperialist Powers. In spite of all the factual and theoretical considerations, if you still prefer to call it an imperialist war, then, don't claim to be expounding a more scientific theory than that of our thesis. You have a popular notion of imperialism, and you prefer the term 'imperialist' as a matter of fashion. Strictly speaking, an imperialist war is an inter-imperialist war. The present war is certainly not of that type. It is not an inter-imperialist war. In characterising a phenomenon, all its causes must be taken into consideration. This war has been precipitated by Fascism. That fact must determine its character. In so far as Fascism is not imperialism, it is not an imperialist war in the scientific sense.

So much about the fashionable term 'imperialist war'. Before I pass on to the next point, I wish to remind you once again of the determining factor. Theorising is all right. But here we are meeting also as political workers. Therefore, the character of the war must be determined pragmatically as well as theoretically. If it is an imperialist war, we should be indifferent to it. What do we care if one or the other imperialist State is defeated? But who will call himself a Socialist, and yet would say that he is indifferent whether Fascist Germany wins this war or not. Anybody who says that he would welcome the victory of Fascist Germany, whatever may be his reason, is a counter-revolutionary, even if he has read all the volumes of Marx. Only a counter-revolutionary can welcome the victory of Fascism.

Now the term 'accident'. The doubt on this score also will be dispelled by a careful reading of our thesis. Indeed, it is not necessary to read the whole document. Read only the two or three relevant sentences. The word 'accident' does not occur in the most decisive passage. The expression used there is 'a new type of war'. Firstly, we define what is an imperialist war; then we give a description of the background of the present war. It is clear therefrom that the present war has not been brought about by the causes known to be associated with imperialist wars. It is nowhere said that we believe in accidents, or that we believe in things happening without a cause. It is only said that causes like that of the last war are absent in the case of the present war. What, then, are the causes of this new war? It being a new kind of phenomenon, we do not dogmatise. We simply say that the armed conflict did not take place of necessity, but was brought about by a fortuitous combination of circumstances. What is unscientific in that view? Having pointed out that the backgrond of the new conflict was not such as headed necessarily towards an armed clash, the following statement is made: "But when neighbouring countries are armed to the teeth, and are in the midst of a perennial economic crisis, jingoist nationalism may serve as a safety-valve, and armed conflicts of more or less serious nature may be precipitated by any chance event or by some unfortunate miscalculation." That is the fundamental sentence.

We depicted the specific features of an imperialist war, and then gave a description of the post-war period. The two pictures do not tally. Having discovered that the present war has not been brought about by similar causes as in the case of the last, we looked for its peculiar causes. No apparent cause was to be found. On the contrary, there were distinct and persistent efforts to avoid a clash. What were we, then, to say when the clash did nevertheless take place. There having been no deliberate intention or necessity, the armed clash must have been precipitated by some chance or miscalculation. That statement cannot be disputed, except by proving that the present war was planned. In order to do that, you have to dispute known facts. You must give us an entirely new reading of post-war history. You shall have to explain why America threw tons of money into Germany; why the Dawes Plan was adopted; why successively, by one measure after another, the Versailles Treaty was scrapped by the victorious Powers; why the French General Staff allowed General von Seeckt to create an army under their very nose; and how the successive acts of aggression of Hitler were tolerated. You shall have to prove that, when Hitler militarised the Rhineland, France and England could not have stopped it; that the invasion of Austria and Czecho-Slovakia could not be prevented; you shall have to prove that the Munich Pact was a necessity.

If there was a plan, it was to avoid the conflict. The existence of such a plan is the decisive factor, and gives an entirely different character to the present war. We must call a thing by its proper name. The word 'accident' is correctly used. All the facts of the situation are against the contrary view. This is an internecine war. You can challenge the deduction only by proving that the analysis is wrong. And since the analysis is based on facts, you have to disprove the facts. Therefore, all the criticisms of our thesis, and particularly the contention that this is an imperialist war, have no force. To prove your contention and to back up any demand for a revision of our thesis, it is not enough to say that you disapprove of this war, and therefore the term 'imperialist war' is more suitable.

It is true that war is inherent in Fascism. In that sense, the war was planned by Germany. But it is known that Germany also was anxious to avoid the war. Moreover, Nazi Germany is not an imperialist country in the sense we have defined imperialism. Fascist Germany, not being an imperialist country, could not have planned the war with an imperialist purpose. Hers was a predatory purpose. But any predatory war cannot be called an imperialist war, if we do not wish to be indiscriminate in the choice of terms.

By saying that the war has been caused by an accident, we mean that an unforeseen event precipitated it, frustrating all the efforts to avoid it. Our thesis is: "Since the present conflict is not the outcome of a premeditated plan, it must have broken out owing to some accidental cause." The murder of the Austrian Archduke at Serajevo, upon which the last war broke out, was also not anticipated; therefore, it was also an accident. Nevertheless, in the case of the last war, a plan heading towards it can be traced ever since 1901. The accident at Serajevo could be fitted into that plan; it just served the purpose of bringing the plan to the climax. But the sudden events in Poland, upon which the present war broke out, cannot be fitted into the scheme of appeasement which was the fundamental feature of European politics, ever since 1924. The plan in this case was to avoid war at all cost. In pursuance of that plan, concession after concession was made to the Fascists. The latter, on their part, pursued a policy of blackmail, being encouraged by the appeasement diplomacy. Experience led them to believe that, at the last moment, they would always be allowed to get off with something. They were also not deliberately precipitating an armed conflict. They were simply bluffing. Therefore, the sudden outbreak of the war cannot be fitted into the scheme of European politics. It was precipitated by an unforeseen cause which, being not a part of the plan, must be called an accident. That is quite scientific.

Official documents have been published since our thesis was written. In addition to those published, the British Government was going to issue another White Paper. It was to contain so many scandalous informations about the break-down of the Moscow negotiations, that, at the last moment, the Government decided to with-hold it, on the ground that it contained such matters as should not be published for the sake of public interest. Some of those documents have been included in a book entitled "Why This War", written by an authoritative English publicist.

We maintain that the war broke out owing to an accidental combination of circumstances,

One may ask: How do we know that the war was not wanted ? Perhaps Hitler wanted it. Such speculation is idle when we do know that Hitler's policy has all along been blackmail. It is also known that, in critical moments, the German General Staff did not want the war. Now we have the weighty and conclusive evidence of Fritz Thyssen. He broke with Hitler, and left Germany, because he was against the war with Poland. The creator and the highest patron of Fascism himself did not want the war. Fascism is an instrument created by German capitalism. If German capitalism did not want the war, how could Hitler act so rashly at a critical moment ? There is a reason to that.

This brings me to the interesting and intriguing point raised by Comrade Tarkunde, namely, the possibility of a metamorphosis of Fascism. In support of this hypothesis, he mentioned the flight of Thyssen. But we must not confound capitalism with individual capitalists. Dr. Thyssen goes; his property is confiscated. But the property remains private. To-day, it belongs perhaps to Goering, who is now one of the rechest men in the world. So, there has been no attack on private property as such, even if big capitalists have been victimised. There has been no involuntary trend towards socialisation, under the pressure of the contradictions of Nazi economy. No Socialist would maintain that Fascism can desire such a transformation. That incredible contention would imply an entirely different characterisation of Fascism, an entirely different view of its genesis. The only conceivable possibility is that of an unavoidable development, however, is not towards socialisation, but monopoly. Monopoly or even State capitalism, when the social basis of the State does not change, should not be confounded with any tendency of auto-transformation into Socialism. That confusion would lead to the belief in the possibility of capitalism gradually transforming itself into Socialism. The characteristic features of Fascist economy, pointed out by Comrade Tarkunde as the basis for his hypothesis, are the crass expressions of a tendency to be traced in the most highly developed capitalist economy. That tendency, born of the contradictions of capitalism, pragmatically proves the necessity of Socialism. Imperialsm is the safety-valve against that danger. When that device is not available, the danger must be otherwise combated. The tendency towards Socialism must be suppressed for the preservation of capitalism. Fascism is the instrument for that suppression.

In Nazi Germany, private property is only changing hands, from one group of capitalists to another group. One group of capitalists created Fascism, hoping that, upon its establishment, the situation would be restored for the normal operation of capitalism. One may create one's own nemesis. One group of capitalists may be killed or driven out, but only for another group to rise and make profit. Too much need not be made of the fact that a number of big capitalists have been driven out of Nazi Germany. For one thing, others remain, and new ones have grown. Secondly, it should be remembered that, already six years ago, two years after Hitler's rise to power, the original Socialist tendency in the Nazi Party was stamped out through the murder of the representatives of that tendency. Gregor Strasser, who represented the "Socialist" trend of National-Socialism, was assassinated as for back as 1934. The advocates of the "second revolution" were eliminated at the behest of the capitalist patrons of the Nazi party. Thyssen goes only in 1940. If some of its original patrons are to-day falling out with the Hitler regime, that does not indicate any trend towards Socialism. Hitlerism liberated itself from the handicap of its original Socialist demagogy already six years ago. As Fascism is by no means Socialism, just so it is not simple capitalism. It is Fascism, quite a peculiar form of capitalism. If one group of capitalists does not like its manifestations in the long run, another group will adjust itself and profit by them.

Let us now return to the point of fact. The flight of Thyssen proves this. A powerful group of German capitalists created the Nazi movement, placed Hitler in power and themselves remained the dominating factor behind the new regime. They not want this war. Hitler could not have done it without their consent. A war may be precipitated by the rashness of a dictator, but it cannot be planned over a number of years, except with the consent of those controlling the economic life of a country, and thereby dictating State policy. Thyssen and his group were for remilitarisation of Germany; firstly, because flourishing armament trade enabled them to overcome the industrial crisis; secondly, the

Nazi regime must be firmly established as a powerful bulwark against the danger of revolution; and thirdly, under the threat of war, international disputes could be settled in favour of the German ruling class. The conclusion from this analysis of the relation of forces in Germany is that the present war was planned neither from the one side nor from the other. Both prepared for it, but none wanted it. Both tried to avoid it until the very last moment.

There is still another reason for our being carried away by this idea of imperialist war. After all, there is a psychological reason for Indians to be pro-German. The enemy of our enemy is naturally regarded as friend. Indian revolutionaries were pro-German during the last war, when there was nothing to choose between the imperialist Powers. Since then, many of them have become Marxists; yet, even some amongst these latter have not ceased to be pro-German. They have swallowed the propaganda that England was throttling and encircling Germany and would not give her the necessary "Lebensraum". Some superficial observers divided the European Powers into "haves" and "have-nots". Germany was placed in the latter category, and her claim to get something out of the pocket of the "haves" was regarded as legitimate.

Germany was a very decent country until 1928. All the economic development, for which many are inclined to admire the Nazi regime, took place during that time, before Fascism came to power, and without any colonies. Because Germany suddenly demanded colonies, she is now called an imperialist country. The Nazi doctrine of living space, however, is not an imperialist doctrine. It is nationalist jingoism. After the advent of Fascism, German industries were built upon the basis of war production. Thyssen and others like him did not want war. They made enormous profits in the beginning. Germany could not sell sufficient goods, in the world market; the home market had contracted in consequence of the upper classes having passed on the burden of war preparations to the masses. The post-war currency inflation had ruined the middle-class. The home market for consumers' goods could be expanded by reducing capitalist profit, so as to increase the purchasing capacity of the masses through higher wages and lower prices. That the capitalists did not want.

Therefore, nationalist jingoism was fomented as the means for overcoming the crisis of German capitalism. It quickened the production of war materials. The entire industrial machinery was set in motion. Metal and chemical industries not only flourished, but began to expand. The Fascist State subsidised them. The entire national income, for two generations, was mortgaged for the purpose. The Fascist State is the administrator of capitalism, based upon war industry. Older capitalists, like Thyssen and others, feared that the whole artificial structure would crash in the face of a large-scale war. Therefore, they were against it. But the war machine, once created, must move in its fatal course. The new type of Fascist capitalists, like Goering, has grown out of the process of building up an economic system based upon war industry. They control the State now. There has been expropriation, but capitalism has not been abolished. Only, the new type of capitalism (fully Fascist economy) is altogether anti-social.

Once the big army, with its huge armaments, was created, it had to be put to some use. Otherwise, it would be frozen capital. There is a saying that one can do everything with a bayonet except sit on it. Therefore, once a huge army is created, there must be war. The reason for its existence must be proved. As soon as neighbouring countries are armed to the teeth, there is pressure from the militarists to start a war. Antagonisms are always there, to provoke one. The people do not want the war. The more clever section of the ruling class may also shrink at the dreadful possibility of a defeat. They may prefer to make profit out of peace. But the professionals are there. War is their trade. They have been given wonderful arms which are supposed to perform miracles. They are eager to see how the miracle works. Therefore, while emphasising the fundamental trend of appeasement politics, at the same time, we pointed out that, since Europe had become a powder-magazine, any spark might cause a conflagration upsetting the whole appeasement apple-cart. But such unexpected causes were not part of a plan; they ran counter to the whole scheme of appeasement politics. Therefore, we are of the opinion that the fundameatal feature of an imperialist war is absent in the case of the present war.

All this has been said in our thesis. I have

read any number of books on the present international situation. Without the slightest desire to exaggerate, I consider our thesis to be the most scientific analysis. It is a historical document. It is bound to be recognised as such by all who understand anything about world affairs. But some of you are ashamed, because it is not said there that it is an imperialist war. It is such a fine document; why not embellish it by introducing the fashionable term? That seems to be the substance of all the arguments advanced by way of criticising the thesis. But we are not composing an essay with conventional phrases. We want a scientific analysis of the situation. And we have made it.

Having proved that this war was not planned or wanted by anybody, (except by the irresponsible professionals), and that it broke out in spite of all efforts to prevent it, we wrote: "This sort of war, however, is not an imperialist war; it is an internecine war." Comrade Pramanik thinks that the term internecine is not scientific. It seems that he does not know the meaning of the word. Someone has helped him by pointing out that an internecine war is a mutually destructive war. Who would say that it is not? Our definition may not be very scientific according to Comrade Prmanik's idea of science. But it is certainly very accurate. We said further: "Such a war is bound to be waged half-heartedly, both the parties striving for an early settlement." The war still continues; so, our analysis was false. Please read the next sentence: "It is an internecine conflict, precipitated by an accident or a miscalculation. While the probability of its continuing is not altogether excluded, and even if it is fought until one of the parties is defeated, it is not a typical imperialist war." The direct conclusion from our analysis was that since nobody wanted the war, they might have the commonsense to end it as soon as possible. But we also saw the possibility that, once it had really broken out, the war might continue.

But why has there been no early peace? If they all wanted peace, why has it not been concluded? It is known to all close observers of events that, even when the war broke out, and even after it had been going on for some time, Anglo-French imperialism did not abandon the old policy of appeasement. Poland went; still they sat tight without doing anything on the Western front. Why did not Germany also sit tight? In the beginning, after the Polish compaign, Germany also acted that way. But the economic blockade was tightening. On the other hand, the Allies also could not wait and watch indefinitely. That game went on for six months. War had been declared, but did not break out. In that kind of war, Germany would have broken down eventually. The Nazis did not believe that in such an eventuality the Russians would come to their aid. If Molotov had really said, and meant it, that there was no fundamental difference between Nazi Germany and Soviet Russia, he should be expelled from the Communist International, and be the accused in the next Moscow Trial. In fact, even when war continued, the Nazis expected Chamberlain to perform yet another feat of appeasement and recognise the German conquest of Poland also as an accomplished fact. But meanwhile, it had become a matter of prestige. Both sides waited for the other to say something. As long as nothing serious happened, nobody was in a hurry. But Germany began to feel the pinch; the terror of the economic blockade tightening compelled the Nazis to act.

I may say a few words about the relative military strengths of the belligerent parties. The military strengths of a Power to-day ultimately depends on the economic resources. That has always been so. But to-day, it is more so, because the war is more destructive. The actual military strength of a country—its army and armaments—do not represent all its potentialities. The ability to re-equip the army recurringly represents the real strength of a country. For that, a country must not only have highly developed industries, but also an inexhaustible source of raw material available. Germany does not possess the raw materials necessary for armament industries. She possesses rich coal deposits, but not such essential things as rubber and certain metals. Even the right kind of iron is not available to her in a sufficient quantity. Yet, steel is the foundation of armament industries. Germany has laid in stores. But the stores are not inexhaustible, if they cannot be continuously replenished, either through manufacture at home or import from abroad. case of a large-scale operation, the stores, however great, would be used up in no time. Moreover, even that insufficient storage of raw materials for the armament industry was a great handicap for the expansion of German capitalism.

After the war, the German exports had to go in for the payment of reparations, and later on, for raw materials required for the war industries. On the fundamental point of the ability to re-equip, Germany is weak. The German army may be strong enough to overrun Norway, Holland and Belgium, and perhaps even France. But in a long-drawn war, Germany will be the weaker side, and be defeated sooner or later. All these considerations contributed to the theory of "Blitzkrieg"—the lightning war. It is the decided opinion of German military experts that, in a major war, if Germany cannot win within three months, she will be defeated. As to resources, the newly acquired territories—Austria, Czecho-Slovakia and Poland—do not produce the kind of iron needed for armament industry. Such essential metals as copper and aluminium are not available anywhere. Rubber does not grow in Europe. Then, there is petroleum, a free supply of which vital material is not within the reach of Germany. Without copper and aluminium, aeroplanes cannot be built, and without petroleum they cannot operate. Through her occupation of Poland, Germany has secured access to some petroleum deposits. But that also is very largely at the mercy of Soviet Russia. Moreover, the kind of petroleum available from those sources is not quite suitable for the purposes requiring high-class fuel. So, even after overrunning the larger part of Europe, Nazi Germany is still not in a position to carry on a prolonged war.

Aggression farther eastwards would have brought Germany out of the difficulty. The "Lebensraum" really hankered after by the Nazis was the Ukraine and the Don Basin. There, iron and petroleum in endless quantities would be available, and the Ukraine is the granary of Europe. Someone to-day remarked that Russia was responsible for this war. Such an opinion should not be held by anyone amongst ourselves. The result of the Soviet-German non-aggression pact was that Germany had to give up the hope of acquiring the grains of the Ukraine, the iron of the Don Basin and the petroleum of the Caucasus.

The frustration of their plan of aggression eastwards compelled the Nazis to turn in the other direction. The object of the Norwegian campaign was not to prepare for an invasion of England. It was to keep free the route to the only other source of iron supply. That was in the north of Sweden. Even there, a free sea route must be found. The Baltic is frozen in the winter, and always at the mercy of the U. S. S. R. The other route is along the Norwegian coast, which must be cleared so as to serve as the base for German submarines to keep British battleships away. That was the reason for the occupation of Norway.

The German anxiety to establish themselves in the north of Sweden also explains the suddenness of the Finnish War. The Soviet Union knew that the North was to be a battle-field. Given a real friendship between Russia and Germany, the Germans need not have the Scandinavian campaign at all. But they did not trust Russia to leave the Baltic route open for them. The Russians, on their side, did not like the "Allies" to come too close to the Soviet frontier. They knew that Finland would willingly come under the influence of the Nazis, once they were established in the northern part of Sweden. That, among others, was the reason which compelled the Soviet Government to undertake military operations against Finland, when the Government of that country refused to come to a friendly understanding.

If the British Government really thought that

the invasion of Norway was a move directed against England, it could have been easily checked. The British Navy could have cut off the German line of communication across the Skagerrak and isolated the German forces in Norway. It was not done on the ground that that would have been too risky for British ships. After all, the ships are made for war, and was is a risky venture. Presumably, the British Government did not think that it was worthwhile to risk the British Navy to frustrate the German plan of occupying Norway. The British troops were withdrawn from Trondheim and Norway was thrown to the wolves. But a desperate effort was made to hold the iron ore port of Narvik. That point, however, was even of greater importance for Germany. If Narvik could not be captured, the whole Norwegian campaign would be in vain. One adventure compelled the Nazis to launch another. They were compelled to attack Holland and Belgium, so that the British Navy would be needed nearer home and thus relieve the north of Norway. A possible settlement even after the Norwegian campaign was prevented by the German need for desperate action with the purpose of having the access to the source of iron supply free.

Some of you seem to think that even to-day people make wars like the Rajput King; that the Nazis have, for some reason or other, made up their mind to invade England and they are bent upon that venture, no matter what happens. But why should they invade England? To-day, wars are very costly. Therefore, no Government would under take one just for fun or out of sheer perversity. To invade England, guarded by the most powerful Navy, is an exteremely risky proposition. One should not launch upon that adventure, unless it was a matter of life and death. A free supply of iron is essential for Germany, if the war continues for long. The British blockade puts her in great difficulty in that respect. But she has now access to the Swedish field. What does, then, Germany want from the conquest of England? The occupation of Holland and Denmark relieves her somewhat as regards food supply. In Belgium, there are rich coal mines and a highly developed iron industry. Having occupied all these positions of vantage, conquest of Britain is completely pointless for the Nazis. The motive behind all these moves is to deal a crushing blow which would force the Allies to make an early peace. The Nazis strike wildly here and there with the hope for an early peace. If the war continues, they are bound to be defeated. Therefore, even when their military adventure is in full swing, the Nazis are still striving for a settlement. But the perspective of peace now has become entirely different from what it was just after the outbreak of the war. Indead, it is dreadful to think of it now. We wanted an early peace before things reached the present stage. Someone asked, why should we regard this war as a calamity. I do regard it as such. Because for the moment it appears that the Nazis are going to win. Perhaps to-morrow we shall wake up to read that the Germans are in Paris. Every morning, I open the newspaper with a shudder. I have no love for imperialist France or Britain. But I cannot think of the possibility of the Fascisation of Europe without horror. The rise of Fascism in Germany delayed the revolution for at least a generation. If Fascism succeeds in establishing its domination over the whole of Europe, then good-bye to revolution and good-bye to Indian freedom as well.

There are politicians and capitalists in France who would welcome the Nazi invaders. Daladier was pro-Nazi when he became Prime Minister. Even the new Reynaud Cabinet includes a member of the Fascist party, which until now is an insignificant factor outwardly, in the French political life. How ever, a blood-brother of Hilter is sitting in the French Cabinet even to-day. And what of the Chamberlain School in England ? Who guarantees that even Churchill and his supporters will not soon realise that it takes a thief to catch a thief, and that for fighting with the Fascists you must be a Fascist yourself, just as you must be a Fascist in order to live in peace with the Facsists. A victory of Hilter over France and England would mean the establishment of outspoken Fascist regimes in those countries. There will be a Fascist peace. France may begin, and England may follow soon. Ever since 1924, there have been persistent efforts to organise a European Bloc against the Soviet Union. England took the lead. If Hitler wins, that counter-revolutionary bloc is bound to be formed; only, it will be organised under the leadership of Nazi Germany. On the basis of a Fascist peace, Germany will then return for "Lebensraum" towards the East, with England and France backing her up.

That is the new perspective. Is it not dreadful ? At the time of our last C. E. C.

meeting, we visualised also this possibility of events developing this way. Therefore, we wanted the war to stop, before the situation was aggravated. We were not moved by any pacifist consideration. At that time, a peace would have been restoration of the status quo with the position of the U. S. S. R. greatly strengthened, and the Nazi plan of expansion eastwards effectively checked. Now, the situation is altogether different. Now, peace will mean the Fascisation of Europe. Therefore, the war must go on. And to guarantee that, the fighters for freedom throughout the world must participate in it, so that an eventual defeat of Fascism will still be brought about.

There are other reasons for dreading an early peace which would be a Fascist peace. But that is the spectre which haunts us to-day. Previously, the things were not yet so very dangerous. They did not appear to be heading towards a calamity of such a magnitude. Nevertheless, we did visualise the danger. When the war started, the Soviet Union stayed out. Efforts were still made for a reconciliation in the capitalist camp. On the other hand, there was an effort to involve Russia in the warn on the pretext of the Soviet-

German non-aggression pact. The Indian nationalist press contributed largely to those efforts. It was the loudest in demanded "Red Imperialism" and practically demanded that England should declare war on Soviet Russia. If the war developed, there was danger for the Soviet Union to get involved. She was not yet in a position to defend her southern frontier. Attacked there, she might have been unable to hold her own. We would not have been in a position as yet to prevent India's being used as the base of an attack against the Soviet Union. Indeed, the Indian upper classes, including many Congressmen, would welcome that "holy crusade" and participate in it enthusiastically. Evidently, to prevent that was the duty of all revolutionaries. We tried to do so by advocating an early peace. But with all its professions of non-violence and advocacy of world peace, the Congress would not appeal to the world for peace.

Having analysed the European situation, having seen the various perspectives of possible developments, not unmidful of the development which has actually taken place, (see "India and War", Chapter 'Dangers Ahead'), we came to the conclusion that the present war was not an imperialist war. We came to the further conclusion that we could not be indifferent to it. Pacifism or dogmatic anti-war propaganda is out of question now. We wrote: "No sensible person can talk of freedom and democracy, and at the same time not admit that the fall of Hitlerism and the elimination of the Fascist menace in general will greatly contribute to the triumph of the cause of freedom and democracy. There should he no hesitation in utilising as instruments whoever may happen to serve the purpose. Are we, then, to support imperialism? The question is altogether irrelevant. Here is an occasion wherein astute fighters for freedom and democracy can push imperialism perhaps to the extent of destroying the bloodiest weapon of its own creation, and thus rendering itself vulnerable to the coming revolutionary onslaught."

The fundamentale principl which should guide us in framing our plan of action even in the changed situation to-day remain the same. Perhaps it will have to be differently applied. Safdar has given you a strong dose of dialectics. I will give you a lighter one, so that you might not choke. Who told you that, to wish for the defeat of Fascism, means to wish for the victory of imperialism ? A subconscious fear confuses your thoughts. We want the defeat of Fascism, because we are revolutionaries, because we know that the defeat of Fascism will weaken imperialism. Just think for a moment: What is going to happen, if Fascism is victorious ? A situation would be created, in which the forces of revolution throughout the world will be suppressed, and the cause of our Indian freedom will be also jeopardised. Therefore, we do not want Fascism to be victorious. If we really want Fascism to be destroyed, why should we not do anything and everything to bring about its destruction ? Don't run away with the idea that the Soviet Union is helping Nazi Germany. The Soviet policy is to give the Nazis a rope long enough to hang themselves. The so-called Russian support to Germany is actually hastening the fall of Fascism.

I maintain that our analysis of the international situation was correct. In our thesis, we gave a true picture of the international situation. We did anticipate what has happened. Because we did, we thought that a desperate effort should be made to prevent it. We could not prevent it. We knew the right way. But we could not persuade others to take to it. We are not to be blamed for the short-sightedness and stupidity of others. In any case, the credit of finding the right way belongs to us. We have the conviction that we can see ahead. If we can keep that confidence, and are not swept away by the tyranny of words, by the desire to live up to the standards set by the prejudices of others, we may still get out of this difficult situation. Having that purpose, we can only repeat the proposal we made to the Working Committee at the out break of the war. There is no other way. We cannot do anything else. We do not propose to defend India for British Imperialism. All these considerations are not matters of intellectual gymnastics, but of practical politics. It is a matter of life and death.

PART TWO

LOOK BEYOND THE NOSE

Before this appears in print, the Working Committee will have met and prepared the resolution to be endorsed by the All-India Congress Committee. In the absence of any response from the side of the Government to the gesture made in the Delhi resolution, no substantial change can be expected in the attitude of the Congress Working Committee. Is this diplomatic haggling a wise policy in a highly critical situation like the present? This attitude, taken up, for no other serious reason than a morbid concern for prestige, is fraught with great dangers.

What will happen if the desired gesture does not come from the side of the Government? The best possible consequence will be continuation of the stalemate, which is no stalemate at all in so far as India's participation in the war is concerned. Whatever may be the attitude of the Congress, Indian resources will continue to be available for Imperialism. The Congress has not been able to prevent that. It will not be able to do so even if it decides upon active resistance. The pseudo-moral attitude that the Congress does not wish to embarrass England, while she is engaged in a serious conflict, is only a face-saving device. The fact is that the Congress is not in a position to do so, even if it wanted. The defects of the present leadership has rendered it incapable of any effective action. Therefore, the continuation of the stalemate will only mean greater political inactivity, and the consequent disintegration of the Congress and demoralisation of the struggle for freedom as a whole. What can be done under the present situation to avoid the calamity? That is the question for the All-India Congress Committee.

A waiting game will be worse than useless. That should be evident from a proper understanding of the present international situation. Some may argue: Let us wait and watch the progress of the struggle between Great Britain and Germany. The argument is based on the hope that, in course of time, the British Government will be compelled to pay the price demanded for Congress co-operation. That hope, in its turn, is based on the belief that the war is bound to continue indefinitely, and England will be having the worse of it. That is a false reading of the international situation, and consequently the hope is groundless. If the perspective really was disappearance of Imperialism, the fighters for Indian freedom would have no cause for the slightest concern. But that is not the perspective. At least, there is an alternative perspective which appears to be more likely, for the moment. It is the Fascisation of England, in order to avoid a defeat. Will that increase the chances of Indian freedom ?

But let us take the less likely perspective, that of the war continuing until a possible defeat for England. In that case also, India will not be automatically free. The British Government or other forces in Great Britain have little to do for keeping India in her present political state. The forces, which hold India in political subjugation, are on the spot and they are very largely of native origin, England's defeat in the war, even to the extent of a German occupation, would not, therefore, directly weaken India's bondage. Great Britain might go; she may be Nazified or be occupied by Hitler's hordes; but that will not mean disappearance of Imperialism, as far as India is concerned. The forces of Imperialism being present in India, she will continue in her political subjugation. So, let us give up the fond hope of freedom falling in our hands as a ripe fruit. Moreover, it is not very moral to expect freedom out of the enslavemnnt and misery of the English people. Such an expectation is a feature of slave mentality.

The continuation of the present Congress policy of ineffectively playing the dog in the manger will only increase the already great chances of India remaining under Imperialism, even after the problematical defeat of England. Imperialism is an impersonal system. It knows no patriotism. It has no home. Like the cuckoo, it lays its eggs in other's nest. It has feathered its nest in India. It will not have the slightest scruple to leave England to her fate and make a new home in India. The position of the Franch colonies is an object lesson. The fall of Frence has not liquidated French Imperialism. The French imperial regime has not been liquidated, or even seriously weakened in any one of the French colonies. If that yet happens, the consequence will be only a change of masters.

Liberation can never come by default. Is there any reason to believe that it will be different in the case of India ? Imperialism can hold its own in India, with the aid of native allies, without any help from outside. The present Congress policy, if continued, will contribute to the consolidation of Imperialism in India. It will help Imperialism to entrench itself in *this* country.

The possibility of the British rulers of India deserting the mother-country as a sinking ship and living in this country, high and dry, is not altogether imaginary. We have already drawn attention to the fact of pronounced Fascist sympathy among the so-called Anglo-Indians, official and non-official. They must regard this war as a quixotic crusade. They are fully in sympathy with the Chamberlain School at home which may still bring about peace on the basis of a Nazified England. Should the politicians at home go ahead with the war, they may cut adrift, to free themselves from unnecessary obligations. That is the perspective of India acting as an "Independent Nation"! Only that will be not national independence of India but independence of Imperialism with a base in India.

This perspective has been pointed out from no

less reliable a quarter than the "Statesman". Having quoted the First Lord of the Admiralty pleading that "final victory will be much shorter if we continue to hold these islands," the Calcutta journal appeals that "our Civil Service hierachy in this country will mark, learn and inwardly digest" the above remark. Evidently, the dangerous tendency, revealted by the "Statesmen's" appeal, is not unknown to the British politicians. The tendency is not to be very much concerned with the fate of England.

Having learned from a reliable source that that tendency is shared by the British rulers of India, it should not be difficult to surmise the result of the policy of 'wait and see'. It will be a definite establishment of the Civil Service Raj with a pronounced Fascist characteristic. The position of those would-be "independent" imperialist rulers of India is being consolidated by the present policy of the Congress leadership. While not doing any harm to Imperialism, this policy is actually preparing the ground for India to have a taste of Fascism.

The "Statesman" further writes: "There is a spirit plainly visible in certain quarters, both official and non-official, which argues that only this summer matters. If that were so, there is little that we in this country can do ....We are in any case dependent on the shipping available for anything we can send to Britain. So, there are others, also expecting the possible defeat of England, and are preparing themselves for that eventuality. But if the eventuality will ever come, the Congress leaders will not be invited to join a 'National Government', but will be sent to the concentration camps, unless they would welcome the Fascisation of Imperialism as the new order of their dream.

Now, let us turn to the other, more likely, perspective—that of an early peace. That will mean voluntary Fascisation of England. The forces working in that direction are not negligible in England. Chamberlain still controls the Conservative Party with its overwhelming majority in the House of Commons. The Conservative Party, in its turn, is controlled by the powerful men of the City, who have all along been very obliging patrons of Hitler and Mussolini.

War is a profitable business; but if it goes on indefinitely, it becomes ruinous as well. It is quite possible for England to hold out indefinitely. The invasion of England is not a practical proposition. But large-scale air bombardment and more or less effective interference with overseas trade will greatly upset the advantages of war profiteering. Therefore, those who control the economic life of Great Britain naturally are not at all favourable to the idea of an indefinite war. Then, what is it all about ? It has become completely pointless—for them. If German invasion of England is an impractical proposition, the plan of England, with the problematical American aid, freeing the European Continent from the grip of Fascism is equally, if not more, impractical. The Nazis, at least for the time being, will be satisfied with the position they have captured in Europe. Letely, their propaganda is being carried on with the purpose of strengthening the hands of those in England who desire an early termination of the conflict. If they are left with the domination of Europe, they would not interfere with the British Empire. They cannot do much in that respect anyhow.

On all these grounds, the real rulers of England are striving to bring about an early conclusion of the present conflict. They have nothing against Fascism as such. They do not want its destruction. On the contrary, they would just as soon introduce it at home. Everywhere, it has proved to be a very useful instrument for the defence of capitalism in decay. It should be equally useful in England as well. So, the more likely perspective of the present international situation is a complete or partial Nazification of England, which will continue to be the centre of the British Empire. Will the prospect of Indian freedom be brighter in that situation? Again, the prospect is not of National Government but of concentration camps for all the fighters for freedom.

Either perspective being dangerous for India, the task of the fighter for Indian freedom is to prevent its consummation. The question: Can we do it? is no argument. A supreme effort must be made. Nothing more than that can be done in the given situation. The alternative policy of 'wait and watch' is defeatism, and is bound to end in a disaster.

There are genuinely anti-Fascist forces in Britain. Not only the very numerous working class, but a growing number of others are also seriously alarmed by the spectre of the breakdown of modern civilisation. To strengthen the position of those genuinely anti-Fascist forces in

England, is obviously the duty of the fighters for freedom in India. Some of the former may still think in terms of Imperialism. But, in course of an active co-operation against the common enemy, the relation of forces may change. Who would deny that the prospect of Indian freedom will be brighter if the genuinely anti-Fascist forces in Britain can overwhelm the reactionary clique which dictates British policy to-day?

The continuation of the war will differentiate forces in Britain. Only the politically blind would fail to welcome that development and yet talk of their abbhorrence for Fascism, undying hostility to Imperialism, and of the "New Order." Those, who are waiting for a generous response from Britain, or for the recognition by Britain of India's freedom, should know that their expectation may be fulfilled only in the case of such a development in England. If you really wish the liquidation of Imperialism, don't be satisfied with preaching the Sermon on the Mount. Come down on this earth of complex realities, and contribute to the crystallisation of the forces which may bring about that result. It is not for fighting Fascism in Europe, or for helping Imperialism, that the advocates of

Indian freedom should take up a positive and realistic position in the scheme of the affairs of the contemporary world. They must do so for promoting their own immediate purpose. If they do not know how that can be done, they are misfits and are not capable of leading the Indian people in these fateful days.

(*"Independent India," July 28, 1940*)

WHY WE SUPPORT THE WAR

By Ellen Roy

The case of those opposed to India's participation in the war is based upon the argument that although the war is said to be waged for protecting freedom and democracy, Britain refuses to recognise Indian independence and allow the establishment of democracy in this country.

We do not expect anything or anybody to bring freedom anywhere. Freedom is not brought or given; it is won by the efforts of those who deserve it. We advocate support for this war not because of any expectation that Britain would give us freedom; nor do we wait for her to give us something, not even a promise, before advocating support. It may not be in her interest to give us what we want. But it is in our interest that we advocate support to this war. And that support does in no way prejudice our pursuing the achievement of what we want. There is no contradiction between the two.

The Congress leaders say that they would also like to give their support to the war, but only under certain conditions. We maintain that, on the one hand, these conditions are completely inadequate and their fulfilment is of no avail for the attainment of Indian freedom; on the other hand, if the conditions are rejected, we should have to sit on our prestige and refuse support to the war in spite of our professed opinion that it should be given. The Congress leaders desire "transfer of power" from the British to the Indians, or at least the "recognition of India's right of independence." We maintain that transfer of power cannot take place all on a sudden through a declaration, but is compelled by the development of events influenced by those who want power. And as for the recognition of the right of independence, only facts can be recognised. India's independence is not yet a fact. Nor can this fact be established by the present Congress policy of "semi-benevolent neutrality," which amounts to nothing in terms of the prosecution of the war and self-immolation and stultification in terms of India's struggle for freedom.

We do not mix up things. We do not maintain that India will gain freedom simply by a victory of the British arms. But we do maintain that the cause of Indian freedom can be better promoted by supporting this war, which, as a war against Fascism. deserves support, than by not supporting or even opposing it. Nor is this war likely to end just with the victory of this or that belligerent, with the *status quo ante bellum* re-established, only the scales tipped in favour either of Britain or Germany. That was so in the case of the previous war. For the small man even in England or Germany, then, it made little practical difference who won the war. This time, we can assume that the small man in Britain knows what difference a victory of the Nazis would mean for him. And what quarrel do we have with the Englisn man-in-the-street ? He is not an imperialist. And it is more likely that, if England wins this war, it will be the democratic people who will have won it.

The European *democracies* do not want Fascism. They know to-day that only through a crushing defeat in this war can it be stamped out, and that, unless it is stamped out, they are in for it. The European *imperialists* were not anxious to fight this war. They blundered into it. Mr. Chamberlain might still have corrected the blunder by coming to (Hitler's) terms with Germany, either after the fall of Poland, or of Norway, or of any one of the subsequent victims. Mr. Chamberlain was indeed the better imperialist. But Mr. Churchill does conduct a war against Fascism which the democratic masses must see through, if they want to servive even in their relative freedom, which is still better than an absolute slavery.

No sane man desires war. But pacifism in the face of Fascism is simply grotesque. The common people suffer in the war; but they will suffer more if Fascism wins. The imperialists might have avoided this war. But for their complacency and even connivance. Fascism would have never become the powerful menace it is today. That is another matter. They are atoning for past sin, and are paying dearly for it. No use sneering. History is taking its implacable course. Politics, which is the process of history in the making, cannot be done with emotions. Out of resentment against British Imperialism, we should not allow ourselves to act against our own conviction as regards this war. On the other hand, whatever our attitude towards this war in particular may be, it need in no way interfere with our legitimate fight against injustice. Only, there are ways and ways of doing a thing.

But in order to define our attitude towards this war, we must have an opinion about it. If it is a "bad" war and should not be fought, we should have the courage to say and resist it, and see that our resistance becomes effective. Or, by analysing the character of the war, we come to the conclusion that the best thing to do now that it is on our head is to fight it to the finish and prevent Fascism from winning it. If we do come to this conclusion, we should also have the courage to say so openly and not shrink from acting according to our conviction.

When the Polish "incident" was closed, we suggested that the Congress should appeal for an early termination of the war. We did so because the discrepancy in preparedness for a major war between Germany and the rest of Europe became evident already then, and the perspective of a complete Fascisation of Europe was clearly opened up. Not much prestige was yet at stake on either side; and though return to the status quo would not have improved matters much, yet it would have closed, temporarily at least, that immediate and horrible perspective.

But the war went on. And peace now would mean voluntary Fascisation of Europe, which is in effect no better than forcible Fascisation. Therefore, this war must go on until the perspective of the Fascisation of Europe, and with it, almost inevitably, of the whole world, will disappear with the defeat and overthrow of Hitler. That is necessary in our own interest; and if it happens to coincide with the interest even of the British Government, should we therefore act against our own interest, only to spite the British? After all, anti-Imperialism is not an end in itself. We fight Imperialism in so far as it encroaches upon our freedom. The Fascisation of Europe is the greatest menace to our freedom. Therefore, we must do whatever we can to prevent it.

In analysing this war, one must of course agree on the premises. We start from the assertion that Fascism is the greatest and immediate menace to the forces of freedom and democracy throughout the world including India and including Germany. Nobody would reasonably maintain that the Fascisation of Europe in general, including England in particular, would bring India freedom. Nor is it a matter of indifference to India. Fascism is more efficient and ruthless in suppression than Imperialism. And supposing Hitler wants to crush the British Empire, it is not the small island that he covets; we can legitimately assume that India will be the prize. And if it was not possible until now for india to become an independent country, with Hitler on our neck, the perspective will vanish in dimmest posterity. On this question, we can only agree or differ, not argue; because the facts of Fascism are known. One may find them good, another bad, but nobody can dispute them. We find them bad—worse than anything, worse even than Imperialism ! It is also a fact that it is not generally realised in this country, at a distance, *how* abjectly bad it is, although the facts are there to be known.

There are reasons for mental reservations; there is a traditional pro-German sympathy; and there is the radio propaganda from Berlin promising freedom to India. Such promises from Berlin are not new. We have also heard Hitler praised because he has made Germany great; and is he not a vegetarian and a bachelor, to boot. He, who approves of the methods with which Hitler is supposed to have made his country great, must be a Fascist believing in the subjugation of other peoples by the cruellest means. As regards greatness, how much greater Germany was in her post-war misery—Germany, the land of poets and thinkers, was never greater than in the period of painful and peaceful reconstruction after the last defeat.

The most facile retort to the contention that the defeat of Fascism is our foremost concern, is: "What do we care ? Fascism and Imperialism are one and the same; let them quarrel and ruin each other; or do you want the victory of Imperialism?" No, we are not interested in the victory of Imperialism. Nor do we think that the welfare of the English people is conditional upon a victory of Imperialism. We even think that there may be no Imperialism left if Fascism is finally crushed. But to be quite consistent, let us assume that British Imperialism will be victorious, Germany defeated and under British influence; we shall not have gained anything for India. Still we would at least be left where we are to-day. Under Fascist domination, either through English Petains or, through direct agents of Hitler, we would be worse off. And as for those who think that Fascism and Imperialism are the same, we wish them an experience of the difference. But we do not wish that dreadful experience for the Indian people.

Some argue that victorious Imperialism would be worse that pre-War Imperialism, would even go Fascist itself. Why should it? A country goes Fascist as the last resort for getting out of the perpetual economic crisis threatening to overthrow the established capitalist system. Fascism is not the product of the wickedness or perversity of an individual, however "great"; nor is democracy the attribute of virtuous people. Fascism is the weapon with which a bankrupt system fights for its life. Therefore, it is so deadly.

So, supposing England would come out of this war victorious and unscathed, the hegemon and patron of all Europe, the restorer of French, Dutch, Belgian, Norwegian, Polish, Czech, Austrian independence and recipient of their tributes in the shape of market monopolies, it would feel safe and strong. Fascism is inconvenient even for the Fascists, unless you assume that a whole section of a people can suddenly go sadist; it is an inconvenient necessity for a certain class of people to cling to their power and privileges. For that purpose, it is a necessity. Without that purpose, that is, if power and privileges are not threatened, it can be a nuisance. A victorious British Imperialism would not feel the necessity.

The worst possible result thus will be the status quo of to-day, minus Defence of India Rules. If all the strategic positions will be occupied during the war, that will not only serve the purpose of democratising certain administrative processes, but also that of strengthening the spirit and organisation of the nationalist forces. We are to choose presently; and our decision will decide much of the future of India.

But certainly, if this war is bad and should not be fought, co-operation, even in the sense of occupying strategic positions conquered by the vote of the people, and in India's own interest, should not be extended, if it also served a purpose which is considered to be definitely undesirable. From no quarters, this view has yet been openly expressed. On the contrary, the Congress leaders have all expressed their sympathy with Britain in this war and abhorrence for Fascism as well as profound regret that Britain does "not give nationalist India a chance" to throw in her lot on the non-Fascist side of this war. The position is queer. They would like (*if* they would like)

Fascist Germany to be defeated without imperialist Britain being victorious. Supposing this to be desirable, how can it be brought about, if it is true that Britain is waging an imperialist war against Fascism ?

We maintain that this is not an imperialist war, because, for the benefit of British Imperialism, this war was not a necessity. Whatever the motive may be or may not be, it happens to be a war against the stronghold of Fascism, and in this sense, logically it is an anti-Fascist war.

Nationalist India wants to see Fascism defeated, but does not want to do so without serving its own freedom; that is the most natural and legitimate thing in the world. The question only is: How to do it ? How will the purpose be served by non-co-operation, which can only be a gesture any how, since all are "co-operating": from the princes who give lakhs and soldiers, the mill-owners who produce and sell to Britain all the latter needs for the war, and profit greatly by it, to the workers who produce what the mill-owners sell, and get at least some more employment and slightly raised wages, down to the rural unemployed, who flock as recruits in the army, where they get at least some full meals a day which they otherwise don't. How would the purpuse be served, even if the Congress demand for a National Government at the Centre was accepted by the British Government? What is exactly this demand? The National Government demanded is a contradiction in terms. It is quite meaningless.

We do not regard bargaining as moral turpitude. But we are against bargaining away our freedom to act according to our conviction for a chimeric mess of pottage. If this war is bad, let us say so and resist it. If it is not, and should be fought to the finish, it does not look well to stand by the whole-sale slaughter and exclaim: "Very good war this, indeed! Go ahead, boys, and fight those nasty Fascists! We ourselves have no time just now, because we must go to jail, so that we may emerge from it as heroes, in time for the next general elections. Therefore, goodbye until after the war, then we shall administer your affairs in India again; and don't forget how well we did it!"

If this war has to be fought, not because the British Government happens to have declared it and incidentally declared India a belligerent party, but, because Fascism is a menace to the world, and not to the world of the big imperialists so much as to the greater world of the oppressed and exploited in all countries (including Germany and including India)—then we must have a place in it. It may sound very nationalistic to argue: "What do we care for Fascist menace to the peoples of the world, when the imperialist menace sits on our necks?". But how will the prosecution of the fight for Indian freedom be prejudiced by making India's participation in the war against Fascism, which is to-day an involuntary fact, a voluntary effort—provided, of course, that we are convinced that this war against Fascism must be fought till the end? On the other hand, how will war resistance or non-co-operation promote the cause of Indian freedom?

Another seemingly patriotic argument is: "Why should India as an enslaved country help her rulers in this war against their enemy?" Well, firstly, we maintain that Fascism is also the enemy of Indian freedom. And then, if a slave is locked up with his master, in the latter's burning house, he will fight the fire together with the master, unless he prefers to die with him, thinking: It serves my master right if I die—why did he not make me free? That is what the Congress attitude amounts to. Is it reasonable?

We maintain, from a knowledge of facts, that Fascism, which the British Government only happens to fight to-day, while we opposed it ever since it came into existence, is our own enemy as much as that of British Imperialism; and that, if Fascism is not defeated, we are in for it. Therefore, we advocate participation in the fight against it. We are of the opinion that, even if India were an independent couniry, she should join the fight against Fascism in the most effective way.

Here arises the question which has been put to us repeatedly, namely: "Why, if Fascism is the enemy of democracy, and Soviet Russia the champion of democracy, does not the latter join the fight against the former? And why, if Russia does not deem it necessary, should we go out of our way doing it?" Firstly, we need not go out of our way; the fight against Fascism lies on the road to Indian freedom. And then has not Soviet Russia joined this war, and is she not playing quite a prminent and effective part in it, having inflicted the only defeats on the Nazis in this war, otherwise so dangerously successful for them? But there are ways and ways of doing a thing. This war against Fascism is waged quite successfully on the Russian borders by means of "neutrality".

The effect of Soviet neutrality may be well appreciated by all Anti-Fascists. English Anti-Fascists even in this country have done so. Russia's anti-Fascism is proved beyond doubt. The rest must be left to their strategists, trusting that they know their job. If India was one of the three mightiest Powers on earth and had common or near frontiers with a Fascist country, the right policy for her might also be a "neutral" tiger's clasp like Russia's "neutral" bear's embrace. But as she is not, the right policy for her must be something else, the aim of all truly democratic forces being the same, namely, defeat of Fascism, *by their own efforts.* One can expect to reap the fruit only of what one has sown oneself. Imperialism, being not a democratic force, cannot be expected to defeat Fascisn ultimately. It has somehow got into this war, and, being a powerful military force, should be welcome as an instrument in the fight against Fascism. But having entered the war reluctantly, in the beginning, still with visible appeasement tendencies, the danger still remains that the defeat of Fascism may suddenly appear too big a victory of democracy for the conscious imperialists to stomach. If the democratic forces will want to carry on in such an eventuality, they can do so only if they are in the thick of the fight themselves.

The democratic forces cannot be sure of the outcome of this war, unless they are active agencies in its prosecution. In India, they can, besides what is being done anyhow, do little but mobilise and quicken the consciousness of the people, and prepare them for their role in any development that events may take. And developments may well happen nearer home. Already Hitler is *ante protas* of the East. This war cannot be fought successfully except on the strength of the popular will to fight an enemy of the people; that is true for the people in India as well as in England and elsewhere. If the expression of this popular will in India looks like support for the British Governmant, which happens to fight the same enemy, is that enough reason for us to act contrary to our conviction (provided we have it) ? Can we not think except in terms of "British Government" ? That is to deny ourselves even our spiritual independence ! And if the popular will to fight Fascism is not there, it is for ignorance of what Fascism is; it is the duty of those who know to make others understand. In India, this is quite a big task, it seems. But the task is urgent, for the danger may be nearer home than one dares think. Supposing that Hitler would defeat England, and an English Petain be found to sell out the Empire—are we going to be the slaves of a slave of Hitler ? Are we to refrain from fighting in such an eventuality, for the mere reason that some Englishmen also may have enough sense to fight the same fight ? Should we not rather try to prevent the dire emergency ? If we are complacent now, and escape from the dilemma into jail, what are we going to do, if such a case should arise, with our crown of thorns in the jails ?

POLITICAL GEOGRAPHY

The Congress leaders seem to be forgetting that India is a part of the world, and that remarkable forgetfulness has come to be the badge of partriotism with the average Congressman. Even the erstwhile prophets of the fashionable cult of internationalism are not exceptions. In the midst of a world going up in blazes, India must behave like the frog in the well. This narrow-mindedness to-day passes as militant nationalism. The inevitable consequence is the commission of one blunder after another, covered by the morbid fascination for the call of the wild. Nero fiddled while Rome burned; the leaders of the struggle for Indian freedom sulk while freedom may be any day knocking at our door, and, there being none to let her in, her enemies will strengthen their grip on India. This is really a tragic situation.

The whole of Europe beyond the border of the Soviet Union lies prostrate under the iron-heels of triumphant Fascism. Britain stands trembling on the verge of a similar catastrophe. She is making a desperate effort to escape it. Only nationalist prejudice and the inability to understand the internal structure of human society can deny the fact that Britain *is* fighthing Fascism. The entire British nation is not composed of imperialists or would-be Fascists. The numerous British working class, together with the enlightened and progressive members of other classes, are more hostile to Fascism than the average Indian nationalist who has a sneaking Fascist sympathy. If Britain will be betrayed by her Petains and Weygands, that will not be for any lack of devotion for the ideal of freedom and democracy on the part of the bulk of her population. Indeed, history would hold Indian Nationalism responsible for that possible misfortune of the British people, should the former remain blind to the facts of political geography and fail to understand that the world is living in the age of Fascism which has replaced Imperialism as the bulwark of a decayed social order.

Turning to the East, one finds Fascist Japan extending her tentacles so as soon to reach the frontiers of India. Except for Soviet help, China has been placed almost in a hopeless position. And the extent of that help will be very largely dependent upon the turn of events in far off Europe. Should England fall, the rapacious eye of triumphant Fascism will immediately be turned upon the Soviet Union, and all the might and resolution of the latter will have to be concentrated to face the onslaught of immensely strengthened enemy. Japan will be left with a free hand, Chinese independence will disappear. And with China compeltely under her control, Japan will be casting greedy glances upon India.

British Imperialism may have disappeared in the meantime. Not many will be sorry for that. But the Nazi occupation or Fascisation of England cannot be a welcome perspective for anyone who pertends to cherish the ideals of freedom, democracy and progress. The fall of Germany under the Hitler regime was a bad day for the world. That was followed by a succession of tragic events. The process culminated in the downfall of France which must go down in history as the greatest misfortune for the civilised humanity. If Britain also goes the same way, the world will enter a new dark age with the only hope of any light coming from the Soviet

Union, if the latter will be able to hold its own against the concerted attack of victorious conuter-revolution throughout the wrold. And when we have regard for the danger which will threaten the Soviet Union itself, the dreadfulness of the perspective becomes depressingly evident. Let the Indian nationalist try to visualise that perspective, while they glee fully await the defeat of England and perhaps even the eventual appearance of Hitler on the frontiers of India as the new incarnation of God with the flaming sword in his hand. Only, it will not be the flame of liberty, but the shimmer of dripping blood.

Under our very eyes, the second largest imperialist Power of the *modern time* has fallen. The experience of the colonies of fallen France should be an object-lesson for those Indian nationalist who expect to derive benefit out of the slavery of the English people. Not one of those countries have been able to regain freedom in consequence of the passing of French Imperial ism. Because, French Imperialism has not given way to a better political system. It has been in corporated in the new system of Fascism which to day threatens to hold the whole world in its bloody grip. Fascist regime has been established practically in all the French colonies. It has not been imported from outside by an invading army. The previous colonial administration has simply stood out in its inherently Fascist character. He who entertains the fond hope that India will fare any better in case of the passing of British Imperialism through the Fascisation of England, is living in a fool's paradise.

India may not be robbed of her fortuitously gained freedom by an invading army, although, in view of the developments in the Far East, occasioned by the fall of France, and the critical position of England in Europe, that can no longer be altogether left out of account. However, there are many other slips between the tempting cup and the greedy lips. Again, a little dominationn g of political geography will help the Indian nationalists to see beyond the nose. The power that holds India under imperialist domination is seated in India herself. That power will not be broken by the fall of England. In other words, the fall of England will not very greatly harm British Imperialism; it will only mean slavery and untold other misfortunes for the English people, who have never been an integral part of the Imperialist system

The day-dreaming and narrow-minded militant nationalists are very proud of the record of the anti-imperialist struggle that they believe themselves to have carried on successfully for twenty years. In spite of all the pardonable self-glorification, it should be admitted that those successes have not been very real. Because, in that case, they would not be still waiting for Imperialism to liquidate itself, for Hitler to make them a gift of freedom by eliminating England from the picture. Indeed, the history of the last twenty years' struggle is punctuated by a succession of defeats. That by itself is not shameful. The point, however, is that those defeats were inflicted by the forces of Imperialism which are in India herself. They are still there. They will be there even after the fall of England, if that will really take place. Consequently, there is no reason to believe that the Indian struggle for freedom under its present inept and reactionary leadership will be any more successful in the event of a Nazi conquest of England. Will India's slavery be any more tolerable or honourable when she will have England as a partner of the mistortune ?

Even to-day, England cannot do anything to prevent India from breaking away from the

Empire if the romantic militant nationalists really had the power and courage to strike the blow. Why do they not then do that ? Why wait any longer, since the relation of forces will not appreciably change when England will fail to defend herself against Nazi invasion ? The militant nationalists prefer to indulge in tall talks and count upon the mercy of a dreadful future, simply because of their inability to cope with the forces of Imperialism which are in India. Since they are unable to-day, they will be equally unable in a future, when the forces of Imperialism holding India in subjugation will remain intact, whatever may be the fate of England. Indeed, they will be in a much worse situation in that case. Because, to meet all possible contingencies, the forces of Imperialism seated in India will reinforce themselves by enlisting the support and cooperation of all the native reactionary elements. It is thus easy to see how the fall of England will not mean the end of British Imperialism. British democracy will be destroyed. But British Imperialism will continue, metamorphosed as Fascism. Exactly this is happening in all the French colonies; and it will happen in India also.

Under the new regime, the "peacefull" economic exploitation of Indian resources by Imperialism will be replaced by a bloody suppression of all popular movements and the brutalisation of the Indian people except the few who will become an integral part of the new regime. There may be nationalists who would regard that as freedom. They should be called by their real name. They are not nationalists, but Fascists. The danger of Fascism, as far as India is concerned, is represented by those "patriots". It is with their help that the imperialist rulers of India will hold the masses of the Indian people in slavery, while allowing the British people to be tyrannised and brutalised by a Fascist regime, either made at home or imported from abroad.

Is it so very difficult to see that the alternative perspective of a real freedom for India is opened up by the success of England in resisting Fascism? A considerable section of the British ruling class is known to be pro-Fascist, and is even to-day striving for a reconciliation with triumphant Fascism. That being the case, in order to continue the fight against Fascism, England must place herself under a new leadership. That is all the more necessary if she wishes to help the rest of Europe liberate herself from the tentacles of Fascism. That can be done only with the active co-operation of the Soviet Union. The pro-Fascist section of the British ruling class is opposed to such a co-operation. Therefore, the fight against Fascism will develop an anti-imperialist struggle in England herself. England must outgrow Imperialism if she wishes to fight Fascism successfully. There can be no doubt that the majority of the British people want to fight Fascism. Therefore, the majority of the British pepole is the ally of the Indian people in the anti-imperialist struggle. That alliance cannot be made through sentimental attachments or school-ties. That will be cemented in course of the common struggle against Fascism. It is neither fair nor honourable to expect the English people to fight their battles against Fascism, and declare India free, when Imperialism will have ended in consequence of their success in the anti-Fascist struggle.

The only possible question that the really democratic Indian nationalists can ask, is: "What can we do?" The answer is: Act independently; get rid of your slave mentality; don't wait for others to declare you free; apply yourself to the task of working out your own salvation. In the accomplishment of that task, you will find yourself closely allied with the British people fighting against Fascism, and together with them put an end to Fascism and its foster-father Imperialism."

"Independent India," August 18, 1940

ANTI-FASCIST MASS MOVEMENT

Appeal for Observance of First War Anniversary.

It is very encouraging that a lively discussion is being carried on by Radical Congressmen throughout the country about the bold and truly revolutionary stand that we have taken regarding the war. The fundamental principles of our policy are stated in our Thesis "India and War." Those principles as well as the analysis of national and international situation, in the light of which they are formulated, were reviewed and discussed at length during our Summer Camp at Dehra Dun. The All-India Conference of the League of Radical Congressmen reaffirmed the principles and policy formulated in "India and War" by a resolution on the international situation. In pursuance of that resolution, we have been trying to persuade the Congress leadership to adopt a course of action suggested by us from time to time. Unfortunately, our efforts have not been successful.

Although the decision of the next meeting of the Working Committee may precipitate an undesirable and highly dangerous situation, we shall have to keep on hammering our point of view, hoping that sooner or later good sense will prevail and Indian politics will be conducted in a really honourable and fruitful course. We need not under-estimate the difficulties. Even to-day, ours may be a cry in the wilderness. Yet, we should have the courage of conviction necessary to swim against the current of set habits, political backwardness and prejudice.

I am decidedly of the opinion that the road to Indian freedom lies through an active participation in the struggle against Fascism. I have come to know that some of our comrades do not fully share this conviction. There can be only one reason for that. It is an insufficient appreciation of the danger of Fascism. To talk of a choice between Imperialism and Fascism is altogether an erroneous approach to the problem. Those romantic Indian nationalists, who have been advising Imperialism to liquidate itself for the benefit of India, are blinded by their prejudice, and therefore cannot see that Imperialism is liquidating itself in as much as Fascism is becoming the politics of decayed Capitalism throughout the world. Therefore, the fighters for freedom, whatever they may be, to-day have only one enemy to face; that is Fascism.

The present is not England's war. It is a war for the future of the world. If the British Government happens to be a party to this war, why should the fighters for human liberty be ashamed of congratulating it for this meritorious deed, perhaps inadvertently committed, and recognise it as an ally in a noble cause? The old saying that adversity brings strange bed-fellows, is not altogether meaningless. If it was justifiable for the Soviet Government to make the non-aggression pact with Nazi Germany, why should it not be equally permissible for the fighters for Indian freedom to support the British Government so long as it is engaged in a war against Fascism?

All these obvious considerations are not seen by those who are not inspired with the ideal of the liberation of the oppressed and exploited throughout the world. Conscious or unconscious Fascist sympathy on the part of the average nationalist makes him blind to the dangers of the situation. Radical Congressmen should be free from such narrow-mindedness and prejudices.

The realisation of the danger of Fascism is the condition for the development of a truly democratic and progressive movement for the freedom of India. Those, who have already realised that, should take the initiative to make others conscious of the danger. An anti-Fascist mass movement is the crying need of the day. All the truly democratic and progressive elements in our country are bound to be crystallised in course of that movement. On the other hand, by developing such a movement, the fighters for Indian freedom will make their contribution to the world fight against Fascism.

September 1, the anniversary of the outbreak of the war against Fascism, should be the most propitious day for launching the movement. The League of Radical Congressmen is the only organised force in India to-day which can take the initiative in this respect. I hope you will approve of the proposition, and make of our next independent action as big a success as on the occasion of the anniversary of the French Revolution.

I shall issue a public appeal in this connection. Meanwhile, I advise you to get in touch with all who are likely to co-operate in the demonstration and do all the other necessary preparations. Let the Anti-Fascist Day, celebrated by the League of Radical Congressmen, mark the beginning of a new stage in the struggle for Indian Freedom.

August 17, 1940.

DOWN WITH FASCISM!

An Appeal to all Freedom-loving, Progressive and Demoractic Indians!

A year ago, Europe was plunged into the cataclysm of the present war by the expansionist greed of Nazi Germany. Since then, staggering events have taken place, and to-day practically the whole of Europe lies prostrate under the iron-heel of Fascism. Those dreadful events are taking place at a long distance. Therefore, their far-reaching significance has until now been realised only by a few in our country. Popular organisations, particularly the Congress, have indeed condemned Fascist aggressiveness and expressed sympathy with its victims. But nationalist pre-occupations and the fact of Britain's being a party to this war, have prevented them from doing anything practical by way of contributing to the struggle for the future of the civilised humanity against the greatest menace of our time.

No doubt, their own freedom is the first

concern for the Indians. At the same time, they must bear in mind that no single country can be free, or remain free, in the midst of an enslaved world, driven back into the darkness of mediaeval barbarism. Therefore, all regional or particular fights for freedom, irrespective of their specific objectives, have to-day become integral parts of the world-historical fight against Fascism, and can be fought effectively and successfully only as such. All the activities of the fighters for Indian freedom must be determined by that realisation.

To the great bulk of the Indian population, Fascism is practically unknown, perhaps except in name. What it really stands for is very little known, even to the average educated public. Its bloody history of nearly twenty years is also known only partially. On the other hand, its philosophy and some of its social and political doctrines have found expressed sympathy and even admiration among a certain section of educated Indians. That being the case, Fascism is not a distant danger, either in terms of space or in terms of time. The danger is in our midst, here and now. If it is not checked before it is too late, India will have to experience a worse tyranny, brutalisation and retrogression, instead of advancing towards the goal of independence. The desired check can come only from a clear understanding of the nature of Fascism. That understanding will make the Indian people alive to the danger and awaken in them the determination to participate voluntarily, free from all prejudice, in the world-wide struggle against it.

Fascism is negation of all the positive outcomes of modern civilisation. The liberating significance of modern civilisation is indeed not appreciated by a certain type of Indians. They may pretend to be patriots, but they do not stand for the freedom which the people of India as a whole must have. They even do not represent the true spirit of ancient culture. The past can be evaluated only as the foundation of the future. The glorification of the past, which compels one to turn his back on the future, represents a betrayal of the positive and ennobling values of past tradition. Fascism is such a betrayal of all human values, created not only in the modern time, but throughout ages. It is a negation of all the ideals of man striving for political freedom, social justice, cultural progress, intellectual emancipation and spiritual elevation. Therefore, it is the very anti-thesis of everything which must inspire all true Indian partriots.

World domination is the declared object of Fascism. It has overrum practically the whole of Europe. It will not stop there. Its greedy glance is cast upon the vast continents of Asia and Africa. The doctrine of the superiority of the White Race is a pronounced feature of Fascism. It does not even pretend to "civilise" the non-White races. It regards the latter as inferior beings, to be subjugated by the chosen people of God. If Fascism emerges triumphant out of the present struggle in Europe, the mechanised hordes of the modern Attila will before long be set in motion for conquering the riches of the Orient. This dreadful possibility, which may not be very remote, shows how intimately are the fighters for Indian freedom conçerned with the armed conflict in Europe.

The countries of Western Europe, all overrun by triumphant Fascism, the British people are engaged in a desperate struggle against that menace not only for the freedom of their own country, but also for human liberty and human civilisation as a whole. Their possible subjugation will not help the cause of Indian freedom in any way. On the contrary, their success in checking the victorious march of Fascism long enough, so that other forces might be brought to bear upon the situation, will ultimately contribute to the downfall of Fascism and the survival of modern civilisation from the most severe crisis ever experienced by it. They deserve not only moral support and platonic sympathy, but active co-operation of all who entertain the ideals of progress and freedom.

On the other side, there stands the Soviet Union as the bulwark against Fascist expansion eastwards. If England is defeated, the Soviet Union will become the next object of Nazi aggression. The subjugation of the whole of Europe, followed by the fall of England will mean such a tremendous accession of power for Fascism, that the very existence of the Soviet Union will be endangered. What will happen to India and other countries of the East, if Fascism can score still more victories, is too dreadful even to imagine.

Therefore, let us be conscious of the danger lurking in our midst and knocking almost at our door. Only the closest co-operation of all the forces of freedom throughout the world can save the world from that imminent calamity. Let the fighters for Indian freedom be conscious of their responsibility, and play their role creditably. Let this first year of the war, precipitated by Fascist greed, close with the heartening news for the European people in distress, that the oppressed people of India are a willing and voluntary party to the World Anti-Fascist Bloc which must be formed with the object of rescuing the world from its present distress, and leading it towards the future of a greater freedom and a higher civilisation.

August 23, *1940.*

FIRST THING FIRST

A circular addressed to all Members of the L. R. C.

I have noticed in the correspondence of our comrades and even in some contributions to 'Independent India' a tendency of being apologetic for our stand regarding the war and the view that for the moment the concentration of the entire energy for helping the fight against Fascism is the correct thing for all the fighters for freedom to do, wherever they may be. This tendency expresses itself in associating the proposed Anti-Fascist Movement with the ideas of "the final struggle" and "seizure of power". The analysis of the national and international situation, which had led us to our present position, excludes the possibility of realising such ideas in the near future. Therefore, no useful purpose will be served by talking about them, when we should apply ourselves to an immediate task of supreme importance, which is to fight against Fascism.

Even from the Bombay, Bengal and Maharashtra resolutions, as well as from individual correspondence, I gather that we are unanimous in that connection. Then, why all this star-gazing and fortunetelling ? The reason for this repetition of certain stock-phrases can only be that we are not sufficiently convinced of correctness of our view that the supreme task of the movement is to organise an Anti-Fascist Movement; we want to reassure ourselves that we are much more revolutionary than "mere Anti-Fascists." That is a wrong point of view, and I am writing to urge that such unnecessary apologies and romantic ideas should not creep into our demonstrations on September 1.

To participate in the fight against Fascism being our task and responsibility, we must find the most effective way of doing so. We cannot imitate the Congress leadership and wait for the British Government to give us the chance. We know how to do it. We have undertaken the task of mobilising popular opinion in support of the world struggle against Fascism. That task should have been undertaken by the Congress. It cannot be done by the present Government for obvious reasons. But there are numerous elements in the country who may be expected to join us in this task. We shall alienate them by introducing in our Anti-Fascist propaganda distant ideals and political ideas, which may not secure their approval. A broad-based mass movement can be created only on the basis of the largest measure of common agreement. Nothing should be done which would prevent our securing the largest possible co-operation in the Anti-Fascist Movement. If we are not careful, our purpose will be defeated. That is not opportunism, it is a categorical imperative of political strategy.

I should also discourage drawing historical analogies. The analogy of the Kerenski Government has nothing to do with the Indian situation. Neither is Churchill a Kerenski, nor are we preparing for the October Revolution. If a historical example is required, for justifying our stand, which does amount to support to the British Government, that will be found in Chiang Kai-Shek. He has committed greater outrages against the Chinese people than Churchil has ever done to India. Yet, when he was driven into a fight against Japanese Imperialism, the Communists forgot all his past crimes and extended to him the fullest possible co-operation without any condition or reservation. Who would say that Churchill is no more earnest in his fight against Fascism than Chiang Kai-Shek against the Japanese invaders of China? The argument that Chiang Kai-Shek is a Chinese, whereas Churchill is no Indian, is completely irrelevant. The point is that, just as it was the duty and the correct policy on the part of the Chinese Communists to help Chiang Kai-Shek and the Kuo Ming Tang, in spite of their bloody record, against Japanese vandalism, just so it is the duty and correct policy for all honest fighters for Indian freedom to take up a similar attitude towards Churchill and the British Government in the present fight against Fascism.

However, the idea I anxiously want to convey is that we should do the first thing first. The present should not be spoilt by dreams about the future. Let us take care of the present, and the future will take care of itself. Let no vacillation or apologia interfere with our single-mindedness which will guarantee success regarding our immediate as well as the ultimate goal.

August 26, 1940.

ENEMIES OF HUMAN FREEDOM AND PROGRESS

Summary of the speech at a Public Meeting in the Town Hall of Dehra Dun on the Anti-Facist Day, September 1, 1940

A year ago, to-day, Nazi Germany invaded Poland, and consequently plunged Europe into a gigantic armed conflict which may bury modern civilisation in ruins caused by wholesale death and destruction. Only faint echoes of the tragic events occurring in far off Europe reach us in India. Generally, the feeling is that India is not interested in this quarrel which does not concern her. It is even believed that Nazi Germany alone is not responsible for this war which has been precipitated by a conflict of imperialist interest. One need not be an apologist of Imperialism to say that that is an entirely wrong reading of the situation. Whatever might have been the desire or designs of other Powers, this war is the result of the aggressiveness and expansionist greed of the present regime in Germany. Therefore, the entire responsibility for having plunged Europe, and incidently the whole of the world, into this orgy of wholesale death and destruction, belongs to the Nazis. Since this war is bound to cause incalculable injury to all concerned, those responsible for it must be regarded as the enemies of human freedom and progress. From that point of view, this war is entirely different from other wars. None concerned with human welfare, whoever he may be, wherever he may be, and however he may be placed, can therefore be indifferent to its outcome. Fascism has proved to be the greatest danger to human welfare. Therefore, for the sake of the future of mankind, it must be defeated. On this anniversary of the war against Fascism, we should declare our determination to make every possible contribution to the attainment of that purpose.

But to the average Indian nationalist, the situation does not appear like that. The obvious arguments in favour of the necessity for a determined campaign for the destruction of Fascism do not appeal to him. We have our contribution quarrel with British Imperialism. It is only natural that the average Indian nationalist should be unwilling to do whatever may promote the interest of British Imperialism. But some understanding of the present international situation makes it clear that British Imperialism did not want the present war. As a matter of fact, the non-Fascist Imperialist Powers never had any serious quarrel either with Nazi Germany or Fascist Italy. On the contrary, successive acts of aggression, brigandage and blackmail, committed by the latter, were tolerated and even condoned by the former for no other reason than to avoid a war. Appeasement was the policy of the British Government for a number of years. There is ample reason to believe that even this war would have been avoided through the continuation of the policy of appeasement, which would mean further concessions to Nazi Germany, had the latter not practised the successful tactics of blackmail somewhat too rashly. The British Government was ready to persuade Poland to accept the German demands. But the Nazis, flushed with one easy victory after another, would not wait even for a few hours. They invaded Poland, and the war was precipitated in spite of the expressed anxiety of the British Government to avoid it and to make further concessions to Nazi expansionism at the cost of Poland. Those facts prove that this war has been brought about not by a conflict of imperialist interests, but exclusively by the expansionist greed of the Nazis.

That section of the British ruling class, which never hand any quarrel with Fascism, and pursued the policy of appeasement, for avoiding a war, with the object of checking Fascist aggressiveness, would naturally try to come to terms with Nazi Germany at the earliest available opportunity even after the war had broken out. The Fascist Powers had all along carefully avoided any serious encroachment on the interests of British Imperialism. Therefore, the latter had no reason to go to war against them. But the imperialist interest of any country is not identical with the interest, sentiments and ideals of the entire people of that country. As a matter of fact, there is a conflict between the two. Previously, the British people had misgivings against the policy of appeasement. But they did not do anything more than express occasional disapproval. But that passive attitude towards a danger which had previously appeared to be a distant one, changed as soon as the Nazi hordes began to sweep one European country after another. The

English people felt the necessity of fighting that danger which loomed larger and larger, the nearer to their home it came. Those responsible for the appeasement policy, which had created the Fascist Frankenstein, had to make room for others who could be relied upon for waging the war against Fascism uncompromisingly. To-day, it is not British Imperialism which is waging a war for conquering foreign territories or subjugating other nations. It is primarily a war of self-defence which, if successful, will contribute to the downfall of Fascism, waged by the British people in the face of the anxiety of British Imperialism to come to terms with triumphant Fascism. The Fascists, on their side, also have nothing against British Imperialism. They are also willing to come to an understanding. If they are left with the domination of Europe, they would not touch the British Empire. That has been the substance of Hitler's peace offer. Had it not been for the determination of the British people, to fight Fascism until the world is free from this menace, Hitler's peace offer might have been accepted, and the world would have seen Europe sinking into barbarism, while the colonial empires thrived as ever.

All the prejudices and natural scruples would disappear, if only those fighting for the freedom of India could realise what Fascism really means. Many suffer from the handicap of a sympathy and admiration for Germany's contribution to the scientific development of the modern world. Those contributions are indeed great. But they were made before Germany was overtaken by the misfortune of Nazi domination. Perhaps it is not generally known that those, who made Germany great in the realm of science and culture, have no place in Nazi Germany, and the names of great Germans who are dead are struck off the pages of German history interpreted by the Nazis. In other words, the Nazis should not be identified with Germany. It is not a war between the English and Germans. It is a war between the freedom-loving world and the Nazis, who, having destroyed freedom in Germany and other European countries, want to destroy it throughout the world.

The Indians may seek shelter in the hope that, whatever may happen to Europe, the Fascist hordes will never be able to reach our country. But Fascism is no longer confined to one country. It has become an international force, and as such it threatens the entire world. If we have a clear idea of what Fascism is, we shall find the danger near at home. It is no longer an imported commodity, made in Germany or Italy. Practically every country has its home industry producing it. India is not immune from that danger. If we realise the far reaching implications of the menace of Fascism, and are determined to fight it, we shall have to begin at home. Those taking that view, will not be tormented by the question how India can prepare to defend herself against Fascism, as long as Imperialism does not give her the opportunity. They should know how to create the opportunity. What is essentially necessary is a burning hatred for Fascism and the determination to stamp it out wherever it is to be found.

If we do not feel it to be our duty to help the British people in their fight against foreign Fascism and the intrigues of the friends of Fascism at home, we talk of freedom in vain. It is perverse to believe that the slavery of the British people, or the Nazification of England, will in any way promote the cause of Indian freedom. If it was a war of British Imperialism, I should not be in any way interested in it.

Indeed, I would oppose India's helping it in any way. But it is the people's war, and as such, the people of India are vitally concerned with it. The mobilisation of the Indian people in a world struggle for the defence of human liberty and human progress cannot take place through the efforts of a Government which, by its very nature, cannot appeal to patriotism, nor claim to be the custodian of popular freedom. That task, therefore, must be undertaken by others. We, who fully realise the magnitude of the menace of Fascism, are determined to shoulder that responsibility. We are convinced that making the masses conscious of the menace of Fascism, mobilising them to co-operate in the world struggle against Fascism, to help the British people defend their liberty against Fascism, external and internal, we shall promote the cause of Indian freedom. We should not entertain the vain hope of deriving freedom from the enslavement of the rest of the world. We should not have the delusion that the destruction of democracy in Europe will help its establishment in India. India will gain her freedom by virtue of contributing to the defence of the world freedom.

Narrow-minded nationalism may derive perverse pleasure from a possible defeat of England. If it were downfall of British Imperialism, no fighter for freedom would be sorry for that. But a defeat of England would not necessarily mean any great injury for those who derive benefit from Imperialism. It will mean only enslavement for the masses of the British people. And what will India gain from that? She will remain in her chains which will be all the more galling, because, defeated by Fascism, Imperialism will stand naked in its Fascist character. On the other hand, the victory of the popular forces in Britain will mean disappearance of Imperialism and freedom for India.

HOW AND WHY ?

Even those who realise, or concede for the sake of argument, that India, either for her own enlightened self-interest or for larger international issues, should participate in the war against Fascism, ask the question. How can she do so ? The question is asked with an air of finality, on the assumption that it cannot be answered without disregarding the consideration of India's honour and dignity. It is believed that this question should put an end to all controversy regarding India's participation in the war, answered of all other arguments in favour of participation. Even if India decides to participate in the war, she cannot do so with honour and dignity. That is the conclusion.

In the last analysis, the question is found to be resulting from an inhibition which, in its turn, may be regarded as natural in so far as any inhibition is natural. The inhibition is that co-operation with Imperialism is a political sin. Not being a free country, India cannot wage a war on her own account. Situated as she is to-day, she she must fight on the side of England. Her participation in the fight against Fascism, under the present circumstances, cannot be direct. It must take place through an intermediary which happens to be Britain. That being the case, participation in the fight against Fascism for India means to co-operate with British Imperialism. This idea is repugnant to the nationalist mind which, during the last twenty years, has been trained to think exclusively in terms of co-operation and non-co-operation. Assuming that India should participate in the war against Fascism, in order to do so, she will be required, in the first place, to do something which she should not do, namely, co-operate with a party which has deprived her of freedom. A sort of political untouchability thus prevents India from acting according to her anti-Fascist conviction, assuming that the conviction is there.

It seems that Indian nationalism must undergo a psycho-analytical treatment, before it can develop a healthy political outlook. The inhibition preventing it from acting according to the supposed conviction must be eradicated. For that purpose, another more fundamental question must be answered. Why should India participate in the war against Fascism and why is this war at all necessary ? Once this more fundamental question is satisfactorily answered, that is to say, in the absence of any doubt regarding the necessity of the war against Fascism and of India's contributing to it, the other question becomes irrelevant. Given the will, the way can always be found. A firm conviction generates the courage to act accordingly.

If the Indian nationalist leaders are taken on their word, it would appear that there is no doubt regarding the fundamental question, why Fascism must be fought. The corollary to the realisation of the necessity of that war is that India should also participate in it. That bring us up against the inhibition against co-operating with Imperialism. The following considerations should remove the inhibition which prevents India from doing something which she realises must be done.

Names are meant to express the nature of things. But in course of time, names themselves become things. Its purpose earned for British policy the name Imperialism. The British Government came to be known as an imperialist government. The attitude of Indian nationalism is a reaction to those hateful names. Things change, though names remain. Carried away by the reaction to names given to the British policy and Government, Indian nationalism does not see if any change has taken place in the thing itself. The fact is that, since the war broke out, important changes have taken place in the relation of forces in Britain. As a matter of fact, the very fact of declaring war against Nazi Germany was a negation of the British imperialist policy in connection with the latter. But the decisive consideration is that the nature of the Government of a country necessarily changes in consequence of a shift in the relation of forces in the country. From this point of view, the present Government of Britain is not imperialist strictly in the same way as the previous governments were.

The Chamberlain Government pursued an imperialist policy. That is to say, a policy calculated to promote and safeguard the interests of British Imperialism. Appeasement was the policy of the Chamberlain Government. A war with Nazi Germany was not necessary for the purpose of British Imperialism. Therefore, it is obviously erroneous to say that the present war is an imperialist war. Appeasement and war cannot serve the self-same purpose.

Nothing happened in the autumn months of 1939 to bring about such a radical change in the years' long relation between Fascism and British Imperialism. The declaration of the war was the result of a fortuitous combination of circumstances. British Imperialism was compelled to do what it had tried to avoid systematically even at the cost of prestige. The previous policy did not necessarily represent any love for Fascism. But the latter functioned as an effective instrument for defending an economic system which constitutes the basis of Imperialism. Therefore, its destruction could not be desired by Imperialism. That was the underlying motive of the appeasement policy pursued by the imperialist Chamberlain Government. The rejection of that policy was not voluntary. It was forced. The compulsion to declare a war, which was sought to be avoided at all costs, therefore, amounted to a departure from imperialist policy objectively. In any case, it was a defeat of the policy of Imperialism.

The present British Government resulted from that departure from the imperialist policy in relation to Fascism. The formation of the

Churchill Cabinet, therefore, is to be regarded as at another defeat of imperialist policy as regards Fascism. Therefore, the Churchill Cabinet and its predecessors are two different things, though bearing the same name. Democratic and progressive forces in Britain, which had all along disapproved of the policy of appeasement, asserted themselves in the crisis precipitated by the fortuitous outbreak of the war, and the present Government is very largely their creation. It represents the anti-Fascist forces as aganist thə pro-Fascist tendency in the public life of Britain. In so far as Fascism is concerned, the present British Government is not imperialist, because the destruction of Fascism would mean a severe blow to the economic system which constitutes the very foundation of Imperialism. The personality of Mr. Churchill or the presence of Mr. Chamberlain in the present Government is of no decisive importance.

It is true that there has been no change as regards the Indian policy of the British Government That is an important fact from the point of view of Indian nationalism; but it is irrelevant for judging the value of the present British Government as a weapon against Fascism. Therefore, for the purpose of fighting Fascism, it is permissible to co-operate with the present British Government. It is assumed that Indians want to fight for a conviction, and not to render services for a payment. Only in the latter case, the question of dignity or honour arises.

Since the Churchill Cabinet is waging a war which was not necessary for imperialist purposes, and is indeed against imperialist interest, to co-operate with it as the only possible way for India's fighting Fascism is quite permissible. That would not mean helping Imperialism. The result of such an action on the part of India, on the contrary, will strengthen the forces which have compelled a rejection of imperialist policy as regards Fascism. Therefore, such action will not only be in consonance with the professed conviction regarding international affairs, but actually promote the nationalist interests of India.

The above considerations should remove the inhibition. There is nothing to be said if the opposition to India's particiation in the war results from some other motive, if it is a wilful policy. The question, why India should participate in the war against Fascism, having been answered, the question: How ? can be easily disposed of. It is a matter of concrete steps: What concretely is to be done ?

The first thing to do is to recognise the fact that India is already participating in the war. Let that be done consciously and voluntarily with the purpose of fighting Fascism. Secondly, the war efforts of the Government can be democratised by the formation of popular ministries in the provinces. That can happen only upon expression of the desire to do so. The activities of the so-called War Committees to some extent do amount to coercion. The burden is not always placed on those who can easily bear it. It is passed on to the common folk, although the money realised that way can hardly be any substantial asset for financing the war. This undesirable state of affairs can be changed by the operation of popular ministries. The War Committees can be the organs of popular anti-Fascist sentiment, and be instrumental in converting the war into a people's war. They can also create a guarantee against the incipient forces of Fascism at home.

Another fact to be faced is the presence of strong Fascist tendencies in certain official as well as non-official circles. The mobilisation of the democratic forces under the direction of popular ministries will create a Home Front, so to say, against Fascism. That is of decisive importance. The Fifth Columm is the most effective part of the Fascist hordes. That instrument must be broken before any country can be secure against Fascism. The Fifth Column operates in India in various ways, one of its expressions being the widespread Fascist sympathy and the hope for German victory. Fighting on this front, India will make a very important contribution to the world struggle against Fascism.

All the activities on the above lines taken together will prepare India to hold her own in the case of England's defeat or of the severance of the lines of communication between England and India. In either case, efforts are bound to be made for establishing a dictatorial regime in India on the pretext of her being in an extraordinarily dangerous position. That is how Fascism will most probably come to India, if the democratic forces are not mobilised and marshalled before that situation is precipitated.

The question, how India will be benefitted by participating in the war, is also answered by the above considerations. Any detailed answer to this question is not necessary, because the queston, how India can participate in the struggle against Fascism, is given on the assumption that this latter quesion is raised by thoso who realise the danger and wish to fight it. However, in a few words, it can be indicated how India will be directly and immediately benefitted.

The process of the change in the relation of forces in Britain in one year of war can be reasonably expected to go on with an accelerated speed during the remaining period of the war which will most probably be rather long. Imperialism would not fight Fascism even when heavy blows were inflicted on its prestige. Because, Fascism is an instrument necessary for the maintenance of the *status quo*. But ultimately, Imperialism could not prevent the democratic and progressive forces from taking up the fight. To that extent, Imperialism has been weakened, and to a corresponding extent, India is benefitted.

The continuation of the war will accelerate the process of the liquidation of Imperialism, begun with the outbreak of the war. The process will not be voluntary: it will take place under the pressure of the democratic forces in Britain. Is it not simple to see how India will be benefitted if the war against Fascism continues until victory is won ?

But something cannot be gained for nothing. To expect that, is neither dignified nor honourable. The very desire to see the end of Imperialism should persuade Indians to contribute to the process of its inevitable liquidation. That contribution, to her own freedom, can be made by India through co-operating with the present British Government in the fight against Fascism. As a matter of fact that co-operation will be a có-operation between the forces of democracy and progress in both the countries. History has tied them together; no use quarrelling with history. The opportunity has arrived when the people of both the countries can work out their respective salvation by joining hands in the struggle against a common enemy.

"Independent India," September 29, 1940.

WHY INDIA SHOULD PARTICIPATE IN THE WAR.

An Open Letter to the Members of the Congress Party in the U. P. Legislative Assembly.

By Kunwar Anand Singh. M. L. A.
Ex-Chief Whip.

The hubbub caused by my resignation from the Congress has clouded the serious political considerations which compelled me to take that step. They were set forth in my letter of resignation clearly enough. I appeal to you to examine them soberly. Abuses will serve no purpose. The examination of our differences can be fruitful if it takes place on the basis of the assumption of an honesty of purpose on the part of all.

Only until yesterday, we were colleagues. For years, we have been working with a common purpose. All of a sudden, we cannot become enemies. Such hard words as "traitor," "coward," "opportunist" etc. should not be used light-heartedly. We are all liable to make mistakes. Therefore, any difference of opinion should be dispassionately examined. The result may be a large measure of agreement based on a collective judgment.

You may ask; why then did I resign from the Congress instead of thrashing out our differences inside the organisation? The reason should be known to you all. No expression of opinion, critical of, or opposed to, the official policy is allowed. On the plea of discipline, freedom of speech is suppressed. One may differ, but he should not express his difference, with the object of winning others over to his point of view. That negation of the elementary democratic principle is regarded as discipline, the standing threat of which compels one to pocket his conviction or to rebel and get kicked out. Not willing to conceal my conviction, much less to act against it, and therefore to be condemned and punished as a disrupter, I preferred to take the more straight forward and honourable course of resigning, so that I could express my views freely and try to persuade others to accept them without laying myself open to the charge of undermining the homogeneity of the Congress organisation.

Apart from the more fundamental questions of ideology, social outlook and programme, the immediate issue is India's participation in the war. Why should India participate in England's war? Before proceeding to answer the question, it is necessary to clear away the confusion about this question.

Since the beginning, the Congress was not opposed to participation in the war on principle. The issue of conscientious objection, which is supposed to result from the creed of non-violence, was raised only in the Bombay resolution of the A. I. C. C. Immediately upon the outbreak of the war, Mahatma Gandhi declared himself in favour of giving unconditional support to Britain. The original demands for a declaration of Britain's war aims and for the recognition of India's independence were abandoned in course of time. The Delhi resolution of the Working Committee, endorsed by the A. I. C. C. meeting at Poona, offered fullest co-operation with the war efforts of Britain on certain conditions. Previous to that, the Wardha Statement of the Working Committee had set aside the creed of non-violence so as to be free to support India's participation in the war. Unless they were firmly convinced of the desirability of India's participation in the war, the majority of the Working Committee would not go to the extent of disregarding Mahatma Gandhi's advice and deposing him from the supreme leadership of the Congress.

All these facts conclusively prove that the Congress leaders have never been opposed to participation in war on principle. They took up the present attitude only when Imperialism refused to pay for the offered co-operation. And what were the conditions for co-operation? Would India's political status be improved in the least if the conditions were fulfilled? What was wanted was a mere promise. What is the worth of such a promise? We had it in the past. Is it permissible for the Congress to ask for, and depend upon, the promise of Imperialism to grant independence, given its long professed principle that freedom cannot come as a gift?

Then, the demand for the "National Government." Was it not a deviation from the goal of complete independence? How could any government be called 'national,' so long as India remained a part of the British Empire? And would she cease to be a part of the British Empire if the Viceroy's Executive Council, possessing no more constitutional authority than at present, included a few Congressmen, and was called a National Government? Yet, those were the conditions for the Congress whole-heartedly co-operating with Imperialism in its war efforts.

In view of these facts, it is baseless to contend that the Congress is opposed to India's participation in the war on principle. That being the case, how can the present policy be justified ?

There is yet another, and more important, fact proving that the present talk of non-co-operation is not only unreal, but actually misleading. Practically everybody connected with industrial and trading enterprises is co-operating with the Government's war efforts, and is making profit therefrom. Congressmen are so connected. They are not condemned for disregarding Congress policy and punished for the breach of discipline. The Birla mills, for example, are manufacturing articles required for the army; yet, the Congress Working Committee meets in the Birla House to pass resolutions against India's participation in the war !

All these facts make it clear that there is no difference on principle as regards India's participation in war. The difference is on matters of details. While the Congress leaders have all along offered co-operation in return for certain nominal concessions, I maintain that it would be more dignified and honourable to render the help unconditionally. That would not be helping Imperialism, but to act according to the Congress profession of abhorrence for Fascism. Moreover, is it permissible for Satyagrahis to take advantage of the enemy in distress? Did not the Congress leaders from the beginning disavow the spirit of bargaining?

Now let me answer the question why India should participate in the war. Leaving aside the larger issues involved, and more fundamental considerations, I shall state only the practical and more immediate reasons:—

1. It is not England's war. Although India was not consulted before she was involved in it, her own future will be determined by the outcome of this war. Therefore, to-day, it has become India's war as well as England's.

2. The victory of the Fascist Powers will decidedly prejudice the cause of Indian freedom. The defeat of Britain will not automatically set India free. Britain may be overwhelmed, and

yet the British Empire remain intact. The British Power in India will not be necessarily weakened in that eventuality. Consequently, the chances of Indian freedom will not be any the brighter. In order to destroy the British Empire, the Fascist Powers must attack its outlying parts and India herself may be invaded in that case. That danger is not remote now. If the Near Eastern countries are overrun, the Fascist forces may advance on India. Conquered by them, India's position would not improve in any way. The British rule would be replaced by a worse system of tyranny and exploitation. We are not free to-day, but in consequence of long years' struggle we are in a position to carry on the struggle for freedom more or less effectively, and the chances of attaining the goal of independence are getting brighter every day. Fascist conquest would mean a tremendous set-back. India will lose even the relative freedom to carry on the struggle for freedom. On the other hand, if the British rulers succed in defending their Indian possession without the willing help of the Indian people, they will naturally be more autocratic than to-day, and that again will also be a great set-back for our struggle for freedom. It is simply idle to nope that the Indian people will assert themselves when the established regime breaks down under the impact of a foreign invasion.

3. Clearly, the question in not whether we shoul help British Imperialism. The future of India hereself is at stake. While the victory of the Fascist Powers would adversely affect the future of India, pushing her way back in the struggle for freedom, her position would not deteriorate in any way if the war ends differently, and specially if she makes a decisive contribution for bringing about that result. On the contrary, by defending the future, if not the present, of our country, we shall certainly strengthen the position of the Indian people in every way, and consequently make a great advance towards the ultimate goal of freedom.

4. While passive non-co-operation, either for the sake of non-violence or on some other ground, is bound to be ineffective in preventing the exploitation of Indian resources for the war, active resistance is neither possible nor desirable. Before the country is actually invaded, India will not be adversely affected by the war. Except for the salaried members of the middle-class, practically all the other sections of the Indian people are

being benefitted, or can be benefitted, by the conditions created by the war. Trade and industry are thriving and can prosper more. The resulting benefit can be distributed to all concerned. Wages can rise to counter the rise of prices. The peasantry can be guaranteed some share in the higher prices of agricultural products. Popular ministries in the provinces can promote people's welfare by introducing measures with the above purpose. Recruitment for the army provides tempting employment. The development of industries, quickened by war emergency, will lay down a solid foundation for the general economic reconstruction of the country. Evidently, a mass movement for resisting India's participation in the war will be antagonistic to general welfare, and, precisely for that reason, it is bound to fail.

The above reasons can be summarised in the statement that participation in the war will, instead of harming India in any way, promote the cause of her freedom in addition to contributing immediately to the general welfare of the people. As regards the question of honour, what is more honourable than to work for the welfare of the people and safeguard their chances of being free, sooner or later ?

Popular ministeries in the provinces are indispensable for making India's participation in the war beneficial for herself ultimately as well as immediately. No amount of complaints and protests will secure the redress of the grievances about the operation of War Committees. Popular ministries, shouldering the responsibility of mobilising mass support for the war, will offer the decisive guarantee against all undesirable methods. But, in the critical moment, the Congress leaders have finally decided to go to the wilderness. Their present policy means laying down of the responsibility which the electorate entrusted to them in the last election. Since this harmful and irresponsible policy appears to be irrevocable, some other way out of the impasse should be found. That consideration compelled me to resign from the Congress, so that I could freely explain why India should participate in the war, and work for the restoration of responsible governments in the provinces, as soon as possible. A dispassionate and serious consideration of the facts and arguments stated above should influence your judgment, so that I may have the privilege of your cooperation in this task I have undertaken, courting slanderous criticism and unpopularity. But I am sure facts will prevail upon fiction, and truth will tell. Otherwise, the future of our country is dark indeed.

Lucknow, October 30, 1940.

THE NEW PATH

Manifesto Issued by the Radical Democratic People's Party

The world is experiencing the severest crisis of modern times. Either the crisis will be overcome by the world entering upon a new period of human progress on the basis of the splendid achievements of modern civilisation, or the latter will break down, and the world will relapse into mediaeval barbarism. This grave menace to the future of mankind is represented by triumphant Fascism.

India cannot claim immunity from this menace. The world crisis affects her as vitally as any other country. Yet, the gravity of the situation is fully realised only by a few among those who are regarded as the makers of her destiny.

Particularly, the premier political organisation of the country has failed signally to measure up to the occasion, and has itself become the first casualty of the crisis. Instead of joining the struggle against the menace of Fascism, the National Congress has adopted a policy which virtually amounts to helping the victory of Fascism. This fatal blunder has been committed on the pretext of anti-Imperialism, which, as it is, represents nothing more revolutionary or progressive than impotent race animosity. Spitefulness is a characteristic feature of slave mentality, which is a poor asset for the grim struggle for freedom.

Having for years condemned acts of Fascist aggression, the Congress to-day refuses to resist it when the danger is knocking at our own door. That is not a curiosity; it is political bankruptcy, inevitably brought about by the reactionary ideas and ideals of Gandhism, which has persuaded the premier nationalist organisation to reject nationalism for a set of individual fads and pseudo-moral dogmas.

In this critical moment, the Congress leaders have turned back on ideals previously professed by themselves, because as a body they never were inspired by the modern ideas of democracy and progress. They are an association of Conservatives, with a decidedly reactionary outlook on social and cultural matters. They believe in the metaphysical precepts and spiritual doctrines, which enter also into the philosophical foundation of Fascism.

A reactionary ideology contradicted the political programme of the Congress, which itself never came up to the modern standard of liberty and democracy. Consequently, the present attitude of the Congress leaders, as regards the war against Fascism, was predetermined. The Congress has succumbed to the crisis, as it were, by fate.

But India must survive. Her future is linked up with the future of the world. The path to Indian freedom lies through a victorious struggle against Fascism. While the Fascist hordes are nearing the Indian borders from both sides, Fascism is raising its ugly head in our very midst. The democratic and progressive forces must, therefore, fight simultaneously on two fronts. The fight on the home front must begin immediately. The decisive battles for the political freedom and social emancipation of the Indian masses will be fought on that front.

In this critical situation, old slogans have lost their meaning. The hatred for Englishmen can no longer be the token of patriotism. It is positively reactionary and harmful for the welfare of the Indian people, in so far as that sentiment coincides with the willingness to welcome the Fascists as liberators. This sentiment is very widespread. It represents neither patriotism nor nationalism; it expresses either a slave mentality, or heralds the rise of home made Fascism.

Anti-Imperialism loses all revolutionary significance, if it goes to the extent of preferring Fascism. Yet, that is the case to-day, not only with many Indian nationalists, but curiously enough, also with those who call themselves Socialists or Communists. Fascism, or Fascist sympathy, to-day, provides a common platform to all the reactionary forces throughout the world, including India. Therefore, destruction of Fascism has become the immediate task for all the opposing forces. The failure to measure up to this momentous task, on any pretext, amounts to a betrayal of the ideal of freedom, whether national or social.

These considerations must determine further development of the struggle for freedom. The Radical Democratic People's Party rises on the ruins of the Congress to blaze a new trail, to lead the Indian masses towards the goal of national freedom and social liberation, which cannot be reached before the world is freed from the menace of Fascism. By mobilising the Indian people to participate in the world struggle against Fascism, the Radical Democratic People's Party will further the cause of Indian freedom.

Our party is not a new-comer in the field of Indian politics. Its pioneers, for years, tried to transform the Congress into a political organisation, inspired with the ideals of popular freedom and controlled and guided by the collective will of the masses. They believed that the rise of such a party was indispensable for the attainment of the goal of national freedom and social emancipation. The contradiction between Gandhism and Nationalism prevented the Congress from developing into party of the people. Thanks to its internal contradictions, the Congress degenerated into a close association of a numerous group of people owing personal allegiance to one man and accepting his idiosyncrasies and divinely inspired wisdom. Consequently, its mass basis decomposed. Not only the Muslims and the so-called Depressed Classes left the Congress, but even the bulk of the Hindus turned against it. Progressive intellectuals were repelled by the irrationalism of Congress politics and the religious othodoxy which dominated it. Already so degenerated, the Congress could not possibly survive the severe repercussion of the present world crisis.

The realisation of the programme of political freedom and national reconstruction, however, is not possible without the joint effort of the entire people, led by a party commanding the confidence of the masses, irrespective of religion or community. The Radical Democratic People's Party rises to perform the historically necessary function of such a party.

Its programme is the same as should have been adopted by the Congress, if the latter could be transformed into the political party of the people.

Politically, the Radical Democratic People's Party will strive for the establishment of a genuinely Democratic State, under which effective political power will be vested into the masses of people.

The party will advocate a comprehensive programme of social reconstruction, which must be undertaken by the free Democratic State of India to promote the progress and prosperity of the nation as a whole.

The fundamental feature of that historically necessary reconstruction of the Indian Society will be the transfer of the ownership of land from the feudal rent-receiver to the cultivator.

Another cardinal point in the programme of social reconstruction, advocated by our party, is rapid industrialisation of the country, with State aid and under the control of the democratic State.

Generally, the party stands for the radical reconstruction of the Indian society, which is conditional upon the removal of all antiquated institutions, the disruption of all oppressive relations and the rejection of all reactionary ideas which together obstruct the free economic development of the country and impede the progress of the nation towards a high level of the modern civilisation.

This programme of economic reconstruction puts a concrete content into the concept of national freedom which until now has been nothing more than an empty term shrouded in all sorts of mystery.

It will secure the interests and promote the welfare of the vast majority of the nation irrespective of religious or communal affiliation.

Therefore, it expresses the sentiment and incorporates the aspirations of all the democratic and progressive elements belonging to all the communities. These elements must now come together to assert themselves actively on the situation with the object of leading the Indian people in this fateful moment of history. The Radical Democratic People's Party is the rallying ground for all those elements who are destined to be the real makers of the future of India.

The movement for Indian freedom must discard false ideals and come out of the rut of conservative ideas hidden behind misleading slogans. It must be inspired with the spirit of our time which calls for a ruthless revaluation of traditional values, as the basis for a new era of human progress.

The entire world is in the throes of a re-birth. An order, based on the power and privilege of a few, thriving at the cost of the rest, is breaking down under the impact of a terrific clash brought about by the contradictions inherent in that order. India cannot remain unaffected by that clash. She must sink or swim together with the rest of the world.

The Fasicsts and their sympathisers are the

defenders of that passing order. They are endeavouring to prevent the inevitable collapse of a worn-out and antiquated system through the violent suppression of the forces of progress which have opened before mankind the perspective of a higher civilisation and greater freedom. The fight against Fascism, therefore, is the paramount task of the moment. India must participate in that fight, simply because she is a part of the world and her future is linked up with the future of the world. In course of that immediate struggle, the Indian pepole will acquire the power and develop the will necessary for enforcing the programme of National freedom and social emancipation.

Let the progressive forces come forward to shoulder the responsibilty of shaping India's destiny. Let them build up the political party of the Indian people engaged in the historic struggle for the freedom of the world as well as its own freedom.

Lovers of democracy and progress! Join the Radical Democratic People's Party!

Fighters for Indian freedom! Take your rightful places in the rank of the new party which holds high the banner of that freedom and is determined to carry it forward through the vicissitudes of the immediate struggle to ultimate victory !

November 15, 1940.

MY DIFFRENCES WITH THE CONGRESS.

Speech at the Allahabad University, November 27, 1940.

While we were in such a situation, the world was plunged into a war, and India, by the misfortune of being a part of the British Empire, was involved in it. In that position, what should have been done by the leadership of the party which commanded the confidence of the masses and which could lead the masses in any way it wanted? There is a very common saying that, when my enemy is in distress, I am given a very good opportunity to advance my own objective. We have been trying to free our country from the domination of a foreign power. That power got involved in a very serious international conflict. At that moment, the Congress to some extent controlled the governments of a number of provinces. I was of the opinion that the control of those strategic positions should be held, and in course of time, when the war developed and the position of the Government became more and more shaken, those points of vantage could be utilised for really developing our struggle forfreedom.

But the Congress leadership thought otherwise, and decided in favour of withdrawing its ministers from office. I do not know what was the object of that move. But everybody knows what was the result. The result was that in a number of provinces the administrative machinery was handed over to the bureaucratic officials, and the consequence is all these extravagances in the name of the prosecution of war against which we complain to-day. I believe that, if Congress Ministries had remained in office, the situation would not have been like this. They could have protected the masses of the people from extortions and exactions that are our grievances to-day. Apart from other considerations, one of the considerations for the Congress Ministries resigning was said to be that India had been involved in this war without being consulted. On the face of it, that may look very plausible. But the Congress Ministries did not resign when India was declared a belligerent party. Why did they not resign instantaneously when that happened? They resigned only several weeks afterwards. Besides, the Congress was prepared to participate in the war on certain conditions, in spite of the fact that India had not been consulted before she was declared a belligerent party. Thus, that could not have been the real cause. Then, it is said that the Congress does not want to participate in this war, or co-operate with the British Government, because it is an imperialist war which is no concern of India. That contention again cannot be borne out by facts. The famous declaration of the Working Committee, immediately after the outbreak of the war, offered co-operation on certain conditions. Gradually, that policy of responsive co-operation culminated in the Delhi resolution of the Working Committee, which was endorsed by the A. I. C. C. at Poona. With those resolutions in our hand, I do not think we are justified in maintaining that the Congress was ever on principle opposed to co-operation with British Imperialism in this war. So, let no high-sounding principles be made out of what has actually become a counsel of despair. There is no disagreement on principle at all. Therefore, it is no use arguing that the Congress does not want to participate in an imperialist war, while others want to do so, and therefore, all Congressmen are good patriots, and all others are damned rascals.

There is yet another aspect from which the question can be approached. For a number of years the Congress has been passing resolutions, and individual Congress leaders have made declarations to the effect that India is deadly opposed to Fascism and Fascist aggression wherever it occurs, and that we detest and abhor Fascism. But now, when Fascism comes nearer and nearer to our country and the question of ourselves fighting it arises, for one reason or another, we should say: No. We are neutral in this fight against Fascism! I do not know how others will justify the position. I think that this is a very unreasonable position, to say the least. When for years we have declared our opposition against Fascism how can we refuse to fight it when it actually threatens our neighbours and thus ourselves? The point that the British Government gives us no opportunity to fight Fascism, or does not trust us, is completely irrelevant. We have to determine our attitude independent of what the British Government thinks or does or would like us to do. Fascism has been growing in Europe over a number of years, and while it was growing, we have been condemning it. It has now overrun the whole of Europe and is knocking at the doors of Asia. What shall we do in this situation? Can we say that we are indifferent to the march of Fascism eastwards? Can we even say that we are indifferent to the fate of the rest of the world? If *you* say we can, I cannot say that. I believe that there should be some connection between profession and practice. If we are against Fascism, and Fascism is threatening the whole of the world, it is our duty to do what we can to fight Fascism.

Now comes the question how we can fight it. As long as the war was confined to the far-off corners of Europe, we might have been indifferent and might have said that it was not our business to save England. But that is no longer the position. Fascism has appeared within 400 miles of Indian borders. The Fascist hordes may sweep farther, and before long India may be within the range of Fascist guns and bombers. What are you going to do then?

Then war will end one way or the other. One party will be victorious. If England is defeated, we need not be very sorry, perhaps. But we shall have to see what will happen to India in consequence of it, that is, how that outcome of the war will affect India. Our policy, our attitude, our action in the given situation must be determined by that examination. We are interested in the future of our country. An opportunity has come. Unfortunately, we cannot do much just now. But at least we should see that we can prevent our position from getting worse than it is already. If Fascism wins, it will get worse. If anybody would maintain that the Fascist Powers will smash the British Empire and give freedom to India, I think there is little to argue with him. It would be a case of irreconcilable disagreement. If the British Empire is broken up by a Fascist victory, India will not be free. Even if all lines of communication between India and England are cut off, British Imperialism would still remian in India unless the Nazis take it into their head to rule India directly. British Imperialism has its roots in India. It is firmly in the saddle here, and has at its disposal the help of a powerful section of the Indian upper classes. This is not a hypothesis. We have seen France, Belgium and Holland collapse, but Fernch, Belgian and Dutch Imperialisms are not dead, and their colonies have not become free. England may go the same way, but the Brittsh power in India may not be dislodged; it may be exercised on behalf of, or in co-operation with, the Fascist Powers, or if at all it will be dislodged, it would be dislodged either by German or Italian or Japanese forces. In either case, we would have a Fascist regime. That is what will happen to us if things will continue as they are going on now. Any alternative is preferable to this. And the alternativer which I suggest may be a very bright one.

In saying this, I am speaking purely from the nationalist point of view. But I believe that many of you have been influenced by a broader vision, by Marxist and internationalist point of view. Inspired by this broader vision, we have been talking about the solidarity of the working class all over the world. The working class of entire Europe is groaning under the bloody heels of Fascism to-day. Can we claim honesty of our internationalist and Marxist profession, and still say that we are indifferent to the struggle going on in Europe and to the outcome of the present war; that we do not care a hang if Fascism wins or loses this war? If Fascism wins, I do not know what will happen to the British Imperialists and I do not care; but I do care what will happen to the British and the entire European working class; I cannot be indifferent to the fate that will befall them in such a case together with all the toiling masses and progressive forces in Europe and all over the world. If you choose to call our efforts to do whatever little one can to prevent that from happening, "co-operation with Imperialism", I cannot help it; nor can I help you. But I strongly feel that whoever refuses to make the effort is either a fool or a knave or both.

There is a national as well as an international approach to things. The two cannot be separated to-day. They lead to identical conclusions. If Fascism wins, not only will the world go to the dogs, but together with the world, India will sink into barbarism. Therefore, not only for the freedom of the world, of the victims of Fascism abroad, but also for the very chances of the eventual success of our own struggle for freedom, we must see that this greatest menace to all freedom is destroyed. And if some Englishmen today, for whatever reason, will fight side by side with me against Fascism, which is my enemy, perhaps more than theirs, why should I refuse to fight? We have not advocated anything worse than this and this is in my opinion the only honourable and dignified and logical thing for the Indian people to do.

On this question of India's relation to the war, the differences, I always had with the Congress leadership, broke out into such a conflict as could not be reconciled any more. If the present policy of the Congress will be carried on to its logical conseqnence, it will means a virtual support to Fascism. And as far as it depends on me, I shall not tolerate that. If the present policy of the Congress could lead to the freedom of India aud enable her to intervene in the present world conflict more effectively as an independent nation, I would follow it unhesitatingly But if it starts a so-called struggle, which does not ffect British Imperialism at all, but has only the you effect of helping Fascism, I shall not be a party to it. And if you are really inspired by the broader vision of Marxism and internationalism, which you so passionately professed for years, you will come to the same conclusions as I have, and you will aet as I have acted,

INDIAN FREEDOM AND FIGHT AGAINST FASCISM

Presidential Address at the Inaugural Conference of the Radical Democrtic People's Party, Bombay, Dec. 21, 1940

The attainment of national freedom was the professed object of the Congress. But national freedom is not an abstract conception. There is absolutely no reason to believe that the masses of the Indian people will be free to make social and cultural progress upon the replacement of the present political regime by a Government controlled by the present leadership of the Congress. The freedom necessary for the advancement of the masses of the Indian People is conditional upon a radical social transformation such as was experienced two hundred years ago by those European communities which stand in the forefront of the modern world. The present Congress leadership is not inspired by the ideal of such a social transformation. As a matter of fact, it represents a spirit of reaction practically to everything which the modern civilisation stands for. One needs only realise the obvious implications of Gandhism, as stated in the famous constructive programme, to come to that conclusion. Owing to this reactionary social and cultural outlook, nationalism, as represented by the Congress leadership, lacks the machinery, urge which manifested itself in the mass awakening during the last twenty years.

Politically, it stands for some superficial change in the administrative machinery, notwithstanding the high-sounding demand for complete independence. The profession of democracy only serves the purpose of fomenting racial antagonism. The removal of the present political regime will be of no benefit for the common people of this country, unless political power will be utilised for a thorough democratisation of the economic and social life of the nation. Such a democratisation is not visualised in the scheme of nationalism as represented by the present leaders of the Congress. As a matter of fact, they are very sceptical about the benefit of political democracy, and are frankly hostile to the blessings of modern civilisation. They preach a cult of revivalism in the social as well as in the cultural aspect of life. They want political power not to open before the

Indian masses all the avenues of progress,. in order to catch up with human advancement in all the walks of life, but to lead India back to mediaevalism and the simplicity of a legendary Golden Age. But the masses of the Indian people cannot be inspired with the spurious ideal of simplicity, which will mean perpetuation of their present poverty; they want to live a fuller and richer life; they want to enjoy all the fruits of human creativeness. That is the ideal of nationalism, in so far as the bulk of the nation is concerned. Gandhism admittedly does not want India to travel that road of material progress and spiritual emancipation. Therefore, it is antagonistic to the objective urge underlying the popular movement which has until now developed under the banner of the Congress. The antagonism between the reactionary outlook of its leadership and the objectively progressive urge of the movement prevented the Congress from developing into an instrument for attaining democratic freedom. Having failed to assert themselves within the organisational framework of the Congress, the popular forces must strike out a new way. Hence the necessity for the rise of the Radical Domocratic People's Party with the object of giving a concrete and conscious expression to the progressive urge of the popular masses.

The reactionary non-democratic nature of nationalism as represented by the present Congress leadership has become evident during the present world crisis. Fascism has appeared on the scene as the avowed enemy of all the political, social and cultural ideals cherished by the civilised humanity ever since Europe merged out of the darkness of the Middle Ages. Objectively, Indian nationalism is striving for the realisation of those ideals by the people of this country. Therefore, Indian nationalism should regard Fascism as its mortal enemy. For years, the Congress professed antipathy for Fascism, and expressed sympathy for its victims. To-day, Fascism threatens to destroy human freedom throughout the world. Practically the whole of Europe lies prostrate under its iron heels. The British democracy is putting up a stout resistance to the Fascist menace. Having failed to subdue Britain, triumphant Fascism has turned its attention towards the direction where it does not expect to meet a very serious resistance. Consequently, India herself has come within the range of a Fascist attack which may be delivered from the East as well as from the West. In this dangerous situation, the leadership of the Congress takes up an attitude which cannot be reconciled with the professions of freedom and democracy. In the light of this attitude, the doubtful nature of those professions stands revealed. It is hardly necessary to examine the arguments advanced as justification for this attitude. The issue involved being a fight against Fascism, nothing can justify our refusing to participate in the fight against it, when the whole world is threatened with the danger of coming under its domination. The attitude is all the more grotesque when it disregards the danger to India herself. Only the other day, the Congress President declared that the Congress would not defend India against Fascist invasion, because that might be helping to keep the imperialist interests intact. Is there, then, no Indian interest to be defended? Will the Fascists come to India only to destroy Imperialism, and give freedom to the Indian people? Nobody in his senses would dare answer this challenging question in the affirmative. Yet, not only the leaders, but the great bulk of Congressmen, maintain that Fascist conquest would not in any way make the position of India worse. This curious attitude can be taken only by those who attach no value whatsoever to the political, social and cultural achievements of modern civilisation which the Fascists are out to destroy and have destroyed in a number of European countries.

The present attitude of the Congress is determined neither by an enlightened consideration of national interest, nor by any regard for the principles of democracy and freedom cherished by the advocates of human welfare. Nor is it determined even by a short-sighted and narrow-minded nationalism based simply on animosity towards the British. Because, it is evident to the simplest commonsense that the destruction of the British power in India by an invading army will deliver India to the mercy of that new-comer. It is equally easy to choose between the continuation of the *status quo* in India and the establishment of a Fascist regime, which will certainly follow upon the overthrow of the British rule by a Fascist invasion. The reactionary social and cultural outlook, which is the outstanding feature of nationalism, as represented by the Congress leadership, is the real cause of the present attitude of the Congress.

We have all along criticised this reactionary outlook with the object of freeing the Congress from its influence. We always maintained that, so long as the Congress remained dominated by a reactionary social and cultural outlook, it could not possibly become an instrument for the estab- lish ment of pohular freedom. Nevertheless, the reactionary doctrines of Gandhism, often expres- sed through apparently harmless fads and high- sounding moral dictums, gained such a decisive harmless it in the Congress that it ultimately replaced nationalism as the creed of the Congress. In order to make the reactionary doctrines of Gan- dhism prevail upon the progressive urge of nation- alism, democracy inside the Congress was com- pletely destroyed. The leader cult is a characteris- tic feature of Fascism. The anti-democratic prac- tice runs rampant in the Congress. There is very little difference between the Fascist subservience to the super-man and the unconditional obedience to the Mahatma which every Congressman must swear. An organisation which completely dis- regards domocracy in its internal administration cannot possibly be an instrument for estab- lishing democtratic freedom. As a matter of fact, there is a striking similarity between the mode of operation of the dictatorial leadership of ihe Congress and the well-known practices of Fascism.

Demagogy and the exploitation of the prejudices and the primitive emotion of the backward masses are the out standing features in both the cases. On the pretext of discipline, enforced ruthlessly, not for maintaining the integrity of the organisation,but for reinforcing the position of the authoritarian leadership, a veritable dictatorship has been established inside the Congress. It makes no difference whether the dictatorship operates through moral coercion or through other methods of terrorisation. The result is the same. The Gandhist leadership of the Congress stands neither for democracy nor for progress. Therefore, it has taken up the present attitude as regards the war against Fascism.

The reactionary social and cultural tendencies, represented by the present Congress leedership and imposed upon the entire organisation through the dictatorial methods of moral coercion, are the breeding ground of Fascism. With those tendencies, a nationalist movement is bound to degenerate into Fascism. Exactly that has happened to Indian nationalism, in so far as it is represented by the Congress. The natural antipathy for the British Government is being exploited for fomenting the admiration for Fascist methods. Anti-imperialism has become a deceptive garb for Indian Fascism. The danger of Fascism, which is the foremost enemy of the forcesof freedom and progress throughout the world, therefore, is raising its head in our very midst. In this critical situation, frank speaking and courageous action are urgently needed. Having failed to check the degeneration of the Congress into a breeding ground of native Fascism and an ally of the same enemy abroad, we must now shoulder the grave responsiblity of combating that organisation which can still deceive a large section of our population by false pretences and fraudulent doctrines.

What is the justification of the present policy of the Congresss? There are two—one political and the other moral. The political justification is that the fight for democracy cannot have any appeal for India, so long as she remains deprived of the blessings of freedom and democracy. Theoretically, it sounds very plausible. But there are practical considerations which cannot be disregarded by people whose vision is not clouded by prejudices. The practical application of this argument is the refusal to help the defence of India even in the case of an attack by Fascist Powers. In a recent statement, the Congress

President said that the Congress would not defend India against Fascist invasion for keeping imperialists intact. As if there was nothing but imperialists. But the refusal is not absolute. Time and again, the Congress leaders have expressed their readiness to participate in the war on certain conditions. It is deplorable that the Government could not find its way to fulfil those conditions. The attitude of the Government may or may not be justifiable. But should we allow India to become a victim of Fascist aggression just to spite the Government? That is obviously a short-sightedess, which is equally, if not more, deplorable. The Government may have its illusions; but the fact is that India cannot be defended against an invasion either from the East or from the West, except with enthusiastic and determined action on the part of the Indian people. Anything done for paralysing that action will amount to helping the invasion of India. Will that contribute to the liberation of India? The present Government may disappear; but the chances of the Indian people attaining freedom will also disappear. In view of these very simple considerations, the political justification of the Congress policy cannot be regarded as at all valid.

The moral justification is even less valid. Whatever may be the personal opinion of Gandhiji, pratically all the other leaders of the Congress have declared time and again their readiness to help the prosecution of the war. That being the case, it cannot be claimed that the Congress policy is motivated by any conscientious objection to war as such. But assuming that the Congress policy is the application of the principle of non-violence, it does not cease to be any less harmful for India as well as for the rest of the world. In that case, the possibility of the Congress participating in the war against Fascism, even for the defence of India, under any condition, should be ruled out. Should India follow the lead of the Congress, and her attitude would influence world events, the result could be easily imagined. Practising the cult of non-violence, India would deliver herself as well as the whole of the world to the mercies of the Fascist Powers who are blatant votaries of brute force. A doctrine which is bound to have such a result cannot be regarded as very noble and, therefore, is not at all valid as a justification for the present policy of the Congress.

In either case, whatever may be the justification of the Congress policy, the result would be the same, namely, helping Fascist victory. This implication of the Congress policy must be clearly understood by all who want the freedom of India. They should realise that no one single country can remain free, or aspire to be free, in the midst of a world dominated by the enemies of all the ideals of democracy, freedom and progress cherished by the modern humanity. Having realised that, they must act accordingly. They must act so as to prevent that catastrophe overtaking India. In the prevailing atmosphere of emotional effervescence, whipped up by demagogic propaganda and deceptive actions, fundamental issues are confused. They must be clearly formulated. To-day, India must fight not so much for attaining freedom, but for preventing the destruction of the very chances of her being ever free. The chances will be destroyed if the Fascist Powers come victorious out of this conflict. Therefore, for her own interest, if not for larger considerations, India must contribute to the defeat of Fascism.

The argument "What can we do, if the Government does not give us any opportunity ?" betrays a slave mentality. Shortsightedness on the part of the Government should not compel us to take up an attitude which will ultimately be more harmful for ourselves. Moreover, if we realise the gravity of the danger of Fascism, and are determined to fight it, the Government cannot prevent us from doing so. As far as India is concerned, the fight must begin at home. The alarming growth of Fascist tendencies and the wide-spread Fascist sympathy under the cover of nationalism and anti-imperialism, should be combated by all means. The realisation of that responsibility must compel all who sincerely stand for freedom, democracy and progress to join hands with us in building up the Radical Democratic People's Party, which rises to lead the Indian people to the cherished goal of freedom through active, voluntary and purposeful participation in the world struggle against Fascism.

We declare not only our determination to fight Fascism, but offer a concrete plan for mobilising the Indian people in that struggle. Pronouncements from high Government quarters, as well as of leading public men, show that there is a good deal of wishful thinking. It is dangerous to seek comfort in the belief that India detests Fascism and the great bulk of her population stands behind the Government in this critical time. It is dangerous, because that is not the case. The present war efforts of the Government can produce only deceptive results. Those efforts cannot touch the masses of the people who are influenced by the whispering propaganda of voluntary or involuntary Fascist agents. For the moment, there may be reasons for complacency. But it would be foolish to believe that India is free from the danger of invasion. The favourable turn in the situation in the Near East only gives us a respite, which should be utilised for preparing to meet future emergencies which are sure to be graver. The Congress resistance, even if it is put up on a larger scale, will create little difficulty for the Government in so far as purely military preparations are concerned. But more than military preparations will be necessary for defending India against the possible danger of Fascist invasion. The entire popular energy and enthusiasm must be mobilised for the purpose. That cannot be done through the present war efforts of the Government. Those efforts must be democratised and popular elements must be associated with the administration of the country in the provinces as well as in the centre without any further delay. The Congress attitude should not prevent the Government from doing so. It would be a grave mistake for the Government to believe that the present constitutional position can continue indefinitely without seriously perjudicing the defensive power of India. On the other hand, it is equally dangerous to lose precious time with the expectation that the Congress leaders would recover their senses after they had thought over the situation soberly in the quietness of imprisonment. A party, which betrays the popular trust for the sake of group prestige, and openly declares indifference even to actual Fascist invasion of India, forfeits the claim to represent the interests of the people. In any case, the present unsatisfactory situation must continue yet for a considerable time, if it is to be ended by an understanding between the Congress and the Government. In the meantime, the situation is bound to deteriorate. Fascist sympathy is bound to spread among the people; and it is easy to imagine how favourable that atmosphere will be for the operation of organised "fifth columns" of Fascism. Those who are concerned with the defence of India against the danger of Fascist invasion must learn from experience that the decisive factor in case of such invasion is not the military might of the invading army, but the agents of the enemy undermining the defence. Having regard for the alarming reality of the psychological atmosphere, that prevails in India to-day, one should not tolerate any procrastination, complacency or wishful thinking.

As against the Fascist conviction in a certain section of the nationalist movement and the wide-spread Fascist sympathy, fortunately, there are other Indian patriots and public men who strongly disapprove of the policy of the Congress, and are prepared to shoulder the responsibility of combating the menace of Fascism and mobilise popular support for the purpose. With their help and co-operation, the constitutional deadlock in the provinces can be terminated, and popular opinion can be associated with the administration of the country, so as to conterbalance all resistance from the direct and indirect allies of Fascism. As far as we are concerned, we anticipated the danger of Fascism even before the war broke out. Therefore, we shall carry on the struggle against this danger, wherever it is found, irrespective of the attitude of the Government. But in the face of the common danger, all genuine anti-Fascist elements must get together to act according to such a plan as can be executed under the given situation. Let there be no illusion or wishful thinking.

The majority party having refused to play the game, others must shoulder the responsibility of protecting popular interest by occupying the vacant offices in this critical moment. It is immaterial whether Congress members of the Provincial Legislative Assemblies are outside or inside the jails. The fact that they have declared their refusal to participate in the defence of the country is decisive. Moreover, they laid down the offices voluntarily, and, having stayed out of office for more than a year, have at last sought refuge in jail. Given their ambiguous and doubtful attitude towards Fascism, it will be highly dangerous to welcome them back to power. We do not know how the Government feels about it. But we Indian anti-Fascists cannot longer trust the Congress leaders. If their profession of non-violence is sincere, they should act according to the advice their patron saint offered to the European victims of Fascist aggression. The more sincere they are, the more dangerous they will be. If they are not sincere, no reliance can be placed on their other professions. Therefore, no Indian, concerned with the future of our coun try, can any longer hope that any good will com out of the Congress policy.

NATIONAL DEMOCRATIC UNION

Summary of Speech at the Inauguration of the National Democratic Union by the Conference of independent pnblicmen Calcutta, December 31, 1940.

We have gathered here not for exploring the possibilities for joint action. There is a general agreement. That can be stated as follows: It is evident that the prospect of Indian freedom and progress as well as the future of the rest of mankind will be seriously prejudiced by the victory of Fascism. Before long, India herself may be directly menaced from all sides. In this situation, non-cooperation with the war efforts of the Government cannot be the standard for Indian patriotism, and a pacifism must be regarded as a positive danger. In the midst of a world enslaved by triumphant Fascism, the chances of India attaining freedom will be more remote than ever. She will even lose the very possibility of carrying on her struggle for freedom. Therefore, all Indian patriots, who are not blinded by false ideals or petty considerations, should for the moment work with the sole purpose of defeating Fascism. But they cannot play their part with honour and credit, unless the Government of the country comes under popular influence as far as possible in the given situation, and the responsibility of defending India passes on to the Indians themselves.

Given this agreement, the question is how to act accordingly. We have assembled here in order to answer this question and place our collective opinion before the country. It is generally maintained that the Government does not want non-official co-operation. I do not know the mind of the present rulers of India. But whatever may be their prejudices and predispositions, ultimately their action will be compelled by the development of events. Therefore, instead of wanting the Government to do this or that, before we do whatever we can for contributing to the fight against Fascism, we should be guided by the fact that sooner or later the Government is bound to realise that the war cannot be won without the fullest and enthusiastic support of India. At the same time, we must bear in mind that India is vitally concerned with this war, irrespective of the attitude of others. It is only natural for those in possession of power to be reluctant to part with it. Therefore, it is idle to make a grievance out of the policy of the Government. Nevertheless, the policy of drift hitherto pursued by the Government is deplorable. A warning must be sounded against the complacency and wishful thinking on the part of the Government. We should emphasise the urgency of the Government securing the active co-operation of all who, in the first place, wish the defeat of the Fascist Powers.

It is evident for all realistic and far-seeing politicians that the present situation affords great opportunities for the Indian people to assert themselves and grow up to the stature of a free and powerful nation. Unfortunately, some have failed to seize the opportunity. The welfare of the nation demands that others should come forward to take the lead. There is no use complaining that the Government do not take any notice of others than the Congress and the communal organisations. The Government may be compelled to change its attitude.. In order to do that, patriots who do not approve of the Congress policy should have confidence in themselves. For the moment, they all appear to be paralysed by the feeling of helplessness. There is no reason for that helplessness. Now that the Congress has definitely chosen to go to the wilderness in order to avoid the responsibility of facing a complicated situation, it is the moral as well as public obligation of others to shoulder the responsibility. We believe that the Congress attitude to wards the war does not truly reflect the welfare and the aspirations of the Indian people. Therefore, the Congress majority in the provincial Legislative Assemblies has become an empty formality. That formality can no longer terrify us or bind our hands. The British democracy was confronted with a similar situation. Nevertheless British politics is dominated by Labour to-day, although there is a formal Conservative majority in the Parliament.

There is no reason why other popular representatives should not take office in the provinces where Congressmen have chosen to desert the trust placed in them by the electorate. Technical difficulties can be easily overcome by an agreement between the executive authority and the popular representatives willing to shoulder the responsibility of office. Patchwork like Interim Ministries won't do; neither would the appointment of non-official advisors improve the situation. There must be a complete realignment of forces. That can be done by setting up Emergency

Ministries in the deadlocked provinces. The immediate task of the Emergency Ministries will be to democratise the war efforts and to prepare the country for a general election as soon as possible. The idea of general elections should not be terrifying. The popularity of the Congress is very largely due to the fact that no other party has appeared on the scene with a programme which can appeal to the people. Every party cannot have a Mahatma. But it is possible to do what the Congress has failed to do. The expectations aroused by the Congress Ministries were not nearly fulfilled. Consequently, there is a seething discontent. The Congress attitude towards the war does not represent the interests of the vast majority of the Indian population, who are participating in the war, directly or indirectly, in one way or another. So far they have not lost anything owing to that participation. On the contrary, they have been all gaining, more or less. Therefore, the popularity of the Congress has become entirely artificial and can be easily challenged. For that purpose, another popular party should appear on the political scene. Those present in this meeting, and others sharing our views, to-day happen to belong to different political groups. A fusion of all those groups is not suggested. The suggestion is tne formation of a National Democratic Union composed of all the parties and groups and independent public men who realise the great possibilities of the present situation, and have the courage to explore them for the welfare of the Indian nation. The constituents of the proposed Union will retain fullest independent as regards all controversial issues, to be settled in due time. They are expected to act jointly only for the common objects, which may be enumerated as follows:

1. Defeat of Fascism, and rapid development of the resources of India for that purpose;

2. Realignment of political forces for opposing those who have been preventing the association of popular representatives with the Government of the country in these fateful days;

3. Re-election of the Legislature in the provinces which remain without popular Governments owing to the obstructionist policy of the Congress;

4. Establishment of Emergency Ministries in those provinces pending the general elections;

5. Inclusion of independent popular representatives in the Viceroy's Executive Council.

6. Democratisation of the war efforts, in

order to make India's contribution voluntary, purposeful and therefore more effective.

The formation of the proposed National Democratic Union is bound to influence the attitude of the Government. On the other hand, it will provide the people with another vehicle for the expression of their opinion. The Government can no longer delay in doing what it must do for its own interest. It can get men and money for the purposes of the war. But Powers waging a totalitarian war cannot be defeated with men and money alone. The energy and determination and the will to victory of the entire people must be mobilised for the purpose. That cannot be done through the present war efforts of the Government. These efforts are utterly inadequate for combating the wide-spread Fascist sympathy and whispering Fascist propaganda under the cover of ill-conceived nationalism and spurious anti-imperialism. Complete democratisation of the war efforts is urgently needed for combating this grave danger which will seriously undermine the striking as well as the defensive power of India. If all the progressive and democratic elements of the Indian population declare their intention to undertake that task, and make a concerted organised effort with that purpose, the Government is sure to respond, and India will consequently become a bulwark against the Fascist menace.

I am sure that this meeting of ours will open up a new vista before the Indian nation, and raise new hopes for its future. Let us not be diverted by remote issues. Let us concentrate upon the immediate tasks. It is easy to see how the communal problems and constitutional issues, which appear to be so very baffling and complicated to-day, will be simplified by the accomplishment of the immediate task of organising joint efforts for increasing the defensive power of India, for freeing Indian public life from unwholesome influences, and for placing the Indian nation where it will command the respect of the world by virtue of having contributed to the titanic struggle for the freedom of mankind as a whole.

IMPERIALISM, FASCISM AND WAR.

Speech at the University Institute Hall, Calcutta, January 15, 1941.

It is a curious phenomenon that even those who, by the logic of the ideology they profess, should be ardent supporters of the war to defeat Fascism, are taking up an attitude which amounts to weakening the forces fighting Fascism. Ever since it appeared on the European political scene more than twenty years ago, Fascism was combated by the Socialists and Communists, together with all other advocates of freedom and progress, as the greatest menace to all the ideals of modern civilisation. It was recognised by them that Fascism meant war. For years, they agitated for mobilising public opinion to resist what was called the danger of Fascism and war. It was anticipated that, by its very nature, Fascism was bound to precipitate wars which could be avoided only by destroying the system which bred wars. Yet, when eventually the war was precipitated by Fascist aggressiveness, many avowed anti-Fascists suddenly went back on everything that they had said previously, and took up an attitude which could only help Fascism.

I am not one of those who ascribe mean motives to all political behaviour. The curious attitude taken even by those, who cannot make any mistake about the nature of Fascism, is determined by their inability to analyse the situation dispassionately. Therefore, I propose to analyse the forces involved in this war, so that its nature may be scientifically appreciated, and all those interested in the historic task of building up a new world order on the foundation laid by the achievements of the last two-hundred years may intelligently determine their attitude towards this epoch-making struggle.

The nature of a conflict is determined by the forces involved in it. The forces can be characterised by different standards. The problem can be approached from different points of view. The nature of the present war is to be determined in the light of 1, the social and political character of the forces involved; 2, its alternative lines of development and 3, its possible outcomes.

The fundamental fact of the situation is that the present international conflict takes place on the background of irreconcilable social and political conflicts inside the nations involved in it. There is a relation between these two conflicts, and the development of the military conflict on the international front may be determined by the anxiety of the ruling classes of the countries, directly or indirectly involved in the international conflict, to hold their own in the civil conflict at home. The more deep-seated social conflict is not limited by national boundaries. It takes place on an international scale, cutting across the antagonisms and rivalries between National States.

This fundamental fact determined the international relations during the years preceding the outbreak of the war. The outstanding feature of those relations was to smooth over antagonisms between National States. Persistent efforts were made to avoid a large-scale armed conflict at the cost not only of a series of small and weak nations, but even of the prestige of powerful imperialist States.

In view of that background of international

relations, it is not permissible to start from the mechanical assumption that the present conflict is the outcome of the rivalry between two groups is imperialist States for the domination of Europe or of the world. This view is based on a simplification of matters. It does not take into account the complex under-currents of the international situation, and ignores the specific features of the economic structure of the two systems, namely Imperialism and Fascism. It is a superficial view: Imperialism is the last stage of Capitalism; Fascism is the most brutal form of capitalist dictatorship; ergo, Fascism and Imperialism are identical. The fallacy is obvious. Even the superficial analysis reveals that Imperialism and Fascism represent two different stages of Capitalism. Therefore, they cannot be identical. Nevertheless, from this simple formalist syllogism, it is deduced that the present war is not is a war between imperialist States, and therefore to be distinguished in any way from previous wars.

In reality, however, the relation of forces is not so simple as all that. Fascism, indeed, is a phase of Capitalism. It is also true that in contemporary Europe, the terms Capitalism and Imperialism can be inter-changeably used, because all the leading capitalist countries have attained, to a greater or lesser degree, the stage of Imperialism. But from that it does not necessarily follow that Fascism is identical with Imperialism in the strict sense of the term. Owing to their expansionist tendencies, the Fascist States have been called Imperialist States. Such characterisation may serve propagandist purposes; but that is hardly a scientific view. Territorial expansion is not the characteristic feature of modern Imperialism. The United States of America is a typical, first-class modern imperialist country; yet, to conquer colonies politically has not been as a rule its policy.

Surplus capital for export is the economic foundation of modern Imperialism. That was the case with Garmany before the last great war. That was not the case with post-war Germany. Germany recovered from the severe economic crisis immeniately after the war as a dependency of American capital. Between 1924 aud 1928, the period of reconstruction of the German industrial system, a vast bulk of foreign capital was invested in Germany. Industrial reconstruction and expansion led to the accumulation of capital German foreign policy manifested neo-imperialist tendencies. But at the same time, Germany remained under the obligation of paying the interest on borrowed foreign capital which was large enough to absorb practically the entire new capital accumulated in her industries. In those days, Germany represented a peculiar, unprecedented, unforeseen type of economy. It was imperialist and colonial at the same time. Eventually, she came out of that peculiar position by simply repudiating not only her obligations under the Versailles Treaty, but also commercial obligations voluntarily incurred. That was an act which gave a staggering blow to capitalist ethics as well to capitalist economy. It was a large-scale repudiation of the right of private property, the rock-bottom of capitalist economy. A system that rose violating the ethical and economic principles of Capitalism could not be normally capitalistic and, therefore, did not contain the germ of modern Imperialism. Fascist expansionism may be analogous to Roman Imperialism, but certainly not to modern Imperialism.

Even after repudiating her financial obligations abroad, Germany had little capital to export. Neo-militarism, inaugurated with a feverish speed after the advent of the Nazis, promoted a new expansion of heavy industries, absorbing all the newly accumulated capital which might have been exported. Thus, the rapid growth of military power and the manifestations of extravagant expansionism coincided with a financial weakening of Germany. Growing as a formidable Fascist Power, she became negligible as an impeialist rival. Excessive expenditure on account of the army, navy and air-force left in Germany so little exportable capital that she was even unable to pay for the raw-material, indispensable for her war industries, imported from abroad.

Autarchy is the peculiar principle of Fascist economy. Self-containedness and expansionism are mutually exclusive. Autarchy is the economics of Capitalism in an insoluble crisis, in an advanced stage of decay. Modern Imperialiam is the outcome of capitalist prosperity. Therefore, Fascist economy provides no foundation for modern imperialist expansion.

Such being the specific features of the economic structure of Nazi Germany, they could not be a serious rival of British Imperialism. Instead of any rivalry, there indeed was a systematic co-operation between England and Germany ever since the signing of the Locarno Pact in 1924.

The initial stages of the economic recovery of Germany had taken place with financial aid from America. With a financial hold on Germany, the United States could eventually dominate the whole of continental Europe. The Versailles Treaty had established French diplomatic supremacy and military hegemony over the European Continent. France emerged out of the war not only as a formidable military power, but also as a great industrialist country with tremendous imperialist potentialites. There was a possibility of a Franco-American alliance. England was naturally alarmed, and wanted to maintain the balance of power. Germany was the obvious ally. But introducing Germany in the League of Nations, and having her recognised as a Great Power, British diplomacy headed off the danger of an alliance between the Soviet Union and the German Republic.

That being the diplomatic background of the present relation of forces in Europe, it is an altogether unfounded theory that Europe is experiencing another imperialist war brought about by the antagonism between the imperialist interests of England and the imperialist ambitions of Nazi Germany. It is well known that, since the invasion of Abyssinia, England refused to raise a finger to resist repeated Fascist aggression. On every single occasion of those successive acts of aggression—Abyssinia, Spain, Austria, Czecho-Slovakia-England could call a halt if she wanted. Terribly alarmed by the growing military power of Germany, and also by the expansionist policy of Italy, France would have readily joined England in any action against Fascist aggression. The Soviet Union was always there, ready tothrow in her weight on the side of freedom and democracy. Yet, it was British diplomacy which prevented any concerted anti-Fascist action.

Territorial acquistions are of little practical value, unless they can offer channels for profitable investment of capital exported from the conquering country. Nazi Germany having little capital to export, new territories cannot be transformed into valuable economic assets, unless the capital came from some other quarter; and in that case, the real profit of territorial expansion would not belong to the conquering State, which should be satisfied with the empty glory of military victory; the real benefit accrues to the third party which has the surplus capital to invest.

The analogy of the last war does not evidently apply to the present conflict. It is not the culmination of a premeditated plan of one Imperialist Power to weaken another. The Nazi demand for colonies was only a Without counter, and served the propagandist purpose of strengthening the Hitler regime by encouraging chauvinism on the part of a certain section of the German people. Therefore, it was never taken seriously. As regards rivalry for world domination, Nazi Germany never really entered the list. Without any economic foundation, the propaganda for world domination is only a matter of words, meant to deceive the people at home to be emotionally attached to an unpopular regime.

Imperialist wars are waged with the purpose of some Imperialist Power or Powers profiting at the cost of others. When the result of a large-scale general war threatens to be such as to be ruinous to the imperialist system as a whole, imperialist wars no longer happen. In the contemporary period of world history, only a war between England and the United States of America will still be an imperialist war. The present armed conflict in Europe does not have the specific characteristics of an imperialist war, which is deliberately prepared by both the parties, and is expected to end in the defeat of one party, whichever party may be defeated, Imperialism as such remaining unweakened.

When neighbouring countries are armed to the teeth and are in the midst of a perennial economic crisis, jingoist nationalism may serve as a safety valve, and armed conflicts of a more or less serious nature may be precipitated by any chance event or by some unfortunate miscalculation. That sort of war, however, in not an imperialist war. The present war is a war of that nature.

A theoretical understanding of the relation between Imperialism and Fascism as well as the events immediately leading up to the outbreak of the war prove that the present conflict is the inevitable consequence of the Fascist system. It is not produced by any clash between Imperialism and Fascism, because there is no such clash. Fascism, being necessary for the preservation of Capitalism, cannot be really antagonistic to Imperialism. Therefore, Imperialist interests cannot desire the defeat of Fascism. Those interests would have stopped this war, if they could. They were prevented from doing so by the intervention of the genuinely anti-Fascist forces. Therefore, the defeat of Fascism will mean not victory for Imperialism, but triumph of the genuinely anti-Fascist forces which, by their very nature, are also anti-imperialist. Whatever may happen in England, a military defeat would certainly mean the overthrow of the Nazi regime in Germany. The repercussion of that event will be felt all over England, That certainly is a result to be desired by all who want the political and cultural ideals of modern civilisation to survive the present crisis. If that is a desirable result, everything should be done to bring it about. That should be the proper approach to the problems of the present international situation, and our attitude should be determined accordingly. On the other hand, the victory of Fascism may eliminate Imperialism, but the positive result will be the subjugation of the world to the worst form of capitalist exploitation. There can be no mistake in making the choice. Let us make the choice. The choice is the defeat of Fascism, which will mean the making of democracy, and the reconstruction of the world on the foundation of the achievements of modern civilisation.

SHOULD ANTI-IMPERIALISM LEAD US TO WELCOME FASCISM?

Speech at the Bengal Provincial Congress of the R. D. P., Jan. 18/19, 1941.

One month after the war broke out in Europe, the Central Executive Committee of the Party, which then functioned as the League of Radical Congressmen, met at Dehradun, and adopted a certain policy with regard to the war, which was later elaborated in a thesis published under the title "India and War". This booklet was a product of collective thinking, which was the necessary pre-condition for collective action, and I believe that even now this book, written more than a year ago, is the most important and valid after all that has since been said about the war. It is on this thesis that all the subsequent actions of the Party were based. Discussions on the question have been going on among members of the Party throughout the country for the whole year, and the time has now come to act according to that policy, and the task of this conference is to adjust and elaborate this policy for application in Bengal.

Although most of you are young in age, all of you have been politically active for many years, working in various organisations and trained in the methods and mode of thinking of those organisations, particularly of the Congress.

In our country, anything, to be acceptable, must be stated as a dogma. You must believe, have faith, in something, in order to act.

The political dogma of the Congress, which dominated the politics of our country so long, is non-cooperation. A Congressman cannot think except in terms of co-operation or non-cooperation; co-operation is bad, and non-co-operation is good. Trained in the atmosphere of Gandhism, people never stop to think that political non-cooperation is possible only in the life of a social Robinson Crusoe. If we want to non-cooperate consistently with the Government, we shall have no other alternative than to commit suicide. Our party has never made a fetish of non-cooperation. Co-operation or non-cooperation is not an issue for us.

The issue is that this war is going to decide the fate of the world, including India, for many years to come. We want a revolution, which means, we want to create a new world order. Revolution may be a necessity, but we should not forget that is is not an inevitability.

To-day, when we say that the fate of the world is in the balance, we mean that revolution, or a new and better world order is no more likely than a relapse of humanity into barbarism. Therefore, we must throw our weight into the balance on the side of the force fighting barbarism; and that means co-operation; we cannot help it; we must want it.

This fight is not the cause of one particular class of human society. All those who feel the necessity of fighting the menace of a relapse into barbarism, which is implied in the victory of Fascism, are to-day the standard-bearers of progress, are in fact defenders of a new and better world order.

Therefore, we have said that Anti-Imperialism becomes a meaningless shibboleth if it implies that the downfall of Imperialism should be welcomed even when brought about by a victory of Fascism. And therefore we have said that we are prepared to co-operate with everybody and anybody in this war for the defeat of Fascism.

This policy of ours is not a tactical manoeuvre. It is based on very fundamental principles, and we have to carry it out with all the courage at our command. And, indeed, it needs courage of conviction to state that, compelled to choose between the conditions as they exist in India to-day, which are the deplorable result of Imperialism, and the conditions prevailing in Germany and Italy and in the countries conquered by them,—who would call himself a patriot and not say that the conditions in India are preferable to those in Fascist Europe?

The fight against Fascism is an objectively revolutionary fight. Bloodshed is not an inherent feature of a revolution. And this is not a new heresy of mine: I can quote scriptures to support this statement. Karl Marx, while developing the theory of revolution, wrote nearly a hundred years ago that in the more highly developed democratic countries revolutions might not take such violent forms, and he mentioned England as a possible instance!

And what else is happening in England to-day than such a revolution? People talk about

Imperialist England, but they forget that England to-day is not only fighting a war against the bulwark of counter-revolution, but actually experiencing a revolution itself. If you have observed the movements of thought in England at present, you will have noticed that a larger and larger section of the English bourgoisie is losing faith in capitalism. This mental state is created by the realisation that fate has overtaken them, and that something is going on that cannot be resisted except by submitting to Fascism, which means losing the war.

Fascism being the embodiment of all the forces of reaction in the world, whoever is fighting against it is an objectively progressive, indeed an objectively revolutionary force. Therefore, Mr. Churchill, who guides to-day the front-rank fighters against the bulwark of world reaction, whatever else he may have in his mind, is a more revolutionary force than all the Congress leaders, right or left, taken together, who are only obstructing that fight. Mr. Churchill to-day signifies the symbol of the English people fighting Fascism. As such, he will be historically appreciated.

On the other hand, the Congress leaders are

to-day doing something that, except by themselves, is appreciated only in Rome and Berlin. In this connection, it may interest you that Rome Radio is heartily abusing me for the policy adopted by our party and the campaign that we are carrying on in India. Now, if M. N. Roy is being abused by Rome Radio along with Mr. Churchill, I refuse to be ashamed of the company. In the fight against a common enemy, I welcome it.

A good old friend of mine told me the other day : "Whatever you are saying is perfectly true; but you have made yourself so unpopular by saying it, that it pains me." I asked him: "Don't you think that the cause for which one fights is greater than the value of one's popularity ? If you cannot include your popularity in the sacrifices of which you talk so much, don't talk of sacrifice at all."

If our fight succeds, India will be saved, and will be placed in a position where she can be one of the determining factors for saving the world.

The decisive battles of this war will be fought in the East. We Indians shall have to fight these battles. It is said that the British do not trust us. Perhaps they don't. But the day will come when they will be compelled to trust us for because these battles, because in this country there is nobody else to fight them unless they are prepared to lose the battles. In this process, India will have to become a first-class industrial and military power, and conditions will be created in which India will be able to advance and prosper as a Free, Modern, Democratic State.

THE IMMEDIATE TASK: DESTRUCTION OF FASCISM

Presidential Address at the Andhra Provincial Conference of the Radical Democratic Party, held at Tenali on Feb. 8, 1941.

The world is passing through one of the most critical moments of its history. Such crises occur as epoch-making events. They symbolise the frantic efforts of a dying world to survive, and also the birth-pangs of a new world. The future of the world is made or marred by the outcome of that struggle. Whenever the efforts of the decayed world to survive succeed, the hands of the clock of history are set back, and human progress is arrested, either generally or in a particular part of the world. The world to-day is confronted with the possibility of such a reaction.

The false optimism derived from a fatalistic view of historical determinism is misleading. It is true that, like physical processes, the march of social events is also determined. But nothing is inevitable. The proposition that everything is possible does not pre-suppose belief in miracles. Determinism does not claim anything more than to indicate the most probable. But what for the moment appears to be the least probable, may any day become an accomplished fact.

These general observations may sound rather abstract and out of place in a political conference. That, however, is not the case. Politics, being a department of social science, cannot be practised properly except with a certain amount of scientific detachedness and philosophical outlook. Emotionalism is the cause of the confusion and barrenness which characterise the political life of our country. Emotion is a part of human equipment. Therefore, politics, cannot be free from emotions. But emotionalism is a different thing. It is the habit of being guided only by emotions. It disregards reason and reality, and has no patience for criticism. There is no sense in organising a new political party, unless it can approach political problems rationally and raise political practice on a higher plane of realism. Therefore, I shall permit myself to dwell a little longer on the general observations.

They will make the grave implications of the present world crisis more easily understandable.

I mentioned that similar crises were experienced in the past. It will be instructive to recollect the more outstanding of them. That will enable us to visualise all the dreadful possibilities of the present situation, and reveal the danger of the comfortable belief that an old order is outstanding the paroxysm of death, and a new order is bound to replace it. This fatalistic belief paralyses action, and motivates a behaviour which may help the least probable to happen. Facism represents the frantic efforts of a dying system to survive. But there is absolutely no reason to assume that the survival is impossible. It is absurd to argue that the triumph of Fascism will mean destruction of Imperialism and, therefore, the rise of a new order on the basis of Socialism. This simplified view of the determined process of social progress persuades one to be indifferent to the outcome of the present struggle. Because the implication of the absurd argument is that the destruction of Imperialism will automatically mean the advent of Socialism, and therefore Fascism should be helped to defeat Imperialism.

But let us revert to the recollection of past crises which show that the determinist laws of social evolution do not preclude occasional relapses of very serious nature. In the antique period, a whole series of civilisations collapsed, even after having attained a very high level. Later on, the Greek culture laid down a very solid foundation for the modern civilisation. The declining period of the Roman Empire was marked by a severe crisis resulting from the conflict between a dying past and a nascent future. The Roman power was certainly autocratic, and the Roman Church had almost overwhelmed the scientific spirit and rationalist thought of ancient Greece. Neverthless, the fall of the Roman Empire did not mean the establishment of a new order in Europe. On the contrary, Europe was plunged in the darkness of the middle-ages which delayed human progress for nearly a thousand years. Fascist victory in this twentieth century will be something like the overthrow of the Roman Empire by the northern barbarians.

India also experienced a similar misfortune which was all the more deplorable because she never experienced the Renaissance as in the case of Europe. The rise of Buddhism was an epoch-making event. Ancient India reached the high-water mark of civilisation during the Buddhist period. Had there been no reversal of the process, she might have retained her place at the forefront of human civilisation. But Brahmanical reaction ultimately overwhelmed Buddhism. Those who helped or welcomed that reaction on the ground that, in its latter days, Buddhism had developed many ugly features, certainly did not help the progress of Indian civilisation. India has still to recover from the staggering blow she received from the triumph of Brahmanical reaction over the Buddhist revolution.

A Fascist victory will mean a great set back for human progress. The misfortune will not remain limited to Europe. The avowed intention of the Fascists is to establish their "New Order" over the whole of the world. Therefore, no one can be indifferent to the development and ultimate outcome of this titanic struggle, and yet claim to be an advocate of freedom and progress. Yet, the Indian nationalist movement not only refuses to help the defeat of Fascism, but is actually trying to resist India making her contribution to that purpose. Notwithstanding this unfortunate and ill-advised policy, the fact remains that the future of India will depend on the future of the world. The ideals of the Indian nationalist movement cannot possibly be attained if the Fascists can establish their "New Order" in Europe and consequently in the whole of the world. In this situation, the rise of the Radical Democratic Party is a necessity. It is not yet strong enough numerically. Its activities are circumscribed by all sorts of difficulties. Nevertheless, the Radical Democratic Party is the only political organisation in the country which realises the responsibility that rests on India in the critical moment of history. It is determined to do everything necessary for enabling India to discharge her responsibility to the world, and, by doing so, win for herself the coveted position of power and prestige.

Although the world crisis presented the occasion for the rise of the Radical Democratic Party, originally it grew out of the crisis in the Indian National Congress. All along, there had been a conflict between the progressive urge of the nationalist movement and tne reactionary outlook of the Congress leadership ever since it came under the domination of the Mahatma. The object of the nationalist movement is not purely political. Every political movement has a social content..

It expresses the urge for economic progress and social advancement. The object of the Indian nationalist movement is to lead the people out of an economic backwardness which has been causing stagnation in every other walk of llfe. But the Mahatma became the leader of the movement in order to put a metaphysical content into the con cept of Swaraj. In course of time, Swaraj ceased to have any political or secular meaning, and was declared by the Mahatma to be a state of mind to be attained through non-political practices. That metaphysical corruption of the nationalist movement was condemned by the pioneers of our Party.

With all its high-sounding pretensions, from the very beginning, Gandhism was an instrument of reaction. Its economic doctrines cannot possibly cure the evils of poverty and mass unemployment, from which the Indian people suffer. Instead of striking at their root, Gandhism would make a virtue out of poverty. That is the meaning of the revivalist doctrine of simplicity and village reconstruction. Politically, Gandhism stands for nothing more than a replacement of the foreign bureaucracy by a native bureaucracy manned mostly by the caste Hindus. That became clearly evident as soon as Congressmen came to office. Tall promises made for catching votes during the election were all forgotten. The much advertised Tenancy Legislation did not give any tangible relief to the peasantry. The Congress leaders were very anxious to placate the landowning classes. Callously in different to the crying needs of the people, they fanatically advocated moral reforms. Prohibition was placed at the centre of the ministerial programme. To justify their failure to implement the Election Manifesto, Congress Ministries pleaded absence of power. The limitations of the Constitution were known previously. Therefore, honesty should have prevented Congressmen from making promises which could not be kept. But while in office, they stoutly maintained that they were all-powerful. They acted like the real rulers of the country. Nevertheless, they failed to do even a part of what they could have done if they really wanted. They were only anxious to prove that they could administer the affairs of the Imperialist State as efficiently as the Englishmen themselves.

The ministerial experience sharpened the contradictions inside the Congress. The divergence between the object of the leaders and the necessities of the rank and file become clear. *The hypocritical preachers of the cult of non-violence shot down workers and peasants on the slightest provocation.* The prophet of the cult gave his blessings to those uncalled for acts of violence, on the ground that violence was unavoidable so long as government was necessary. Repressive measures, previously condemned as lawless laws, were enforced by Congress Ministers against Congressmen themselves. Favouritism was practised disregarding the susceptibilities of the minority communities. Communal tension was accentuated by insisting on measures which bore the stamp of orthodox Hinduism.

The Congress Ministries became more and more unpopular. Another year in office would have ruined their chances in the next election. The war presented a plausible pretext. A virtue was made out of a necessity. To guarantee success in the next elections, Congress Ministries were withdrawn. To-day, Congressmen are going to jail for no other purpose than to secure re-election. The object of the present Satyagraha as declared by the Mahatma himself is to save the Congress. But the anxiety is not to save the Congress as a mass organisation, but to maintain a position in which Congressmen alone will be entitled to replace the present bureaucracy.

The discontent created by the operation of Congress Ministries expressed itself for the first time in the re-election of Subhas Chandra Bose as the President of the Congress. That was a vote of no-confidence in the ruling clique. That was a possibility for overthrowing Gandhism. The figure-head of that primitive revolt turned out to be a very weak man. Moreover, at the critical moment at Tripuri, he was betrayed by the so-called leftists. But the banner of revolt was taken over by the confirmed opponents of Gandhism who organised the Leagure of Radical Congressmen with the object of putting a clear political and social content in the concept of Swaraj, and of transforming the Congress into a democratic people's party.

Ever since 1929 we had combated all disruptive tendencies and stood loyally by the Congress, incurring the displeasure of those so-called leftists who to-day worship in the temple of Wardha and act as the advance-guard of Fascism. But the Gandhist leaders did not want democratic freedom. They exploited the superstition and religious sentiment of the masses for their own purpose which could not be served if the masses became politically conscious. The authoritarian leadership rendered the domocratisation of the Congress impossible. Nevertheless, we continued our efforts until the Congress adopted its present policy which cannot be tolerated by the fighters for freedom and democracy.

The present policy, however, was not unxpected. It was pre-determined by the reactionary outlook of Gandhism, by its mediaeval cultural ideals and the leader cult which is so very analogous to the Fascist doctrine of super-man. Moreover, totalitarianism is the distinctive feature of the Fascist political organisation. The Congress frankly represents this tendency. It is not a political party. It pretends to be a parallel State organisation, and it identifies itself with the State which is to replace the present State. The totalitarian pretension of the Congress, however, has made impossible for it to be a democratic organisation of the Indian people. It has alienated all the communities except the Hindus and even a considerable section of the Hindus themselves who do not accept Gandhism as the quintessence of Hinduism. Consequently with all its totalitarian pretensions, the Congress has degenerated into a minority organisation. Still it claims to represent the whole of India, and pretends to be the mentor of her destiny. That is a peculiarly Fascist characteristic—a vocal minority terrorising and explains the majority. Gandhism contradicts all the legitimate aspirations of nationalism. Yet, the association of Gandhists claims to be the only nationalist organisation.

The ideological and organisational affinity with Fascism explains the present policy of the Congress. The policy may appear to be harmless. Because, the present Satyagraha movement cannot be taken any more seriously than a third-rate comic opera. Nevertheless, it has very dangerous implications. The practice of non-violence may go the extent of an abject surrender to Fascist aggression. This is not a fantasy. Having applauded Quislings and Petains for their betrayal, and advised the British people to put up no resistance to Fascist aggression, the dictator of the Congress cannot possible allow his followers to participate in the defence of India. Should the Congressmen disown the desire to surrender India to the Fascist invaders, they could not be credited with any honesty as regards their devotion to the Mahatma. The latter, on his part, would forfeit his claim to the living faith in non-violence, if he would allow the formation of the National Government to shoulder the responsibility of defending India. Yet, the fact is that even to-day all Conressmen are eager to return to office. As a matter of fact, their loyalty to the discredited organisation is retained by the hope that before long Congress Ministries will return to office, and a whole army of Congressmen would have their shares in the loaves of office. Otherwise, there would be no sense in the present Satyagraha movement. It does not create any difficulty for the Government to get all the money and men required for the war. It even does not prevent the vast bulk of the Indian people from participating in the war. Whatever may be the desire of the Congressmen, they should not be allowed to return to office. Because, assuming some honesty on their part, they can be expected to do only one thing on the strength of being in office. A National Government controlled by them should act according to the advice that the Mahatma has been so freely giving to the victims of Fascist aggression in Europe. Therefore, those who do not believe that voluntary submission is the highest of virtues, and regard Fascism as the negation of all the cherished ideals of civilised humanity, must prevent the Congress leaders from regaining the positions of power and vantage, from which they could do incalculable harm to India as well as to the rest of the world.

For that purpose, there must be a really popular party which could challenge the Congress totalitarian claim. The situation is very favourable for the rise of such a party. All the other political organisations and groups disapprove of the Congress policy. Notwithstanding the formal majority in the provincial legislatures, the Congress to-day really represents only a minority. In this situation, the totalitarian claim of the Congress can be easily challenged if all the other political groups, communities and independent nationalists will get together with the object of giving the country a new lead in this critical moment. Therefore, our party has taken the initiative regarding the formation of a National Democratic Union. Although the artificial popularity of the Congress and its powerful propaganda machinery still have a paralysing effect on many organisations and individuals, yet the movement for the formation of a National Democratic Union is gathering strength. To develop this movement is the immediate task of our Party. But the National Democratic Union should not be confounded with the Radical Democratic Party. The programme of the National Democratic Union is to lead the country out of the present crisis precipitated by the mistakes of commission and omission on the part of the Congress. Strictly speaking, it is to protect the country against the Fascist menace as represented by the pacifism as well as the totalitarianism of the Congress. The Congress having persistently refused the responsibility of administering the country in these critical days, and the implication of its opposition to India's participation in the war bring so very dangerous, other representatives of the people should come forward to shoulder the responsibility. The fact of the Congress controlling majorities in a number of provincial legislatures should no longer stand in our way. In the first place, the majority is only formal; and secondly, in office, it may sabotage the defensive as well as the striking power of India. As a matter of fact, the majority creates an emergency situation. Therefore, emergency measures must be adopted for overcoming the crisis. The formation of Coalition Ministries in the provinces where Congressmen have resigned office is, therefore, a perfectly legitimate as well as contitutional procedure. The Radical Democratic Party must fully endorse this demand of the National Democratic Union and concentrate all its enery for mobilising popular support for this demand. The formation of Provincial Ministries, composed of those elected legislators, who favour India's participation in the war, is also necessary for transforming this war into a people's war.

Our agitation for the formation of Coalition Ministries is condemned as an alliance with the reactionaries. Not professions, but practice, indicates who is a reactionary. Those who, on some pretext or other, refuse to participate in the fight against Fascism, are the worst reactionaries. We have parted company with the Congress because it has come under the domination of such reactionaries. As determined fighters for the political freedom and social liberation of the Indian masses, we cannot have any scruple in allying with all who are to-day actually engaged in the struggle against the avowed enemy of freedom, democracy and progress. We never shared the reactionary social ideas and compromising political views of the Congress leaders. Yet, for years, we worked as Congressmen, because, objectively, the Congress promised to be a platform for a democratic alliance. Similarly, to-day we are prepared to ally with all anti-Fascists, irrespective of whatever may be their reaction in other matters. In the midst of the fight against Fascism, the democratic forces will be strengthened and organised, so as to hold their own against any possible reaction after the fight against Fascism is won.

The Radical Democratic Party, with its programme of democratic political freedom and social emancipation of the masses, is the pivot of the plan for a re-alignment of forces on the Indian political arena. Its programme is far-reaching, although it is not the programme of Socialism. It is far-reaching because it visualises the radical re-adjustment of social relations which is indispensable for opening before the Indian people the avenues of economic prosperity and social progress. The parliamentary democracy has exhausted all its possibilities. The victory over Fascism will enable Europe to attain a higher level of democracy. It is not necessary for India to adopt parliamentary democracy just when it will be discarded by the more advanced nations of the world. By parliamentary democracy, I mean the system which grants to the masses of the people formal political rights without any effective power. This sort of formal democracy does not establish popular freedom, that is to say, real democracy. Without social democracy, that is, equality of opportunities in the economic field, political democracy is bound to remain a formality. Our party is called the Radical Democratic Party, because it will not be satisfied with formal democracy. *It stands for a thorough reconstruction of our national life. Its object is the establishment of democratic freedom which will invest effective political power in the masses of the people.* It is the political organisation of the common people to be controlled by themselves and conducted according to their collective will. It stands for Swaraj, the establishment of a government of the people by the people, instead of dreaming of a legendary Ramraj. It advocates modernism in every waik of life, as against revivalism. It is the torch-bearer of enlightenment which will dispel obscurantism in the political as well as the spiritual life of the nation. It wants the disinherited to come to their own, and enjoy the richness and fullness of life on this earth. It wants man to be the master of the world and the maker of his own destiny,

These are ideals which must be cherished by all advocates of human freedom and human welfare. They reflect the conscious aspirations as well as the unconscious urge of the Indian masses. Therefore, the Radical Democratic Party legitimately claims to be the party of the Indian people. As such, it is determined to apply itself to the immediate task of mobilising the Indian masses in the stuggle against Fascism, which is not a danger coming only from aborad, but is growing visibly in our very midst. By accomplishing this immediate task, the Radical Democratic Party will acquire the right of leading the Indian people farther in the struggle for freedom. But the future depends on the present. No use dreaming of a bright future, if we cannot measure up to the tasks confronting us to-day. Let us remember once again that nothing will happen inevitably. It is idle to believe that we shall have the opportunity of building up a new order after

Fascism and Imerialism have destroyed themselves. The builders of the new order must help the passing of the old, and there should be no mistake in recognising in Fascism the instrument of the old order struggling for survival. The possibility of the survival remains so long as Fascism is not defeated. Therefore, the destruction of Fascism is the task of the present, and the future will be conditioned by the fulfilment of that task. Only those who will contribute to that task will be the rightful builders of the future. Therefore, the Radical Democratic Party is determined to mobilise the Indian masses to take their due share in the fight against Fascism.

A NEW LEAD

Summary of Speech at a public meeting a Coconada, 6th Feb. 1941

Two reasons are generally given for the anti-war campaign of the Congress. Firstly, India has been made a belligerent party in this war without being consulted; and secondly, India believes in non-violence and is therefore opposed to war on principle. None of these arguments holds good on closer examination. The conscientious objection of the Congress to war has only come as an after-thought, after the Congress had offered its active co-operation in the prosecution of the war for a whole year, although on certain conditions. Assuming that those condi-tions were granted by the Government, if Congressmen were opposed to war in general, or to this war in particular, how could they have reconciled this attitude with active participation in this war, which they would have been obliged to do if the conditions had been accepted? A straight-forward answer to this question reveals the inconsistency of the Congress attitude. If the war is bad, a National Government would not have made it any better, nor would it have given any more substantial power to Indians. It would perhaps have satisfied the prestige of the Congress and strengthened its monopolistic and authnritarian claims. But it would have made no difference to the Indian people, and it would not have brought us a step nearer to the goal of freedom. In short, it is quite clear that originally the Congress leaders had no objection to co-operate in the prosecution of the war; but they wanted to do so on conditions which served their own purpose, and in pressing for those conditions they overplayed their hands. They believed, that if the Congress Ministries resigned, the Government would immediately come down on its knees and implore them to come back on their own terms. But when that did not happen, it was too late for the Congress leaders to climb down, they had to stick to their conditions and the Satyagraha movement is an ineffective gesture to enforce them.

The other argument with which Congressmen justify their anti-war attitude is that India had not been consulted before she was declared a belligerent party. That is a fact, and only those who laboured under the illusion that Congress Ministries had brought Swaraj could be surprised by it. India is still a subject nation. But that does not mean that foreign domination should also enslave our mind and intelligence. If we are still far from political domination at least we can do our independent thinking and have an independent approach to the problems confronting us. If this war is bad, even a National Government will not make it any better. But if we come to the conclusion that it is necessary to fight this war for a certain object, the mere fact that it had first been declared by England and England has dragged us into it, does not alter that conclusion, does not remove the necessity of dragged this war. And if it is true that Fascism is the greatest menace of our time, then it is necessary to fight it.

For many years, along with all progressive elements throughout the world, the Indian nationalist movement was opposed to Fascism. Time and again, Congress expressed their abhorrence for this menace to human civilisation, and passed resolutions condemning Fascist aggression and sympathising with the victims of Fascism. From press and platform, the British Government was accused for conniving with the Fascist dictators, for betraying democracy in Spain, in China, in Czecho-Slovakia. It was pointed out that, when Hitler was still weak, and it would have been easy for England and France to stop his agressive conniving and they did not do so and thereby helped the growth of Fascism to the terrible menace it has now become. It was also pointed out that the imperialist Governments acted in this way because they were afraid that upon the fall of Hitler, revolutions might break out on the European Continent, and they would rather put up with Fascism than with revolutionary movements. When at last this war broke out, Fascism had already grown so strong that it resources to be almost too late. When France surrendered, it appearedthat Fascism would conquer the whole of Europe and perhaps the whole of the world. At that moment, it was imperative for all the fighters for freedom, democracy and progress throughout the world to pool all their resources for a desperate effort to defeat the Fascist monster, because a victory of Fascism, or even appeasement on the terms of the Fascist dictators, would make the whole world a victim of Fascist terror and brutalisation, and would throw back humanity into the dark ages of mediaevalism. If we have condemned Fascist aggression in Spain, in China, Austria and Czecholovakia and sympathised with the victims, and even supported them to the extent of sending men and money and medical aid, why should our attitude suddenly change in the present gigantic fight against the bulwark of Fascism in Europe?

But leaving aside the larger issues and the fate of the world, how is India herself concerned with this war? We have been under British domination for many years. We have resented this domination and fought for our freedom. We were still in the midst of this fight when the war broke out. Having failed to win our freedom until now, we are to-day seeing our opponent engaged in a deadly fight, and the primitive reaction on the part of many Indians is a desire to see him beaten by somebody else. That may be a very natural, but not a very dignified, attitude; because it implies that, unable to win our freedom ourselves, we expect somebody else to win it for us. But let us look at it a little closer. Supposing the Fascist Powers succeed in defeating England and the English people also fall a victim to Nazi barbarism—how will that help us? Having sympathised with the previous victims of Fascist aggression, should we not rather sympathise also with the English people in such a calamity? On the other hand, it does not appear likely that the Fascists will succeed in conquering England herself. If they want to win the war, they shall have to strike at other parts of the British Empire, and every day you find indications in the press that they are turning East. Within a short time the main theatre of war may be shifted very near to the frontiers of India. Communications between England and the East may be interrupted or altogether broken. The Fascist armies will sweep through the Balkans and the Near Eastern countries, and who is going to stop them? In this part of the world, they can be stopped only if India throws in her whole might, her man power, her resources, her fighting spirit, her fervent determination to defeat Fascism and win freedom. A defeat of the British power in India by Hitler's armies can happen only when those armies will actually invade India and overthrow the British Government here with the might of their arms. And who would be so foolhardy as to suggest that the Nazi hordes will come to

India and overthrow the present Government, only to declare India free and march back home with the satisfaction of liberators? Such things do not happen. There are of course those who think that would not matter whether we have the English here or the Nazis; that it would only be a change of masters. But for such an attitude one can have only contempt. It is an expression of slave mentality. I can tell you from my own experience that the difference would matter a lot. It is bad enough that we must still fight for our freedom from imperialist domination; but under Fascist rule, even the chance of fighting for our freedom will be lost.

Therefore, if for no other consideration, even if we do not care what happens to the rest of the world, for the sake of the very chance of ever becoming free, we shall have to fight Fascism, we shall have to do whatever we can to prevent a triumph of Fascism, and that can be done only by a crushing defeat and overthrow of the bulwark of Fascism. In pursuance of that object, we cannot be delicate in choosing our means and allies. Whoever chooses or happens to fight this battle, he cannot but be our ally.

Apart from the fact that, for sake of the very

opportunity of carrying on our fight for freedom, we must contribute to the defeat of Fascism, the prosecution of the war itself does in no way intertere with our fight for feedom. On the contrary, in the course of the war efforts, for the sake of the prosecution of the war itself, India will have to be increasingly industrialised and militarised. Only if the defensive and striking power of India is thus strengthened, can India be an asset in this war and make a decisive contribution in winning the battle against the Fascist menace. Once this war is won by the decisive contribution of an industrialised and militarised India, it will depend solely on the Indians to retain the powerful position thus gained, nor would there be anybody likely to challenge it. That is the opportunity offered to India by the present war. The Congress has failed to recognise it. But there are many others, at least as patriotic and representative of the people as Congressmen, who are prepared to grasp the opportunity and take an active part in the shaping of India's desttny. Going to jail at this moment is only an escape. It has neither the negative value of preventing India's participation in the war, nor the positive value of bringing her anywhere nearer the goal of freedom. It is admittedly meant to serve solely the purpose of self-preservation of the Congress and the return of its candidates in the next election. But given the attitude of the Congress towards the war, this object is not in the best interest of the country, indeed, it would be decidedly harmful. Therefore, I appeal to all the rational, intelligent, far-sighted patriots to get together, rid themselves of the stupor of the deadlock, and give a new, determined and organised lead to the country, so that India, in the process of contributing to the liberation of the world from the menace of Fascism, may come to her own and take her rightful place in the future commonwealth of the free nations of the world.

BETWEEN DEVIL AND DEEP SEA

Presidential Address At the Maharashtra Provincial Conference of the Radical Democratic Party, Poona, 22nd & 23rd March 1941

We had to break with the Congress on the issue of the war, because the Congress policy on this particular issue happened to be the logical consequence of the counter-revolutionary ideology, reactionary social cutlook and political opportunism, which we had combated all along. The difference is not regarding the relation with Imperialism. One must be very credulous indeed to assume that the Congress policy regarding the war is motivated by irreconcilable anti-Imperialism. The Congress as represented by its present leadership has never had that motive. It was always ready, indeed eager, to come to terms with Imperialism. That is its position even today. That was the meaning of the Poona resolution, and the Mahatma has again lifted his ban on that plan for a settlement with Imperialism.

As a matter of fact, the Congress has never opposed India's participation in the war, on principle. The latest Mahatmic pronouncement bears testimony to that. It completely repudiates the previous statement of the same supreme authority that, committed to the doctrine of non-violence, the Congress could not have anything to do with the war. According to the latest statement of the Mahatma, the Congress would help British Imperialism in the prosecution of the war on certain conditions.

The significance of the Congress policy is confused by laying emphasis on the conditions. What is overlooked is that, on the fulfilment of the conditions, the Congress would co-operate with Imperialism. The essential thing is the readiness to co-operate with Imperialism. Evidently, there is little of anti-Imperialism in such a policy. Therefore, it is misleading to say that our view about India's relation to the war means rejection of the anti-Imperialist policy of the Congress. One cannot oppose or reject what does not exist. The Congress policy is not anti-Imperialist therefore, its rejection is not pro-Imperialism.

The difference is about India's attitude regarding the outcome of the war. We believe that, together with the rest of the world, India also will be adversely affected if the war ended in a victory of the Fascist Powers. That belief is based on the appreciation of Fascism.

The obvious implication of the present Congress view is that, except upon the fulfilment of certain conditions, which admittedly would not free her from British Imperialism, India should not participate in the war, even if her non-participation weakened England to the extent of helping the victory of the Fascist Powers. Such a view can be held only by those who do not believe that the victory of Fascism will be harmful for the world and affect India adversely. That is the real difference between our Party and the Congress, and the Congress view is shared more or less by other nationalist organisations. It is a difference in the appreciation of Fascism. It is a difference in the attitude towards Fascism. And this difference results from the old difference in ideology, social outlook and political ideals.

The issue of the war cannot be isolated. As a matter of fact, our attitude to the war is determined by the programme of our Party. The realisation that the programme of our party, which is the programme of political liberation and social emancipation of the Indian masses, will have no chance of being put into practice in a world dominated by Fascism, compels us to the conclusion that, for the sake of her own freedom, India must participate in the world struggle for destroying the menace of Fascism. A recapitulation of the main items of the programme of our Party will make that clear.

The Radical Democratic Party stands for a thorough reconstruction of the national life. Its political object is the establishment of democratic freedom, which will mean effective political power for the people. It stands for that kind of Swaraj, instead of dreaming of a legendary *Ramraj*. It strives not only for national freedom, but also for the social emancipation of the toiling masses. It is the torch-bearer of enlightement which will dispel obscurantism in the political as well as the spiritual life of the nation. It advocates modernism in every walk of life as against revivalism. It wants the disinherited to come to their own and enjoy the richness and fullness of life on this earth. It wants man to be the master of the world and the maker of his own destiny.

Concretely, our Party holds that land should belong to those who made it bear fruit. It demands that rent abd taxes should be reduced so as to relieve the burden on the poor. It demands control of usury, and provision of cheap credit, so as to protect the peasants, workers and middle classes against the exactions of the money-lenders. It stands for the development of modern industries for relieving the pressure on land by creating new employments and causing increase of national wealth through the productive investment of accumulated riches. It demands adequate payment for labour and legislation for promoting the welfare of the working class and salaried employees. It demands free schools, hospitals and supply of water for drinking and irrigation.

Only those who wish to sway the masses by cheap slogans will find this programme inadequate. Such a programme is bound to have an irresistible appeal not only for the toiling masses, but also for all others who stand for democratic freedom and general progress. The relation between this programme and the fight against Fascism is also evident. Fascism stands for the destruction of all the political, social and cultural ideals incorporated in this programme. If Fascism triumphs, and India comes under its domination, those ideals will become inaccessible to the Indian people more than ever. The devotion to those ideals of freedom, and the determination to attain them as soon as possible, inspire us to favour India's participation in the war against Fascism. Those who believe that the fight for Indian freedom, as depicted in the programme of our Party, can disregard the issue of the war against Fascism either do not realise the gravity of the menace of Fascism, or entertain fraudulent ideas of freedom. We are not deluded on either score and therefore we have realised the necessity of fighting the battle for Indian freedom on the anti-Fascist front. We earnestly hope that all those, who, sincerely stand for the masses, will, see the logic of our position and join us in the common struggle.

A brief review of the evolution of our policy will show that we are neither obsessed with any preconceived notion, nor are we actuated by any base motive. Our policy has been determined, step by step, by the development of international events. As soon as the war broke out, we made an exhausive analysis of the situation, in order to estimate its character and visualise its possible development. In the beginning, it appeared that the war might end soon or remain localised in Europe. Therefore, our first resolution, adopted in October 1939, was " to strive for an early termination of armed hostilities in Europe, by issuing an appeal to the people of England and France to demand discontinuation of the war, the laudable object of checking the danger of Nazi aggressiveness having been attained to a large extent by the military and diplomatic moves of the Union of Socialist Soviet Republics." And " to declare that, in case of the war continuing in Europe, even after the laudable object, which secured India's spontaneous sympathy, has been largely attained, the most honourable attitude on the part of India will be that of neutrality which of course cannot be absolute as long as India remains part of the British Empire."

Unfortunately, neither our recommendation nor the profession of non-violence could persuade the Congress leadership to issue the appeal for the termination of hostilities, although at that juncture such an appeal might have found a powerful response from the peoples of England and France. At that time, the Fascist menace did not affect India directly and immediately, and therefore we advocated a policy of neutrality.

Moreover, the subsequent sweeping victories of Fascism could hardly be anticipated at that time. But events took the less expected turn, and the war tended towards developing into a world-wide conflict. The new situation was reviewed by the All-India Conference of the League of Radical Congressmen held at Dehra Dun in the beginning of June 1940. The resolution on the international situation adopted by that Conference stated:

" The League of Radical Congressmen is still of the opinion that a triumph of Fascism and the establishment of its domination, directly or indirectly, all over Europe, will mean a serious setback for the forces of revolution throughout the world, and will constitute a great menace for the Union of Socialist Soviet Republics. Therefore, without desiring the victory of the Imperialist Powers, to-day engaged in an armed conflict with Nazi Germany, it is not permissible for the fighters for freedom, democracy and progress to act in such a way as may contribute to the imminent victory of Fascism. The activities of Radical Congressmen will be determined by this consideration. The conflict in Europe continued even after Nazi aggression eastwards was checked by the clever Soviet foreign policy, and consequently the present fierce clash has been precipitated. The situation has developed in such a way as makes an early peace no longer desirable, because an early peace now will be a peace dictated by Nazi Germany, or a peace sought by Nazified England and France. That is the danger which theatens the world to-day. Since an indefinite continaution of war will be equally ruinous for both the parties, the suspension of hostilities on the back-ground of a Nazified Europe appears for the moment to be the more likely perspective. A far-sighted, well-calculated, realistic plan of action on the part of the fighters for Indian freedom may change that gloomy perspective. We shall prevent the reorganisation of the forces of international counter-revolution under the domination of Nazi Germany."

In the summer of 1940, events moved rapidly in Europe, and within a few months one country after another fell victim to Fascist aggression. Ultimately, the fall of France was the most staggering blow. With practically the whole of Europe under its domination, victorious Fascism cast its ominous shadow on the entire world. No fighter for freedom and democracy anywhere in the world could remain indifferent to the dreadful perspective of all the achievements of modern civilisation being destroyed by the dark forces of reaction mobilised under the banner of Fascism. In that critical moment, the Indian National Congress adopted a policy which virtually amounted to helping the victory of Fascism.

Consistent with our declared conviction, we could not possibly approve of that policy. The time for the inevitable parting of ways was reached. The Central Executive Committee of the League of Radical Congressmen met at Meerut at the end of October 1940 to consider the situation. On the basis of the opinion crystallised in course of a thorough discussion which had been going on for three months among the Radical Congressmen, it was decided to break away from the Congress, and to organise a new political party with the name of the Radical Democratic People's Party. Our view regarding India's relation to the international situation, as stated in the Manifesto declaring the formation of the new Party, marked yet another stage in the evolution of our present policy.

In that Manifesto, subsequently endorsed by the Inaugural Conference of the Radical Democratic Party, held in Bombay two months later, the following declaration was made: "The world is experiencing the severest crisis of modern times. Either the crisis will be overcome by the world entering upon a new period of human progress on the basis of the splendid achievements of modern civilisation; or the latter will break down, and the world will relapse into mediaeval barbarism. This great menace to the future of mankind is represented by triumphant Fascism. India cannot claim immunity from this danger. The world crisis affects her as vitally as any other country. Yet, the gravity of the situation is fully realised only by a few among those who are regarded as the makers of her destiny...Having for years condemned acts of Fascist aggression, the Congress to-day refuses to resist it when the danger is knocking at our own door. That is not a curiosity; it is political bankruptcy, inevitably brought about by the reactionary ideas and ideals of Gandhism which has persuaded the premier nationalist organisation to reject nationalism for a set of individual fads and pseudo-moral dogmas. In this critical moment, the Congress leaders have turned back on the ideal previously professed by themselves, because as a body they never were inspired by the modern ideas of democracy and progress. They are an association of Conservatives with a decidedly reactionary outlook on social and cultural matters. They believe in the metaphysical precepts and spiritual doctrines which enter also into the philosophical foundation of Fascism......The present attitude of the Congress leaders as regards the war against Fascism was succumbed war The Congress has succumbed to the crisis, as it were by fate. But India must survive. Her future is linked up with the future of the world. The path to Indian freedom lies through a victorious struggle against Fascism. While the Fascist hordes are nearing the Indian borders from both sides, Fascism is raising its ugly head in our very midst. The democratic and progressive forces must therefore fight simultaneously on two fronts. The fight on the home front must begin immediately. The decisive battles for the political freedom and social emancipation of the Indian masses will be fought on that front. ....Fascism or Fascist sympathy to-day provides a common platform to all the reactionary forces throughout the world including India. Therefore, the destruction of Fascism has become the immediate task for all the opposing forces. The failure to measure up to this momentous task, on any pretext, amounts to a betrayal of the ideal of freedom, whether national or social. These considerations must determine further development of the struggle for Indian freedom. The Radical Democratic Party rises on the ruins of the Congress to blaze a new trail, to lead the Indian masses towards the goal of national freedom and social liberation, which cannot be reached before the world is freed from the menace of Fascism. By mobilising the Indian people to participate in the world struggle against Fascism, the Radical Democratic Party will further the cause of Indian freedom."

Having undertaken the task of mobilising the Indian masses for voluntary, active and purposeful participation in the war against Fascism, we had to rely on the available ways and means for doing so. Apart from the fact that practically all classes of the Indian people were actually participating in the war, directly or indirectly, there were political parties and groups as well as numerous independent individuals who did not approve of the Congress policy and deplored the initiative for bringing all those elements together on a common platform, so that a realistic lcad could be given to the country in the critical moment. While favouring India's voluntary participation in the war against Fascism; our Party maintained that the energy and demandedtion and the will to victory of the entire people could not be mobilised through the war efforts of the Government. We characterised those efforts as utterly inadequate for combating the wide-spread Fascist sympathy and voluntary pro-Fascist propaganda, under the cover of nationalism or anti-Imperialism. We demanded complete democratisation of the war efforts and systematic anti-Fascist propaganda to be conducted non-officially. But we realised that nothing could be done in that respect before the constitutional deadlock was terminated and the government of the country, in the Centre as well as in all the provinces, came under popular control, as far as possible, under the given circumstances. The Inaugural Conference of our Party, therefore, recommended the establishment of Emergency Ministries in the deadlocked provinces, and inclusion of independent popular representatives in the Viceroy's Executive Council. It further resolved to strive for the formation of a National

Democratic Union, composed of all the parties and groups and independent individuals opposed to the futile policy of the Congress.

The National Democratic Union was inaugurated by a conference of independent public men practically from all the provinces in the closing days of 1940. Its recommendations for the ending of the constitutional deadlock and for the democratisation of war efforts have since been popularised by the untiring efforts of our Party, and have been securing increasing support from organised groups and numerous individuals.

Thousands and thousands of workers have attended rallies, held under the auspices of our Party, together with their respective Trade Unions, to express solidarity with British democracy engaged in the resistance of Fascist aggression. Labour organisations, embracing about two hundred thousand workers, have pledged their support to the anti-Fascist campaign carried on by us and are co-operating with our efforts for the formation of an anti-Fascist People's Front in India, as well as an International Labour Front. The All-India Scheduled Castes Association has joined the National Democratic Union. The Non-Brahmin movement of South India has extended its fullest co-operation. Thus, the exploited and oppressed masses of India are joining the anti-Fascist People's Front. There is every reason for us to be encouraged by this achievement made within such a short time.

But at the same time, experience has brought us up against some organisational difficulties which arise from the regrettable fact that practically all the political organisations are more concerned with communalist and particularist interests than with the general welfare of the Indian people as a whole. Anticipating these difficulties, our Party in its Inaugural Conference resolved to go ahead with the task of mobilising popular opinion in support of the war against Fascism, while making efforts for securing the co-operation of other organisations on the basis of the recommendations of the National Democratic Union. Realising the grave danger of the wide spread Fascist sympathy and whispering Fascist propaganda, seriously undermining the striking as well as the defensive power of India, the Inaugural Conference of our Party resolved to co-operate with the war efforts of the Government by carrying on anti-Fascist propaganda in every possible manner, and join the War Committees and Civic

Guards, wherever and whenever local conditions would be found suitable for fruitful activities.

That remains our position even to-day. With our firm conviction that the attainment of Indian freedom as conceived in our Party programme is conditional upon the defeat of international Fascism, we stand to-day between the devil and the deep sea, so to say. Narrow-minded nationalists carry on a campaign of abuse against us, because do not understand the issues involved, nor can they appreciate the values at stake. On the other hand, the Government is suspicious, because we are avowed revolutionaries. But the courage of conviction and a clear vision of the goal will enable us to steer through the dangerous waters between Scylla and Charybdis.

It is natural that avowed revolutionaries should be feared by those who still cling to the forlorn hope of maintaining the *status quo* even after the war. Let the *status quoers* find a morbid pleasure in their dream. But they are foolish to quesion our *bona fides.* Our readiness to co-operate with all and sundry in the fight against Fascism has no other motive than the destruction of this menace. But even if our *bona fides* are foolishly doubted, we do not feel insulted by the foolishness of the purblind bureaucrats. We pity their stupidity, because it will ultimately ruin themselves.

There is absolutely no reason to be suspicious about the motive of our present policy. There is nothing new in it. It is the logical continuation of our previous activities in pursuance of our programme. It is the practice of our professed principles. We make no secret of those principles. We belong to the vanguard of the new world order which will be raised on the foundation of the positive achievements of the modern civilisation—the epoch-making conquests of science and the tremendous increase of the creativeness of human mind and energy resulting therefrom. Only those who are inspired by the vision of a new world—with a greater freedom, higher culture and nobler ideals—can be the unrelenting opponents of Fascism, because the latter represents the paroxysm of a social order which has exhausted all its potentialities. If Fascism is to be defeated, its downfall will be brought about by those who have no stake in the passing order; and only they will save the achievements of modern civilisation from the danger of a relapse into barbarism, as the common heritage of humanity. Therefore, let those who would escape the disaster of a Fascist victory be guided by enlightened self-interest, if not by any higher motive.

On the other hand, we are not in the least bothered by the campaign of abuse carried on in the nationalist press. Conscious of the great issues involved, we do not allow ourselves to be swayed by emotion, to be paralysed by prejudices and stultified by spitefulness. We do not believe in political untouchability. We are prepared to co-operate with everybody actually engaged in this titanic struggle against Fascism, no matter whatever may be the motive. Our policy of unconditional participation in the fight against Fascism is condemned by the narrow-minded nationalists as co-operation with Imperialism, and therefore unpatriotic. But what really is the position of the nationalist organisations? All of them are ready to co-operate; they have repeatedly offered to do so. They would sell their services. Unless their offer of co-operation is paid for, they would not care, if India together with the rest of the world is overrun by triumphant Fascism, and all the hopes of modern humanity are dashed, perhaps for ever.

Therefore, it is sheer dishonesty to abuse us as the nationalist press does. We do not think in terms of co-operation and non-co-operation. And if it is co-operation, we are not offering it. In this war against Fascism, the British Government is co-operating with us, who had all along been anti-Fascist and demanded of the Governments, professing to be democratic, an active, united resistance to the growing menace of Fascism. There were others who also supported that demand. Not only the Socialists and Communists, but the Indian National Congress was also one of them. Together with others, the Indian National Congress agitated for the British Government's intervening for protecting Abyssinia, Spain, Austria or Czecho-Slovakia against Fascist aggression. It condemned the British Government for not doing so. It was maintained that the failure to do so forfeited Britain's claim to be a democratic country. To-day not only the National Congress, but others calling themselves Socialists or Communists, are condemning the British Government for acting undemocratically, even when it is doing what they wanted it to do previously. And what is still worse is, that they are refusing to co-operate in a war they wanted the British Government to wage all along.

The incongruity of this position will be revealed if an honest answer is given to a straight question. What would the Indian National Congress and its misguided allies have done if the present war had broken out some years earlier in consequence of the British Government resisting Fascist aggression in Abyssinia or Spain? That action on the part of the British Government would have been directly in compliance with the demand of the former. Therefore, they could not have possibly withheld co-operation much less put up resistance. Why should they then act differently to-day? The familiar answer is that, the British Government is not acting democratically towards India. Is there any reason to assume that the British Government would have acted differently if the war had broken out for resisting Fascist aggression in other countries?

The relation between India and British Imperialism, and that between the Indian struggle for freedom and the world fight against Fascism should not be confounded. Instead of making some adjustments of the former retaiion a condition for Indian participation in the fight against Fascism, it should be realised that the development of the latter relation is bound radically to change the relation between India and Britain. Our policy is based on that realisation. Ours is a fight for principle. The British Government is doing what we wanted it to do. If we are true to our principle, we cannot withhold co-operation. As a matter of fact, it is not for us to offer co-operation, but to welcome the co-operation of the British Government in the fight against Fascism desired by us. Therefore, we need not be ashamed of our readiness to co-operate. Those for whom co-operation means selling services for a price should be ashamed.

While, on principle, our position is clear, honourable and dignified, there may be some misgivings about what we can actually do in pursuance of our policy in the face of the suspicious attitude of the Government. Our present position is difficult. But we should not be daunted by these difficulties. We shall have to go ahead, irrespective of the attitude of the Government, believing that our efforts will be ultimately crowned with success. It appears that, until the attitude of the Government changes, and genuine anti-Fascists occupy positions of vantage, their participation in war efforts cannot amount to anything more than helping the collection of money and recruitment of men. What can we do in this situation ? Are we then to ask the Indian peasants and workers to enlist themselves in the army and contribute to the war fund? The idea appears to be repulsive. But we cannot be swayed by emotions. We are definitely of the opinion that only men and money will not win the war. And for getting that much from India, the British Government can disregard all opposition. On the other hand, recruitment in the army offers employment to a good many unemployed peasants. Therefore, there is no sense in resisting recruitment, except on the ground of opposition to war on principle. That is not our position. Therefore, we should have no objection to helping recruitment. Indeed, in the absence of other possibilities, the recruitment can serve the purpose of anti-Fascist propaganda. We can help the new recruits to be conscious of the political implications of the battles they may have to fight soon. Finally, since we believe that India must participate to the fullest extent in the fight against Fascism, why should we not ask the Indian workers and peasants to join the army with that purpose. The composition of the army and the political consciousness of the soldiers will very largely determine for what purpose it could be used. In other words, if we want a people's army to fight the war against Fascism, foreign as well as indigenous, we must ask the workers and peasants to join the army in large numbers.

As regards the collection of war funds also, our position should not be apologetic. The matter can be judged from two points of view. We have made it clear enough that, in our opinion, mechanical collection of money from the poor may defeat the purpose of the war effort, which should be to enlist popular support for the war. Moreover, the vast amount of money necessary for the war cannot be raised through small contributions paid by he poor. Therefore, we have suggested that the war should be financed by taxing those who are capable of bearing the burden and through loans. But voluntary contributions may be a token of solidarity of the Indian workers and peasants with their brethren bearing the brunt of the war against Fascism in other countries. International solidarity of the toiling masses is one of the fundamental principles of the Socialist movement. Those who sincerely profess this principle should not be ashamed of practising it in the critical movement. We do not want the toiling masses of England to become helpless victims of triumphant Fascism. Therefore, we should be prepared to make any sacrifice necessary for preventing a Fascist victory. Our opposition to Imperialism should not stand in the way to our demonstrating the solidarity of the Indian toiling masses with those in England. And as a token of that solidarity, Indian workers and peasants may be asked to contribute to the war fund. Only, we insist that, before collecting money from them, they should be helped to have the feeling of solidarity.

But it is not true that the deplorable attitude of the Government precludes the genuine anti-Fascists from doing anything more than helping recruitment and collection of money. There is a good deal of misunderstanding about the issues involved in this war, the nature of this war and India's relation to it. Systematic untiring propaganda should be carried on to clear that confusion. The present Government cannot do that. None of the other political parties is interested in that propaganda. As a matter of fact, most of them overtly or covertly are carrying on the contrary propaganda. Our party alone can undertake that task, in spite of all difficulties. It is the only organised anti-Fascist force in the country, and as such it is the only guarantee for the eventual democratic freedom for India. Our party is the only organised anti-Fascist force in the country, because it alone stands for the ideal of political freedom, social emancipation and cultural progress which would be destroyed everywhere irreparably, if Fascism won.

In spite of all the difficulties, we are making progress in the direction of making the intellectually more advanced section of the Indian people conscious of the Fascist menace to Indian and enlisting mass support to our view regarding India's relation to the war. Our party took the initiative for uniting all the anti-Fascist forces in the National Democratic Union, which has placed the following programme before the country: 1. Defeat of Fascism and the rapid development of all the resources of India for that purpose; 2. Sharing the responsibility for the defence of India and with that purpose to press upon the Government the necessity of winning popular confidence; 3. Re-election of the Legislature; 4. Establishment of Emergency Ministries in the provinces at present without any responsible Government; 5. Inclusion of independent popular representatives in the Viceroy's Executive Council; 6. Democratisation of the war effarts, in order to make India's contribution more effective.

The campaign for popularising this programme is organised by our party. I have just finished a four months' tour through a number of provinces. The lesson of that tour is very encouraging. During this period, I have addressed dozens of public meetings, attended by thousands each, often more than twenty thousand. It was generally admitted in the respective places that they were the largest political meetings during the recent years, larger than meetings addressed by popular Congress leaders. People did not come to those meetings for the *darshan* of popular heroes, nor for *tamasha.* Our party does not yet possess a sufficiently powerful machinery, nor the means necessary for ogranising country-wide campaigns. Therefore, the response to our campaign should be regarded as spontaneous. Our views on the war are well known. The

Congress press presents it to the public in the most distorted form. Yet, thousands of people throughout the country gather when meetings are held to present the point of view of our party. And the most remarkable feature is the composition of the audience. It is mostly composed of educated people of independent views, precisely the element which can be relied upon for turning the tide of public opinion. Experience has proved that our party is capable of tackling all the problems that confront India to-day. The decisive factor is mass support. Our party can secure mass support for its point of view, and consequently moblilise Indian resources and energy in support of the war against Fascism, if it is given the necessary facilities. With a long perspective, that is to say, if we had many years to work up, we could win single-handed. But to-day, it is a race with time. The task must be accomplished within perhaps no more than a couple of years. All our difficulties arise from that time factor. But, on the other hand, we must make a supreme effort, because our party alone can save the situation and lead India out of the present crisis. If we fail, the future of India will be dark.

But the Government seems to be afraid of genuine anti-Fascists. We are prepared to shoulder the responsibility which others, with big names and purses, are afraid of. Yet, the Government prefers the ruinous policy of drift, hoping ultimately to secure the co-operation of parties, whose will to fight Fascism is a matter of grave doubt. It is obvious that popular opinion cannot be fully enlisted in support of the war, unless the artificially kept-up influence of the Congress is destroyed. The Congress is fighting the Government; it is opposed to India's participation in the war; yet, the Government is very reluctant to do anything which might seriously injure the Congress. The Congress is the most powerful bulwark of conservatism in the public life of India. Hence the anxiety of the Government to see that it remains intact, and the concern of others to bring about a reconciliation between the Congress and the Government.

As a matter of fact, the Congress influence is limited to a vocal minority. The control of the press and a liberally financed authoritarian machinery are the source of strength of the Congress. The vast bulk of the population is only slightly touched by Congress propaganda. The masses can be swayed by the Congress, because there is no other popular party in the field. If the recommendations of the Inaugural Conference of the National Democratic Union are accepted by the Government, a really popular party will appear on the scene in no time. The success of our campaign during the brief period of a couple of months leaves no doubt on that score. Therefore, let this Conference representing the avowed anti-Fascists of this country urge upon the Government to take up a more realist and far-sighted view and appeal to the British democracy to intervene energetically, so that India's voluntary and effective participation in the war against Fascism may no longer be delayed by bureaucratic stupidity, and reactionry nationalism.

The present policy of drift, which is seriously impairing India's defensive and striking power, is justified on the ground that the Government is helpless in the face of the obstructionist attitude of the major political parties of the country. Is the Government really so helpless? Could it not change the situation, if it wanted to? The forces are there to be mobilised. The genuinely anti-Fascist elements organised in our party are only too eager to shoulder the responsibility. The only thing that the Government need do is to let us have the chance of doing so. We are not offering our services for a price. We believe that this is our war as much as of England. We believe that Fascism must be defeated, if the Indian people are to attain the goal of democratic freedom. What, then, is the obstacle in the way to ending the present constitutional deadlock, so that the war efforts of India may be democratised and therefore be more effective? The Government is really not helpless. It could easily overcome the difficulty of the obstructionism on the part of the major political parties. It seems rather to be paralysed by the fear for the genuine anti-Fascists who, in order to be so, must be avowed revolutionaries. But the situation cannot continue like this indefinitely. The choice will be forced upon it as soon as it will realise that, if the situation is not radically changed, India will be rather a liability than an asset in the critical moments. Relying on the logic of events we shall therefore go ahead with our activities, disregarding the attitude of others.

Our suggestion that there should be a general election on the issue of India's participation in the war is considered to be too optimistic. But obvious facts do not permit any pessimism on that score. Practically all classes of the Indian people are actually participating in the war, and are being benefitted therefrom, directly or indirectly. The Congress majority in a number of provincial Legislatures has become an empty formality. The burning issue of to-day was not before the country at the time of the last election. Therefore, it is correct neither constitutionally nor factually to maintain that the Congress policy reflects the opinion of the majority as regards India's relation to the war. A fictitious formal majority should not be allowed to dominate the situation. The Congress claim to represent the majority should be tested. A re-election of the Legislatures will not be the true test, because only a fraction of the Indian population is enfranchised. But we Indian anti-Fascists are prepared for the partial test of a general election. Of course, we are too realistic to dispute that, if the election is held in the near future, before the opposing popular party has had the advantages until now monopolised by the Congress, the latter would most probably win the election. But even in that case, it is practically certain that its victory would not be as sweeping as on the last occasion, and in some provinces it would lose the majority. Given the means necessary for conducting elections, our party could be expected to put up a good fight, even if the election took place in the near future.

But in the present emergency, it is not permissible to lay too much stress on mere formalities. Before the electorate is asked to give its verdict on the burning issue of the day, it must be exhaustively explained to the country; the monopoly of press shuold be broken, so that an atmosphere be created in which public opinion could be formed intelligently and independently. There can be little doubt about the result of a general election if it takes place after a minimum period of preparation on these lines. Avowed anti-Fascists, who stand for India's unconditional participation in the war, and represent social and political ideals which appeal to the masses, should therefore be forthwith associated with the Government of the country. That position of vantage will enable them to do what they are doing even to-day more effectively, and build up a popular party to challenge the totalitarianism of the Congress.

The Government would be ill-advised to fall

back upon the co-operation of leaders without any following. I must enlist the co-operation of those who can command an organised popular backing, even if they may not have that at present to the fullest extent. The criterion of the choice will be the readiness to face a general election as soon as possible. Our party has repeatedly declared that readiness.

Apart from other considerations, the record of the Congress Ministries is bound to influence the result of the next election, if it is contested by a genuinely democratic party. The Congress Ministries gave stones to the masses, when they were crying for bread, so liberally promised to them during the election campaign. It is true that blind faith fostered by large-scale demagogy has prevented the masses from seeing how they have been deceived. But the complete emptiness of the record of Congress Ministries can be easily exposed. The hypocrisy of pseudo-moral reforms should not be allowed to hide the complete failure to give any concrete relief to the masses. It is easy to show how the so-called constructive programme of the Congress does not even touch the burning economic problems facing the country. The disappointing record of the Congress Ministries was causing popular discontent, and the masses were showing signs of disillusionment. The resignation of the Congress Ministries and the subsequent comedy of individual Satyagrah a were very largely due to the desire to whitewash the record of the Congress Ministries. But even the mast skillful and unscrupulous demagogue, with all the authority of the prophetic Inner Voice, cannot possibly deceive all the people for all the time. Only those who doubt the least intelligence on the part of the masses can believe that the Congress will be able to sweep the polls on the strength of the Satyagraha stunt. The result of a few by-elections here and there indicates which way the wind is blowing. The process of disillusionment must be quickened. That can be done by a popular party which seeks to draw its strength from the political consciousness of the masses.

The criticism of the Congress programme and exposure of the humbug of the Congress policy will have no effect, unless an alternative programme is placed before the country, and a more realistic policy suggested for the realisation of that programme. I have already given an outline of the programme of our party. It is before the country already for several years. In the given situation, the efforts for the realisation of that programme are expressed through the slogans: Industrialisation, Militarisation and Democratisation. The next general election should be fought with those slogans which express the aspiration of all the progressive elements as well as the toiling masses.

Industrialisation will open up new fields of employment, raise the standard of living of the wage-earners and eventually solve all the present economic problems of India. It will provide an expanding field of profitable investment for accumulated wealth. The Government can no longer stand in the way, even if it wants to do so. If the people possessing money invest it in modern industries, they will grow rapidly, now that a market is guaranteed by the exigencies of the war. Whatever may be the attitude of the Government to-day, it is bound to change before long under the pressure of circumstances. In the meantime, efforts should be made to bring the Government under the control of genuinely democratic elements. That will provide a guarantee against war profiteering, and the necessary and inevitable industrialisation will take place rapidly with money raised by the Government through loans.

The slogan of militarisation expresses the idea that in order to defeat Fascism, at home and abroad, this war must be converted into a people's war. Our demand is not for a larger without army. We want that the entire people must be placed on a war footing. The regular army cannot be without limit. It cannot embrace the whole people. Therefore, it must be supplemented by the creation of a National Militia with detachments throughout the country. England already has such a National Militia in the Home Guards. In India, the Civic Guards should be developed into a similar instrument of defence, qualitatively as well as quantitatively. This idea of developing the defensive power of the country through the mobilisation of popular energy has been conceived by our Party. Why, then, should not our Party be entrusted with the task of putting it into practice? As a matter of fact, none else can do that. It is not a mere accident that the Chief Instructor of the two million strong British Home Guards is a famous Communist.

Engaged in a desperate struggle against a mortal enemy, one must have the intelligence to distinguish friends from foes, and have the courage to welcome the true friends, wherever they are found. On this issue of militarisation also, we are not perturbed by the unimaginative attitude of the bureaucrats. We count upon the development of events which will compel the Government to act as we suggest, if they are really serious in this business of defeating Hitler. If they are not, we shall have to fight them also. We must be prepared for all eventualities, because the Fifth Column of Fascism is to be seen in this country in the most unexpected places.

Democratisation will follow industrialisation and militarisation on the above lines. Therefore, we are of the opinion that voluntary and purposeful participation in the war against Fascism will democratise the public life of our country, thus creating the pre-condition for the realisation of the political and social ideals set forth in the programme of our Party.

That is the connection between the programme of National Democratic Revolution and the struggle against Fascism, national as well as international. Keenly conscious of that connection, our Party has undertaken the task of mobilising the popular forces of India to support this war as the task of the moment. By accomplishing this task, our Party will contribute immensely to the final success of the struggle for the political freedom and social emancipation of the Indian masses. Therefore, we can be confident of having all the progressive elements in the national life of our country in the ranks of the Radical Democratic Party. And such a party is bound to command the confidence and the backing of the masses.

Blinded by prejudices and perhaps by even baser motives, the bureaucrats may be afraid of our Party and try to impede its growth by withholding co-operation in our single-handcd campaign against the incipient and insidious force of Fascism inside the country. But our Party, which grows out of the present situation in India, is bound to be a most decisive factor in it. Because it alone, from the very beginning, anticipated developments and suggested how successive events should be met. All the difficulties in our way will disappear as soon as it is realised that the anxiety to maintain an untenable *status quo* only weakens the struggle against Fascism, indeed, belies the very anti-Fascist profession. That realisation is bound to come, because the defeat of Fascim is indispensable for the future of mankind. Those who are in power to-day may be more concerned with their selfish interests than with the welfare of humanity. In that case, they are bound to be swept away from their present position of power, because the urge inherent in the laws of human progress is strong enough to resist a relapse into barbarism, which will surely happen if Fascism comes victorious out of this epoch-making struggle.

So, let us not be daunted by the difficulties. We belong to the vanguard not only of the forces of Indian freedom, but also of a higher civilisation, to be built on the ruins of the *status quo* which is being desperately defended by international Fascism. The Radical Democratic Party is the standard-bearer of the new conception of democracy, which is an ideal worth fighting for. Therefore, it holds out a bright ray of hope in the darkness of the present political situation. The hope it represents, is going to be fulfilled, because Indian people must live and they cannot live and prosper unless they are free and India cannot be free in the midst of an enslaved world.

FOR INTERNATIONAL SOLIDARITY

May Day Manifesto

For the second year, the May Day will not be celebrated in a number of countries. Triumphant Fascism rules there; the working classes groan under the heels of bloody repression; their organizations have been destroyed; their leaders killed, imprisoned or hounded out of the country; political and economic rights, gained in course of the decades of hard struggle, have been abolished. Having reduced practically the whole of Europe to this state, international Fascism is stretching out its merciless tentacles, threatening the rest of the world. In the countries directly menaced, the working class, together with all the other progressive and truly democratic forces, are putting up a valiant resistance.

How can the May Day this year be fittingly celebrated in the countries which have not yet been overtaken by the misfortune of Fascist domination? A mighty anti-Fascist demonstration will now be the concrete expression of the international working class solidarity. Never before was this solidarity so very urgently needed, not only for defending and promoting working class interest, but for guaranteeing the future of human civilization. Never was the slogan "Workers of the World, Unite!" so full of meaning as it is to-day.

It must be a demonstration of the will to fight Fascism—in every possible manner—wherever it is found. Tragic victims of triumphant Fascism, the workers of Europe are anxiously expecting succour from their comrades in the other countries. Nothing short of a shattering defeat for the military forces of international Fascism will be of any help to them. It is vain to hope that by themselves they will eventually rise up against Fascist tyranny. The enemy is much too powerful for them. It must be stricken from outside, before the internal forces can assert themselves. The loyalty to their comrades in continental Europe—to the principle of international solidarity—must therefore be demonstrated by the workers in other countries by making the greatest possible contribution to the military defeat of the forces of international Fascism.

The British workers are bearing the brunt of the burden of resisting the menacing march of Fascism. Had it not been for their determined efforts, Fascism might have triumphed in Britain also. The struggle still continues. Engaged in it, the British workers urgently need the fullest co-operation of their comrades in other countries. That co-operation should be pledged to them on the May Day—the historic occasion for the demonstration of the international solidarity ef the working class.

But the British workers alone cannot possibly defeat international Fascism. Baffled in the battle of Britain, it is striking in other directions, in a madqfury. The Balkan countries have been over-run. Egypt is also menaced. Constantinople and the Straits are within the range of the guns of the Nazi hordes marching eastwards. Troubles are brewing in Syria. It is well-known that the Fifth Column of international Fascism has penetrated the Arab countries. The military *coup d'etat* in Iraq is a portent. Iran is infested with Nazi agents, who are busy even in Afghanistan. Hitler's hordes are actually knocking at the gates of Asia.

The Soviet Union is also in danger. To

destroy it, is the avowed object of international Fascism. A clear diplomacy kept it out of the war as long as possible, so that the fullest preparations could be made for the day of reckoning. But neutrality will not for much longer be the guarantee against the inevitable Fascist aggression. According to well informed military observers, the Nazis will most probably strike for the seizure of the Ukraine and the adjoining industrial districts of Russia, as soon as the Balkan campaign is over, so that the Soviet Army may not be available for cutting their advance through the Near East. In that case, the Asiatic partner of the international Fascist alliance will be sure to attack the Soviet Union from the East. Thus encircled by the sworn enemy, the very existence of the Soviet Union will be at stake, if the forces of international Fascism are not heavily engaged elsewhere by the determined and concerted action on the part of the working class. This year, the May Day should be celebrated by the demonstration of the will for organizing such action.

In India, the demonstration will be of particularly great significance, because the Indian workers can be the decisive factor in this ominously aggravating struggle for the future of mankind. A rapid development of the striking power of India is the sole condition for arresting the eastward march of the Nazi hordes. Enthusiastic and purposeful co-operation of the Indian workers, particularly of those engaged in industrial production, is essential for that process.

Notwithstanding the nationalist prejudice and foolishness on the part of some labour leaders, Indian workers are participating in the process of developing India's striking power, inasmuch-as they remain engaged in industrial production. But they are not acting with any particular purpose. This year, the May Day demonstration should make them purposeful, and thus arouse in them the enthusiasm of international solidarity—of contributing to the success of a common cause.

While demonstratiug international solidarity by declaring the will to fight Fascism in every possible manner, and wherever found, it is only natural for Indian workers to demand facilities such as will enable them to discharge their voluntarily undertaken responsibility more effectively. Simultaneously with her striking power, the defensive power of India must also be developed, in order to guarantee that she would not become a willing victim of Fascist aggression, in case it could not be arrested in the Near East.

The problem of Indian defence is primarily a political problem. The defensive potentialities of India are sapped by a wide-spread sympathy for Fascism and wish for the victory of the Fascit Powers. Those sentiments, associated with reactionary and narrow-minded nationalism, must be combated by mobilising the toiling masses in the struggle against Fascism—on the home as well as on the international front. But that cannot be done unless the Government of the country is democratised by the co-operation of genuinely anti-Fascist elements—those who are prepared to set aside all other issues, in order to concentrate upon the fundamental task of defeating Fascism.

A people's war should be the reaction to the totalitarian war waged by the Fascists. The toiling masses of her people must be put on a war footing, if India, like any other country, is to make a voluntary contribution to the victory over Fascism.

Bitter experience has proved that the regular army cannot resist a Fascist invasion which is invariably assisted by the Fifth Column operating inside the country attacked. In the case of India, the regular army will be even less effective, because it is numerically small and not adequately equipped. Nor can it be enlarged and properly equipped within a short time. Therefore, the responsibility for defending India in the case of an attack will devolve upon the people. Hence the urgent need for general militarisation. The regular army plays a secondary part in the people's war, and this war must become a war of the people, as against the concern solely of a bureaucratic machinery completely divorced from the people, before it will be won.

The will of the Indian working class to defeat Fascism should, therefore, be demonstrated on the May Day with the demand:

Transform The War into A People's War !

That is the general demand of those who believe that the cause of Indian freedom will be vitally affected by the outcome of this war, and therefore are anxious to influence it. The general demand includes the following particular and concrete demands, which must be associated with this year's May Day demonstrations.

1. Democratisation of the Government in

the provinces as well as in the Centre, with the co-operation of those who have all along advocated India's voluntary and unconditional participation in the war against Fascism.

2. Transformation of the War Committees into People's Defence Councils.

3. Free admission of the avowed anti-Fascists, workers and peasants, into the Civic Guards, so that they can become the units of a People's Militia.

4. Increase in the number of Civic Guards to five millions within six months.

5. Systematic and extensive anti-Fascist propaganda as the most essential part of the war effort.

6 No compromise with the opponents of India's voluntary participation in the war against Fascism, even on the pretext of formal democratic practice.

7. Exposure and suppression of Fascist tendencies and war profiteering by Public Security Committees elected by the anti-Fascist movement.

8. Dearness allowance for workers and the benefit of higher agricultural prices to the peasants.

9. No collection of money from the poor until the above demands are fulfilled. The war to be mainly financed by loans in addition to taxes on those who can afford to pay.

10. Rapid development of modern large-scale industries for accelerating the process of general militarisation and creating new employments for labour.

The fulfilment of these demands will enable the Indian workers to co-operate effectively with the workers of Britain as well as of the workers in other countries in this bitter struggle against the common enemy. Therefore, we appeal to the British workers to throw in their influence in support of the demands of the Indian workers. Through this reciprocal action, international solidarity of the working classes will become the unshakable bulwark against the imminent danger of Fascist world domination. Let the tragedy of Europe thus cement international working class solidarity on this May Day. Let the Indian workers, on that historic day, demonstrate the determination to play their part, so that at last international solidarity may be a realised ideal. Let the May Day this year be celebrated by the formation of the Indo-British Labour Front against International Fascism!

RADICAL DEMOCRACY PARTY

April 15, 1941.

WHAT COULD BE DONE

What India needs to-day for her defence is not a suffiiciently large and well-equipped regular army, but a people vitally concerned with that defence and keenly conscious of their responsibility in that respect. That fundamental condition for Indian defence is absent. That is the core of the tragedy which may overtake India any day.

It is simple enough to lay the entire blame for this unforunate situation on the British rulers of this country. Undoubtedly, they are very largely responsible. But immediately, the responsibility belongs almost entirely to those who, on one pretext or another, have created in the Indian people a mentality which renders the defence of the country psychologically impossible. To defend any country is next to impossible when the great bulk of its population is prepared to welcome the invader as the liberator. This mentality is an inevitable by-product of reactionary nationalism; it has been particularly promoted, directly or indirectly, by the Congress policy adopted on the outbreak of the war. All the activities of the Congress during this year and a half have contributed to the erroneous, short-sighted and suicidal view that it is utterly immaterial for India how this war ends; as a matter of fact, the view goes to the extent that the victory of the Fascist Powers will be beneficial for India. Given this view, held by a large section of the people, and promoted by the Congressmen, it is extremely difficult for anybody to prepare the country for defending itself against a powerful invader.

If the Congress parlimentarians are installed in office to-day, and are entrusted with the task of mobilising the Indian people for the defence of the country, there will be a hopeless confusion. They cannot over-night cure the mentality of sympathy, admiration and friendship for the enemy, which they themselves have been promoting for a year and a half. They will have to adopt the same bureaucratic methods, which have been practised until now and have failed to create the vital condition for Indian defence. The first condition for their suceeeding would be to apply them selves to the none too creditable task of undoing the mischief that they have been doing all this time on the pretext of promoting the cause of the country's freedom. If they are really prepared to atone for their sins, for that it is not necessary for them to be installed in high offices, they have the fullest freedom, and all the means necessary, to educate public opinion in the right direction, and thus create the psychological atmosphere which is the indispensable condition for mobilising the people in the defence of the country.

But, on the other hand, by admitting that during the most critical period they have been abusing the popular trust, misleading the people, and thereby laying the country open to Fascist invasion, they will forfeit the claim to be placed at the helm of affairs in these fateful days. Nevertheless, if their anxiety to share the responsibility for the defence of the country is sincere, and their denunciation of Fascism is not a comouflage, that is exactly what they should do. That is the only correct and practical way still open to them, and by travelling that way, they can still help sparing India the misfortune of falling a victim to Fascist aggression.

Whatever may happen in the future, and irrespective of whether the Congress leaders will have the moral courage to act as repentant sinners at this eleventh hour, the fact remains that they have bungled and mismanaged the situation in such a way as has brought India on the verge of a veritable catastrophe. With injured innocence, to-day they ask: What could they do as long as the British Government would not allow them to shoulder the burden of organising the defence of the country?

There are no two opinions on the score that bureaucratic complancency persuaded the British rulers of the country to act in the most short-sighted manner. But the short-sightendness or any other defect on the part of one, does not justify the same mistake on the part of another. It was evident to all critical students and close observers of the international events during the last year, that the war would not remain confined to Europe, and that it would affect India directly sooner or later. Preparations for fully developing the defensive as well as the striking power of India should have been begun well ahead of time, in view of that certain eventuality. The failure of the British Government to do so is no excuse for the Indian leaders to be unmindful of their responsibility. If the

Congress leaders were not labouring under the wrong idea that the defence of India was a concern of her foreign rulers, and therefore Indians should do nothing on that account unless paid by the rulers of India for the services rendered, they could have easily seen what was possible for them to do to face the danger which is knocking at our door to-day.

An honest anti-Fascist conviction, and the consequent determination that on no account should India be allowed to come under the domination of Fascism, would have enabled them to rise above the petty consideration of prestige, and find the correct and practical way. Nor was it necessary for them to take the unaccustomed trouble of taxing their brain and imagination. That was done for them by others who repeatedly pointed out to them what could be done even within the limitations of the given situation.

The suicidal step of resigning office in the provinces was justified *post factum* with the argument that having no power, the Ministries could do nothing. The argument carried no conviction to those not blessed with the virtue of blind faith. Congress leaders must have read the Government of India Act of 1935 before they decided to accept office under that Act. Its defects must have been well known to them. If nothing whatsoever could be done by Ministries under that Act, why did they accept office at all? As a matter of fact, notwithstanding all the criticism of the Act before the assumption of office by Congressmen, once they came into office, they discovered endless possibilities in that "Charter of Slavery". Whenever the failure of the Congress Ministries to do this or that thing was explained by their apologists on the ground that they had no power, they indignantly repudiated such explanation and asserted that they were not only in office, but in power. The object of wrecking the unwanted Constitution was replaced because of the newly discovered possibility of gradually expanding its bounds to the extent of complete independence, which was interpreted as equal partnership within the British Empire.

Although, generally, that was not true, the fact is that the Government never prohibited the Ministers from doing whatever the latter proposed. On course, that liberal attitude on the part of the Governors was determined by the fact that the Congress Ministries did not propose to do anything serious. The obstruction to the legislative and other measures of the Congress Ministries came rather from the Indian vested interests, landlords and capitalists, and they were modified or even abandoned in order to placate the latter.

In any case, there is absolutely no justification for the assumption that after the outbreak of the war there would have been the least interference by the Governors if the Congress Ministries adopted even the most far-reaching measures for mobilising the man-power and resources of India. Here again, the defeatist, incapable of any initiative, would raise the question : What exactly could they do concretely, the Provincial Ministries having nothing to do with the military affairs ? The answer was given already then by those who opposed the resignation of Congress Ministries, and insisted upon their returning to office, reinforced with the co-operation of other popular parties, particularly the Muslim League. Although it is now too late to do what could be done then, yet it may be useful to recollect what the Congress leaders failed to do, so that their claim to be the sole and eternal custodians of Indian interests may be challenged.

If Congressmen remained in office, there would be no such mischievous activities which have sapped the defensive power of India. There would be no anti-war propaganda which inevitably, however much the propagandists may disown the desire to embarrass the British Government, promotes sympathy for Fascism, at any rate for the foreign armies which are likely to invade India in the near future. In the absence of that propaganda, the efforts for educating Indian public opinion in favour of defeating Fascism could be more successful. Given the conviction that the defeat of Fascism is desirable for the interest of the world as well as for the welfare of India, the determination to contribute to that defeat would not be absent as it is to-day.

Concretely, the presence of Congress Ministries would have guaranteed the democratization of war efforts, preventing the present alienation of popular support. War Committees could have become the units of a powerful anti-Fascist People's Front. The Civic Guards could rise as local Defence Corps to be welded into a formidable defensive weapon like the Home Guards in England. All these things and many more could be done by Congressmen remaining in office, provided that, from the beginning, the leaders of a movement, said to be for democratic freedom, realized that the victory of Fascism would be detrimental for the cause of democratic freedom even in India. The Congress leaders did not do what they could have done, not really because they felt that Congressmen in office were powerless, but because they expected to secure some concessions to themselves by embarrassing the British Government in a critical time. They may or may not have succeeded in embarrassing the British rulers of India. But they certainly have succeeded in placing India in a very dangerous position, and have prevented other Indian fighters for freedom, who did know the correct and practical way, from leading the Indian people in that direction.

"Independent India", May 25, 1941.

AN APPEAL TO CONGRESSMEN

Friends and Comrades,

Nearly a year has passed since the Satyagraha Movement was launched. We opposed the decision on the ground that it was bound to fail. Many of you also felt that the movement as originally started, as civil resistance by individuals, could not produce any appreciable result. Neverthless, you joined the movement, hoping that in course of time it would develop into a mass struggle. We did not share that hope. The supreme commander of the movement himself evidently did not desire that it should develop in that direction.

Those who believed in the possibility of the movement, under its momentum, outgrowing the artificial limitations, should have been warned by the replacement of the elected Congress Committees by Satyagraha Committees which were invariably composed of men who would subordinate political considerations to the Mahatma's injunction. The abolition of the elected Committees eliminated the possibility of mass pressure being brought to bear upon the Congress policy. Therefore, the hope of the Satyagraha movement developing into a mass struggle could no longer be mentioned. We pointed that out, from the very beginning.

On the other hand, a realistic view of the given situation presuaded Mahatma Gandhi to eschew the idea of launching civil disobedience on a mass scale. He knew that, on the issue of war resistance, a mass movement could not be organised, and any attempt to do so would be crushed ruthlessly. That would have a very demoralising effect.

A popular sentiment could be created against such measures as collection of war funds, under compulsion. A resistance to such measures might be organised if there were no other considerations to influence the judgment of the people. However condemnable may be the attitude of the Government, and however justifiable the Congress demand, the fact remainsl that practically all classes of the Indian people have been all along co-operating with the war efforts of the Government, not because all of them want to do so, but because they are being benefitted therefrom, directly or indirectly, more or less. That being the case, the masses could not be mobilised in a movement for resisting India's participation in the war even if such a movement were desirable. We pointed out that too when we opposed the launching of Satyagraha.

Now it is no longer a matter of speculation or argument. Your own experience should now guide you. Not only has the Satyagraha movement failed, but the failure has gone to the extent of destroying the Congress organisation. All political activity has stopped. There is a general depression and passivity when just there is so much to do.

No use simply protesting against the method of collecting war funds, if practical ways and means cannot be devised for redressing the grievances of the people. The presence of Congress Ministries could have at least served that purpose. But to-day even the Congress Committees are gone. Things will have to be done all over again.

The beginning must be made with the admission that the Congress leadership has failed the people in a most critical moment. It may be painful to admit that, but the truth must be told. The Congress may survive this crises as a party of parliamentarians, but it cannot again become a mass organisation. The belief in a Mahatma may still sway the masses. But that belief is no political asset. On the contrary, it has decidedly prevented the masses from being politically conscious. A disappearance of that blind faith is the condition for the re-birth of a political mass movement.

The hope of the Congress Ministries returning must also be given up. Although Congress policy has not succeeded in compelling the Government to concede to the demand of a National Government, some sort of a settlement may still take place. But the Congress will not be the sole party to that possible settlement. It will be made together with other parties and provincial ministries, if and when restored, will be Coalition Ministries. The Congress, consequently, will cease to be even the dominating parliamentary group. What, then, has been the result of this waste of time and energy? Nothing. Therefore, it is necessary to strike out a new path, with a new orientation, with a new leadership.

All that must be provided by yourself. We have always advocated initiative from below. It was never more necessary than to-day. We appeal to you to rise up to the occasion. Misunderstanding of our policy and malicious propaganda against us in the Congress press created a gult between you and ourselves. But that will disappear if you will have the courage to learn from your own experience. Then, you will see that we proposed the only policy practicable under the given situation, and that, had our advice been accepted, the Congress would not be in its present plight, and India might have by this time occupied a position of vantage in her struggle for freedom.

The attitude towards India's relation to the war has brought the Congress to grief. The policy dictated by that attitude, therefore, should by revised. The question before you is very simple, Do you want India to be overrun by the Fascist hordes? Are you yet prepared to act according to the advice of Mahatma Gandhi in case of invasion? We are only too painfully aware of the fact that there are people who, even among Congressman, believe that the Fascist invaders will come to liberate India. Can you really share that illusion? If not, then you cannot be indifferent to the defence of India. Indeed, Congress leaders themselves have lately been showing great concern with the question of defence. Only, as usual, they are incapable of taking the initiative.

Our party has placed before the country the proposal for the organisation of Volunteer Defence Corps in every district and eventually in every village. This proposal opens up the perspective of political activity on the largest possible scale.

Our party has also placed before the country a programme of concrete action nccessary and practicable under the given circumstances.

We appeal to you for joining hands with us in working out this programme, the central idea of which is to mobilise the Indian masses to resist attack on all fronts-from all quarters. Believing that you are dissatisfied with the present complete absence of any perspective in the Congress policy, we appeal to you to get in touch with the local units of our Party for discussing the details of the proposed co-operation in action regarding the issues which confront our country to-day. We are sure that the programme of our Party will be acceptable to all fighters for political freedom of the nation as well as the social emancipation of the masses. The war policy of our Party is only a logical consequence of its programme, which is more comprehensive and far-reaching. Therefore, we expect you all to join us in the Party, which has grown out of the failure of the Congress and proposes to accomplish the task which the latter could not do.

Friends and Comrades!

This appeal was written the day before the dramatic change in the international situation brought about by the Nazi invasion of the Soviet Union. The change adds force to the appeal. But a few words must be added to urge upon you the necessity of quick decision.

The war has developed just as we predicted at the very beginning. The issue involved in this gigantic struggle is clear now. The fighters for Indian freedom can no longer remain indifferent to the outcome of this struggle, much less oppose India's participation in it, holding that this is an imperialist war. It was a wrong view; now the march of events has proved that it was wrong.

Nevertheless, your leaders do not seem to be inclined to abandon the policy based on a wrong view about this war, a policy which has signally failed to achieve anything. The supreme commander has not yet spoken; but given his oft-repeated view, he is not likely to allow his followers to participate in any war. Nor can he be expected to feel that the Nazi attack upon the Soviet Union should influence India's relation to the war. Indeed, this opinion has already been publicly expressed by his trusted lieutenants, such as Dr. Rajendra Prasad and the General Secretary of the Congress. They have already said that the Congress should only wait and watch.

Are you prepared to share that attitude, even when the Fascist war machine is fiercely hurling itself against the Worker's and Peasants' Republic, whose achievements have won your admiration and presented to you the picture of freedom you wish to win for the Indian masses?

It is not only the Soviet Union which is in danger. If the Fascist hordes succeed, even partially, in their latest adventure, the danger of India coming within the range of their greedy tentacles will be greater than ever. If they can establish themselves even on the northern shores of the Black Sea and reach the Caucasus, from there, they will surely sweep through Persia and appear at the gates of India.

Can you remain indifferent to that danger? Is it not your duty to do everything possible so that the Nazi hordes could be checked in their mad career, and dealt a crushing defeat?

The familiar question: What can we do, as we are not free?—should no longer justify your passivity and refusal to participate actively in this struggle against Fascism. Because, where there is a will, there is a way !

We have shown above what can be done if you are determined to do your duty, which has now become clearer than ever. Now that the British Government is standing shoulder to shoulder by the Soviet Government in the fierce fight against the common enemy, you cannot refuse to co-opeate with the former and yet be seriousty concerned with the defence of the latter. The British Government has pledged all support to the Soviet Government. How can you still non-co-operate with the war efforts of the Britisn Government, if you wish to help the defence of the Workers' and Peasants' Republics' thereby creating the guarantee against the eventual Fascist invasion of India?

It is no longer possible to shirk the responsibility. Neutrality is not possible nor permissible in a conflict like the present. You must make the choice, and having chosen the side throw yourself whole-heartedly, without reserve, in the struggle. And there cannot be any doubt as to the camp you must join, if you wish to remain true to the ideals you have cherished. You must join the camp against Fascism, where you will be in the best company. Is it not more honourable to be in company of a Churchill, who is fighting Fascism, in alliance with the Soviet Union, than to follow the pseudo-anti-imperialists, who would still continue the policy of extending moral support to Fascism, even though condemning it verbally?

Your present leaders evidently would not abandon the policy which has until now been futile, and henceforth will be positively shameful. Therefore, you must have courage to act according to your conviction. You have to choose between your conviction and those who have misled you long enough.

Friends and Comrades: Let us join hands to build up a powerful party of the Indian people, which will not be emasculated by impractical and questionable ideals, and distracted from the straight path to freedom by pseudo-moral, non-political considierations. The Radical Democratic Party welcomes you in its ranks. History has vindicated the views we held from the beginning of the crisis. It will also vindicate that the way travelled by us in the face of popular prejudice and malicious propaganda is the only way to the freedom of the Indian people.

RADICAL DEMOCRATIC PARTY

June 23, 1941.

THE WAR AIM

Disregarding the indisputable fact that this war was precipitated by the aggressiveness of Nazi Germany, Indian nationalists as well as the so-called Socialists and Communists held that it was an imperialist war, and believed that India could remain unconcerned with its outcome, India's participation in this war was opposed because the Congress demand for a definition of its aim remained unfulfilled. It was maintained that the failure of the British Government to define its war aim to the satisfaction of the Congress corroborated the contention that it was an imperialist war, which was not only waged, but engineered, for promoting the interests and increasing the power of British Imperialism.

The neutrality of the Soviet Union was seized upon as the justification for the Indian "anti-imperialists" not only refusing to participate in the fight against Fascism, but even adopting a policy which might contribute to the victory of Fascism. It was argued that the Soviet Union was staying not because it was an imperialist war. The stupidity went to the extent of believing that the Soviet Union was actually allied with Nazi Germany and aiding it to fight British Imperialism. It was held that the object of the Soviet-German non-aggression pact was to frustrate the conspiracy of British Imperialism to destroy all its rivals.

The Nazi attack on the Soviet Union has placed some in a rather delicate position. They can no longer evade the choice between nationalist pseudo-anti-imperialism and Socialist anti-Fascism, which alone can be honestly and irreconcilably anti-imperialist. An ill-conceived "leftism" landed them in the camp of counter-revolution, just when the forces were being marshalled for the decisive battles in the international class war which has been developing over a quarter of a century. They are now trying to extricate themselves from that discrediting position. The more courageous among them have already shifted their position with the argument that the relation of forces on the international scenee has changed. That is a welome development, but it would be a mistake not to learn a lesson from a rather discrediting experience.

Undoubtedly, the invasion of the Soviet Union is a turning point in the history of this war. But is it a fortuitous events? Was it not possible to anticipate it? Is there no logic in the sequence of historical events? For the parochial nationalist, with his prejudices and natural sympathies, these questions may not arise. But they must challenge the conscience as well as intelligence of those who call themselves Socialists and Communists. Marxism answers those questions categorically. The Nazi invasion of the Soviet Union is not a fortuitous event. It was possible to anticipate it. Historical events are determined.

The whole situation was wrongly appreciated because, while catechising the British Government about its war aims, Indian Socialists and Communists as well as the Nationalists completely forgot to enquire about the war aims of Fascism. Otherwise, the whole process of development could have been easily anticipated, at least in broad outlines.

The nationalists, given their prejudices and natural sympathies, simply believed Hitler when he declared that the British Government was conspiring to check the rise of Nazi Germany as a first-class world power. They simply took it for granted that Nazi Germany was compelled to prepare for, and precipitate, this war with the laudable object of frustrating the British policy of encirclement. But such a view could not be taken by others who, by virtue of their social outlook and political conviction, could not take the Fascists on their words.

About the war aim of Nazi Germany, there could never be any doubt. Hitler had never made any secret about it. From the very beginning of his political career, he declared it from the house-tops, so to say. The tirade against the encirclement policy of British Government was only an interlude. Even when quarrelling with the British Government over the fate of this or that small country, Hitler was always prepared to come to terms. The dramatic flight of Rudolf Hess represented the latest effort. The episode still remains enveloped in mystery. But there have been ample indications of the object of Hess's flight to England. It is now generally agreed that Hess came to England as Hitler's emissary with the object of urgiug upon the British Government, through influential channels, the necessity of an Anglo-German alliance for fighting Communism. Evidently, the Nazis could not expect a still unbeaten British Government to consider any agreement with Germany if that would in the least touch the Empire. For the moment, we need not speculate about the causes of the failure of the mission of Rudolf Hess. But there can be no doubt that it did fail. Otherwise, the Nazis would not attack the Soviet Union only to be confronted with a formidable alliance for the defence of democratic freedom.

Although for the scientific student of contemporary history there could be no doubt about the war aim of Nazi Germany, yet let it be recapitulated so that the point we desire to make may be driven home.

Fascism in Italy and National Socialism in Germany rose as the avowed enemies of the working class and other progressive elements striving for the construction of a social order with higher ideals and greater freedom on the foundation of the liberating forces invoked by the achievements of modern civilisation. That construction was actually undertaken, at least in one country. Therefore, the destruction of the Soviet Union was the condition for the attainment of the purpose with which Fascism and National Socialism were born. Nearly twenty years ago, Hitler declared the war which he is at last waging actually.

But we need not go into past history. The war aim of Hitler's Germany is being proclaimed all over again, and it is the same old story. Arthur Rosenberg is the spiritual monitor of National Socialism. It was he who elaborated this sinister cult in all its details, including the plan for the destruction of the Soviet Union and the extermination of Marxism. Two days after the Nazi invasion of the Soviet Union, he wrote in *Voelkische Beobachter*, the central press organ of the National Socialist Party : "With the decision fraught with fateful results for the whole world, Germany has undertaken the task of overthrowing Bolshevism and freeing this vast region for her historic task." The official organ of the German Foreign Office, *Diplomatische Korrespondenz*, writes: "If German diplomacy at the eleventh hour frustrated Anglo-Russian collaboration in August 1939, it did not mean the abandonment of German opposition to Bolshevism." The entire German press published leading articles with flaring headlines with the central theme that Germany is now leading a crusade to save world civilisation from Communism. The *Voelkische Beobachter* again writes: It is a campaign which does not initiate a new war. The issue between National Socialism and Bolshevism must be fought out." The Diplomatic Correspondent of the London *Times,* no the particular friend of Bolshevism, writes: "In all non-belligerent countries, the Germans are trying hard to stir up the old anti-Comintern and anti-Moscow campaign. All their old plans and tricks, which for nearly two years have been gathering dust in Goebbels pigeon-holes, are being produced." The Foreign Editor of the London *Daily Mail,* known for its anti-Soviet sentiments, writes; "For Hitler, the only question was, when? and for him the answer is, now. Undoubtedly, there is a fanatical sincerity in his hatred of Soviet Russia and all that it symbolises. Anyone who has heard or seen Hitler utter the word Bolshevism, mouthing it with a malevolent hate, knows that this detestation of the Soviet is more than sincere: it is pathological. To shatter the power of Satlin would give him intense satisfaction. He can now reassume his favourite role of crusader carrying his crooked cross to the land of the red infidel. And even in his ideological frenzy, he is still a practical politician. He hopes by attacking Soviet Russia to gain the sympathy, if not the active support, of all anti-Bolsheviks throughout the world."

All this is not new. It is only a fresh announcement of the war aim of Nazi Germany. Yet, in this country it was all forgotten or overlooked intentionally. Perhaps, the nationalist pseudo-anti-imperialists sympathise with the war aim of Nazi Germany. But there are others who could not have done that. Given this war aim of Nazi Germany, the present development was predetermined, and therefore should have been anticipated by them. The situation has not changed. Simply its basic implictaion has unfolded itself.

The war aim and even the peace aim of all who are engaged in the fight against Fascism will be necessarily determined by the war aim of the Nazis. On the one hand, the declared and well known war aim of the Fascist Powers is not antagonistic to Imperialism, and therefore its attainment is not likely to weaken the latter. On the other hand, the necessarily determined, if not voluntarily proclaimed, war aim of the other party cannot possibly promote the interests of Imperialism. All this was evident from the very beginning to those who were neither carried away by an emotionai conception of anti-imperialism, or influenced by Fascist sympathy. The interminable sophistries about the war aim of the British Government, therefore, meant, by implication if not consciously, that it was not worthwhile to fight for thwarting Hitler's war aim.

Generally, the essentially pro-Fascist attitude is still maintained in the nationalist circles. Of course, everyone must follow his natural predisposition. The frog-in-the-well nationalism has become an antiquated cult—an anachronism. But others, who are actuated by higher ideals of freedom, can no longer stultify themselves, or do even worse, on the pretext that the British Government refused to define its war aim.

Lenin backed up his decision for signing the Brest-Litovsk Treaty dictated by arrogant German Imperialism, with the argument that the Treaty had already been signed by the Russian soldiers—with their feet. He meant that the soldiers did not want to fight any longer; they were coming back from the front. The war aim of the British Government similarly has been declared—indeed. Who ever cannot be satisfied with that declaration, which is more convincing than any verbal proclamation, simply look for a plausible pretext for their indefensible attitude prompted by questionable and discrediting motives.

So, let there be an end to this sophisticated controversy about the war aim. The aim of this war is sufficiently known to all who do not want to be Hitler's dupes, or are not Fascists by conviction. It is no longer possible to sit on the fence. The issues are clear. Whoever would not participate in the fight to frustrate the war aim of Hitler's Germany, will be only contributing to the attainment of that aim, and consequently working for the enslavement of the whole world and the perpetuation of India's own slavery.

"Independent India", July 13, 1941

THIS WAR & OUR DEFENCE

At last, the war has reached our doors. It is no longer a distant rumbling. It is foolish even now to maintain that we can be indifferent to it, regarding it as a great show which we can only watch. Before long, it may penetrate our hearths and homes.

How is the average Indian reacting to this danger ? Our country may not belong to us; but we are certainly the owners of our hearths and homes, and to defend that is our responsibility. None can do that for us. It is simply silly to say that the Indians are not even owners of their own homes, and that they have absolutely nothing the destruction of which will directly injure them.

Previously, there was complacency. It was not believed that the war would really come so close. The warning about a danger of invasion was ridiculed as alarmism. Now that complacency itself has become ridiculous, everybody is panic-stricken, paralysed by the feeling of helplessness. None knows what is going to happen tomorrow or in the next hour. None knows how to prevent it, if something dreadful is going to happen.

Measures taken by the authorities are not even half-measures; they fail to create confidence and as a matter of fact, only provoke greater panic. The attitude of the major political parties, and particularly of the popular heroes, reminds one of Nero fiddling while Rome burned.

India is not yet actually in flames. But she is full of inflammable material, and unfortunately not wanting in lunatics who would play with burning torches on a powder magazine. Therefore, the conflagration may break out any day in consequence of an ignition from outside. Air bombardments may serve the purpose, and they need not be even very serious. Or landing of parachutists, which before long may cease to be a distant possibility. Behind the tragic spectacle of a general panic and confusion, there lurks a greater danger, represented by the lunatics who hoping that a non-descript or questionable "new order" might arise out of the threatening chaos, would usher the latter in. Disregarding what happened in China, they would welcome the Japanese invaders as the heralds, if not actually the standard-bearers, of Indian freedom.

The problem of Indian defence is rendered almost insoluble by this under-current of insanity—a deplorable state of political pathology, created by historical reasons and accentuated by the short-sightedness, complacency and lack of imagination on the part of the authorities. How to cure the disease? If there is no cure, as it may appear today, India cannot be defended.

But all talk about these difficulties is irrelevent as long as the most fundamental question remains unanswered. Do we want to defend India? Where there is a will, there is a way. The religious-minded people may prefer the other dictum—God helps those who help themselves; and Indians are said to be a God-fearing people. The ground, physical as well as psychological, will be cleared for action, the possibilities of the situation will be visualised, as soon as the fundamental question is answered affirmatively.

Until now, the average politically-minded Indian has answered the question in the negative, either explicitly or by implication. India does not belong to the Indians; why should they defend her ? In a way, that appears to be a plausible retort.

But that apparent plausibility is contradicted by the actualities of the present situation. If the masses of the Indian population were really indifferent to the possibility of an invasion, the present state of panic would not be there. One cannot like, or even be indifferent to, a thing that he fears. And the outstanding feature of the situation is a general fear of a possible invasion. Therefore, it is quite clear that the masses of the people are afraid of that danger. That being the case, all the sophistries, woven around the apparently plausible question : why should Indians bother about the defence of a country which does not belong to them ?—can no longer paralyse the process of thought and will to act, on the part of Indians who are neither devoid of the sense of public responsibility nor wish to shirk it.

Will not the Indian people lose anything if the cities are bombarded, factories are blown up, dockyards, harbours and industrial plants destroyed or damaged ? Thousands and thousands of wage-earners will be without any means of livelihood. They will be destitute in every sense. Small traders will also find themselves in a similarly painful situation. Young men and women belonging to the higher and middle classes will also lose, because educational institutions may be closed down. Practically the entire people will thus lose and suffer if the country will be invaded. Therefore, their concern for the defence of the country is evident. The anxiety for immediate safety must prevail upon nationalist sentiment. All romanticism about the future is bound to be eclipsed by the rude realities of the present.

These realities are jolting some of the leaders out of the rut of a negative politics. All of them are no longer prepared to watch the great show, even when it threatens to engulf India. But having been so very late in becoming conscious of the sense of public responsibility,—their responsibility to the Indian people—they have got to face the Frankenstein, and seem to be afraid. Therefore, they think of defence only in conventional military terms, just as the Government whose policy is guided by men living in the moon. It is maintained that Indians cannot do anything for the defence of the country, unless an Indian politician, who may not know the difference between a regiment and a batallion, or know a Bren gun from a mine-thrower, is allowed to occupy the most ornamental chair in the Defence Department. Just an obsession! It is neither explained nor thought how the military power of India will grow miraculously, and reach the necessary peak, as soon as the ceremony of placing a stack of paper, called a portfolio, in charge of a certain gentleman, will be performed.

No. It is not as simple as all that. Nor is the defence of a country any longer a matter of mere military technicalities. This war is revolutionising many things, including the methods of warfare themselves. People's war is not a meaningless phrase. Gold ribbons, medals, brass buttons and feathered caps are not necessary for raising a people's army, which alone can wage a people's war. Nor will that be done as soon as some constitutional reshuffling will take place. A people's war can be fought by the people, and the people alone can create a people's army. If the will of the people is not a metaphysical conception, bureaucratic stupidity cannot effectively prevent the people from acting particularly in a critical moment as the present.

The first thing must be done first. Don't worry about arms. Let there be men, with the will to defend their hearth and home, which after all is the concrete shape in which the country appears to the bulk of the people, and which do belong to them—and arms will be found in due course of time. For the moment, there are not many such men. Hence all the helplessness and panic. Those who are seriously concerned with the defence of the country should go ahead with the immediate task of instilling in the people the will to defend their hearth and home, and gathering together men actuated by that will, disregarding whatever may be the attitude of the Government. The unfortunate fact that, in a way, India does belong to non-Indians, guarantees that the Government will ultimately fall back upon the co-operation of a people's army composed of such men. Because, the Government also wants to defend the country. As soon as it will be clear that a purely military machine, divorced from the people, cannot serve the purpose, the Government will be bound to look for other, more effective, weapons. But the Government cannot create those weapons. The people alone can do that. A weapon created by the people can only promote the cause of the people's freedom.

It is said that freedom is our birth-right. But it is forgotten that the children of the soil are owners of the country also by a birth-right. The country is not an abstract conception. It is composed of things which do actually belong to the people. And exactly those things will be destoyed and ruined in case of a foreign invasion. Therefore, the people must shoulder the responsibility of defending the country for defending a birth-right. Let us exercise that prior birth-right, and the birth-right of freedom will automatically be ours.

What is then to be done, concretely? We have answered this question all along, ever since the war broke out. The imminence of the danger is compelling others to realise their responsibility. Any effective action presupposes the belief in its possibility. The vehemence of condemning the Government for have disarmed the Indian people has undermined that belief. It is maintained that, having disarmed the Indian people, the Government has rendered it incapable of doing anything for its own defence. But does emasculation necessarily follow from disarmament? Even in the so-called free countries, everybody does not run about in the street with a gun in the hand. Nor is everybody trained in the use of arms. The lack of the belief that Indians can defend their country is very largely due to the absence of the will to do so. Therefore, to quicken that will is the paramount task of the moment. Nobody can prevent us from accomplishing that task.

Even if the Japanese succeed in breaking through the outer lines of military defence, it will be hardly possible for them to land a very large army in India proper. A determined people can easily put up an effective resistance to such an invasion. And the fight, in that case, will not consist of pitched battles, in which modern weapons of warfare are indispensable. In the last analysis, the method of guerilla warfare will have to be adopted to defend India against any invasion. Human material is the decisive factor in that method of warfare. Guerilla bands can operate, making things very difficult for an army of invasion coming from a distant country, even with very primitive weapons. As a matter of fact, they can be peasants who need not even abandon their peace time profession. That happened in China, and the story of the Chinese resistance to Japanese aggression has become a classic.

The popular terror about air bombardment can also be very largely minimised if it is explained how such a bombardment cannot be very destructive in a country like India. The object of air raids, which the ambitions invader may undertake, will be to undermine popular morale. That object can be frustrated by explaining to the people that they will not gain anything by running away from the cities, fearing that the later may be bombarded. Those who are earning their livelihood in the cities will have to face starvation by running away. Therefore, by running away, they will not find any greater safety anywhere. As soon as that will be realised, they will regain self-confidence and can be easily persuaded to remain where they are, to face the danger and overcome it.

All this work, again, can be done irrespective of the attitude of the Government. Therefore, the attitude of the Government need not make us feel helpless. We shall have to fall back on the time-honoured principle of self-help. Complaints and criticism, however vigorous, cannot possibly equip India in a sufficiently short time with the most up-to-date military machine for defence and air-raid protection. Therefore, we shall have to take a practical view of the situation. We shall have to fall back upon the weapon of popular resistance, and that is a more powerful weapon. Let us forge that weapon, if we wish to defend our country and make it ours by defending when none else can do that. In the last analysis it is the will to resist that counts. Once that will is shared by sufficiently large number of people, then, before long, a powerful people's army will arise, and the problem of Indian defence will be solved. There is no other solution of the problem.

"Independent India", Jan. 13, 1942.

CONVICTION, COURAGE AND DETERMINATION

Summary of Speech at the meeting of the Calcutta People's Defence Committee, Jannary 25, 1942.

The fundamental problem of Indian defence is political and psychological. Official war efforts cannot solve it. On the other hand, the activities of the major political parties and popular leaders have aggravated the problem, instead of helping its solution. Those activities have fostered indifference to the danger of Fascist invasion which, indeed, is regarded by many as not a danger but an agency for Indian freedom. Consequently, the country was not prepared for the present crisis which is causing a wide-spread panic, and a paralysing feeling of helplesness seems to be shared by all. The official measures are ill-conceived, inadequate and inefficient. They do not inspire confidence. But it is not wise to rest content simply with criticising them. We must act—on the basis of popular initiative and popular energy, In critical moments, like the present, great things happen quite unexpectedly; hitherto unknown personalities step forward and are recognised as the leaders of the people.

Although for more than one reason, the necessary preparations were not made, in time, under the impact of the crisis the tide of public opinion is turning. The instinct of self-preservation is compelling a response to the call for self-defence. But still there is a good deal of confusion, and mischievous forces are trying to operate with the slogan of defence. There are those who still entertain the illusion that an invasion by the enemy of Britain will bring freedom to India. That illusion undermines the very possibility of defence. The essential condition for a successful self-defence is the will to resist. That, in its turn, presupposes absence of any illusion about the consequence of the imminent invasion.

These few observations, made on the basis of a realistic analysis of the situation, indicates what is, in my opinion, the task of People's Defence Committees. It is to tackle the fundamental problem of Indian defence—a task that cannot be accomplished by official efforts. The task is to change the popular mentality, so as to quicken the will to resist a greater evil.

Evidently, it is a political task, primarily. A

very widespread campaign of a systematic propaganda alone can create the psychological atmosphere favourable for the mobilisation of popular energy for the purpose of defence; and the propaganda must necessarily be political. Very largely, it has got to be a counter-propaganda.

There is a widespread belief that an invasion by any enemy of Britain would bring freedom to India. This illusion has been created by a propaganda which is still being carried on, covertly as well as overtly. It creates confusion and spreads panic, which baffle all efforts to organise self-defence. Those who are making the mischievous propaganda should be regarded as the advance guard of the invader, and be exposed as such. Simultaneously, information about the practice of Fascism, about the conditions in the countries under the domination of the Axis Powers, should be supplied to the people. Only when the people will realise that invasion by any Axis Power will mean a greater evil, will they develop the will to resist. Thus, the psychological foundation for an effective popular defence will be laid down, and the problem, which to-day appears to be baffling, will be solved.

Therefore, I suggest that, to do what others cannot do and to act as the saviours of the situation, popular Defence Committees should be organised with the following objects:

1. To combat the sympathy for the Fascist Powers and the wish for their victory; 2. To expose those whose activities encourage this mental attitude, as enemies of the people: 3. To explain how a successful invasion by a Fascist Power will be a greater evil, and prejudice the cause of Indian freedom; 4. To promote the popular will to resist the greater evil; 5. To counter act panic by awakening self-confidence; 6. To mobilise the entire manpower to meet all possible emergencies.

I would further suggest that the Committees should be built up from below. The wards of the city should be divided into zones, each with a Committee guiding and co-ordinating the activities carried out by all the citizens of the locality. In course of these activities for organising mutual help, relief, first aid, protection etc., the entire man power will be mobilised. The resources of the entire locality will be at the disposal of each citizen of the locality. Collective action will create confidence and the consciousness of power.

The rest will follow easily. It is difficult to make a beginning. Let us begin with conviction, courage and determination. There is no other way.

INDIA'S DUTY

Summary of a Speech at a public meeting in Calcutta, January 25, 1942.

For two years or more, there was a lively controvercy regarding the nature of the war and its possible consequences. Then, the war was far away from our country. To-day ithas reached the Indian frontiers and may soon be over our heads in the shape of bombing planes. Therefore, discussion has become out of date. To-day, it is the burning question of actual defence which has to be faced. The question is not whether we should help England or not; it is whether we should defend ourselves or not. If it is decided that we should not defend ourselves, there is nothing more to be said. But it is doubtful if there any are many who would say that we should not defend ourselves. There are some who indeed say that we should not bother about the defence of the country, because the invaders would bring us freedom. It is argued that the country is not ours; why then should we defend it? Those who are still thinking in those terms, do not seem to realise that British Imperialism is ceasing to be a factor in the situation. An invasion will mean inability of the present Government to defend the country. That will amount to its practical disappearance. There then will remain two contending forces, the invaders of India and the Indians.

The fact is that this is our country, and the Indians will be primarily injured when military operations will take place on Indian soil. This is no longer a distant possibility. It may happen any day, and we shall have to think in terms of that dreadful happenning.

Yet another question prevents the development of popular initiative for self-defence. It is: "We are not allowed to take any active part in the war; how then can we defend the country?" It is true that the people are placed under all sorts of disadvantages which prevent any serious military operations on their part. It is very deplorable that the Government still refuses to take the people into confidence, including those who have from the very beginning declared their determination to mobilise the Indian people in suppurt of this war against Fascism. But there is another side of the picture. This refusal of the Government to take us into confidence should inspire us to take the initiative, and the present emergency affords us the opportunity.

The possible military developments can be easily visualised. The fall of Singapore is not altogether out of the question. So, the invasion of India is no longer beyond the realm of possibilities. Military events on the eastern front since Japan started belligerent actions do not allow much optimism regarding the possibility of defending India with the help of the regular army in case of an invasion. In that situation, it will be for the people to take into their hands the task of their own defence. By defending the country, when it cannot be defended by the forces at the command of the present Government, we shall not serve our foreign rulers. We shall be only helping ourselves.

Finally there is the question: How can we defend the country? We are unarmed; there is no great chance of arming the people; how can we then do anything at all? The apparent impossibility of answering this question has created a sense of helplessness and fatalism. Last week, addressing the meeting in the University Institute, I gave some idea of what we could do. In some quarters, it has been characterised as a fantastic plan. Therefore, I propose to show that the plan is quite practicable, provided we are really determined to shoulder the task of defending the country.

Air raids do not constitute the whole of the danger which threatens us. They should be regarded as the prelude to a large-scale invasion. When that takes place, the A.R P. arrangements or the Civic Guards, as they are at present constituted, will be of no avail. If the regular army cannot stop that invasion, the burden of defence will have to be shouldered by the people, if the country is to be defended at all. So, immediately after an invasion, it will be a struggle between the invader and the Indian people.

We shall have to think what the latter can possibly do in that situation.

The landing of invading forces on some points along the Indian coast will not yet mean conquest of the country. If the regular army fails, such landing cannot be prevented, and the invaders will seize some important places, possibly including Calcutta. From that time onwards, the situation will be favourable for the defenders, and it will be possible and a very practical proposition to organise an effective popular defence, again provided that the will to resist is there. In the first place, the invading army occupying some places on the coast will be soon confronted with the problem of provisioning itself. Local store will be soon exhausted. They will not be able to get supply from outside the country. An economic blockade of the occupied places will then become a very powerful weapon in the hand of the defenders. And that can be easily organised. If the economic blockade succeeds, the invaders will be starved, and may be compelled to withdraw. They will, of course, not give in so easily. They will try to penetrate the country by force, and for doing so they will have to divide themselves into smaller groups, which will advance along the railways and highroads. The latter pass through hundreds of villages and are thu sopen to interference by popular defence volunteers. For impeding the penetration of the invaders and harrassing them in innumerable ways, modern up-to-date weapons are not indispensable. That can be done with primitive weapons and improvised devices which have been practised by popular defence forces in Spain and China. Bridges can be easily destroyed;

night attacks by small popular forces will do havoc among the invaders. They will find themselves in the midst of enemy country. If all these possibilities are kept in mind, it is not at all difficult to imagine how it is possible to organise popular resistance, and out of it create a People's Army.

But all that depends on the popular will to resist invasion. Therefore, the primary task is to promote that will. Unfortunately, activities are being carried on which undermine that will. If those activities are allowed to be carried on, it is idle to blame the Government for the misfortunes which may overtake us before long. On the contrary, it should be remembered that, by ourselves defending the country, we can make the country our own.

PEOPLES' ARMY

The present helplessness in the face of a possible invasion is undoubtedly a result of the recent history of our country. But more strictly speaking, the effect of that cause is rather the indifference to the danger, and even the inclination to welcome it as a blessing. These direct results, however, affect only a comparatively small section of the population—the so-called politically minded. On the one hand, those few really politically minded do not share the fatal inertia and the dangerous illusion. On the other hand, the feeling on the part of the vast bulk of the population is of helplessness. This feeling is the decisive factor of the situation, and the cause of this phenomenon can be traced far back into Indian history—much earlier than the British conquest.

This is not the first time that India is threatened with an invasion. She was invaded on innumerable occasions, and practically every time she became an easy prey. That is an outstanding fact of Indian history. If it happens once again, the responsibility for the misfortune will not belong only to the Government, whose policy during the last two hundred years has certainly contributed to the creation of the present paradoxical situation.

The situation is paradoxical because it is characterised by a mass psychology which undermines the possibility of what is said to be the popular aspiration, namely, the attainment of national freedom. It is maintained correctly that India belongs to the Indians by birth-right. But, at the same time, it is argued that Indians cannot feel the responsibility of defending their country because it is ruled by a foreign Government. The condition for the Indians shouldering the responsibility of defending their country is the grant of freedom by its present rulers. The conclusion of that argument is obvious. If freedom is not granted, Indians should not defend their country, even if it be in the danger of being invaded by another foreign power. Those who pretend to be fighters for freedom, thus appear to be indifferent to the possibility of a change of masters. Such an attitude on the part of those who claim to represent the popular aspiration for national freedom, is certainly very paradoxical.

However, the absence of the will to resist a new invasion on the ground that it will not be dignified for the Indian people to do so as long as it remains deprived of freedom, or that it will make no difference, is explained by the more fundamental fact of the general feeling of helplessness. The cause of this fact is very deep-rooted in Indian history. Barring exceptional cases, the will to resist has been conspicuously absent throughout the history of this country, and a national virtue has been made out of that absence of the will to resist. The proverbial Indian peasant bowing his head before the storm of occasional invasions, only to raise it again and trudge partiently behind his plough, has been lyrically depicted as the symbol of the Indian spirit undisturbed by the vicissitude if this ephemeral world. Why, then, bother of the time-honoured experience is to be made once again ?

The paralysing feeling of helplessness in the faceof a possible invasion, thus, ist he result of a cultivated mental habit. It has not been cultivated by the people as a matter of choice; it has been cultivated in them. That soul-killing cultivation of inertia is the net result of what is erroneously conceived as the Indian culture. The present position is a cultural heritage. It will not change, however much we may quarrel with outsiders. Indeed, if the latter have been able to do harm to our country, that has also been very largely due to the absence of the will to resist on the part of the Indian people.

The decisive argument (considered to be so by those advancing it) is: How can an unarmed and emasculated people defend itself? A people can be disarmed by force; but emasculation does not happen so easily. If the Indian people have been emasculated, a short period of disarmament cannot be the sole cause of that misfortune. Bravery and other manly attributes are not necessarily coincident with the bearing of arms. The emasculation of a whole people is not a simple physical phenomenon, unless it is nothing more serious than a general physical deterioration caused by insufficient nutrition or other factors. Emasculation as a shameful national characteristic is a moral and spiritual degeneration. It has nothing to do with actual physical condition. Able-bodied men, even strong men, can be cowards. On the other hand, people of average physical strength often perform feats of supreme heroism. What is known as moral courage, is the decisive subjective factor in all human action. Emasculation means absence of moral courage. Therefore, it is palpably incorrect to say that the British rule has emasculated the entire Indian people simply by restricting the right of bearing arms. On the other hand, emasculation in the sense of a mass inertia, in the form of the absence of the will to resist misfortunes, is a national characteristic which was to be found in Indian history much earlier than the British conquest.

When, a thousand years ago, a few hundred Arab horsemen invaded India, and seized a large part of it, there was no foreign Government to disarm the people or to deprive it otherwise of the means to defend the country, Since then, similarly remarkable events of conquest by small bands of invaders took place often enough, indicating the general absence of the will to resist. Occasional resistance here and there was only the exception which proved the rule. Therefore, there is no reason to believe that a change in the attitude of the present Government will increase the defensive power of the country. The psychological condition for a successful defence cannot be created by any such makeshift.

As far as the regular army is concerned, it can be raised by the present Government almost unlimitedly, the only limitation being financial, and the possibility of equipment. That limitation will be operative even in the case of a National Government. So, the question is whether a regular army can defend the country. Experience is creating more and more doubt on that score. Out of that doubt grows the realisation of the necessity of a different kind of defensive force—a People's Army. Evidently, something entirely new is visualised. It is not merely a demand for an endless expansion of the regular army, to be recruited, drilled, armed, regimented and employed in the good old conventional manner. This war is revolutionising everything, including the method of warfare itself; and that implies the structure also of the armed forces.

In the scheme of a regular army, whether conscript or voluntary, there is little room for will. The soldiers, particularly composing the rank and file, have only to be disciplined to obey. They are only to do and die; it is not for them to reason why. Such an armed force may still serve the purpose of an offensive war; but it is utterly useless for defending a country, whether ruled by a foreign Government or by a National Government, in the case of an attack by a modern mechanised army. The history of the present war until the Nazi invasion of the Soviet Union made that abundantly clear. Therefore, whoever is seriously interested in the question of Indian defence, must think in terms of a People's Army and of new methods of war.

The essential difference between a People's Army and the conventional regular army is that, while in the case of the latter will and intelligence are either absent or suppressed, the former presupposes an operation of those very subjective factors of a high level. A People's Army can be created only by the people, or by a People's Government. It will not do to postulate a People's Government as the condition for the rise of a People's Army. Because, in that case, it may never come into being, and, in its absence, the impossibility of the establishment of a People's Government will only recede into an immeasurably distant future. On the contrary, a People's Army can serve as the lever to raise the politics of a country to a higher level, and thus prepare the atmosphere for the rise of a People's Government. It is clear to see how foolish and short-sighted it is to argue that, until we are free, we cannot act for winning our freedom.

Since the general absence of the will to resist is a cultural heritage of the Indian nation, the creation of the psychological atmosphere suitable for the rise of a People's Army should appear to be almost an impossible proposition. In a way, it is; if not actually impossible, at least a very difficult proposition. Under normal conditions, the process would be very long and laborious. The spiritual rebirth of a nation does not take place all of a sudden. But an activist approach may render the problem less baffling, and such an approach is very possible in the midst of the present emergency. The very feeling of helplessness implies a sub-conscious urge of self-help. When the need for self-help cries aloud, because there is none to offer any protection against an impending catstrophe, the sub-conscious urge may suddenly become vocal in an atmosphere of activity. It is possible for the Indian people to make this jump from the slumber of age-long lethargy and fatalism towards initiative and purposefuless.

The possibility and opportunity are afforded by the present emergency.

The freedom that the Indian people sorely need is the freedom from the loadstone of the cultural heritage of an indifference to the vicissitudes of this life. That freedom is the condition for all other forms of freedom. The nationalist movement has degenerated into its present self-contradictory and self-stultifying position under the pressure of this precious cultural heritage. Hatred and bitterness against the foreign rulers and the spitefulness born of them should not be confounded with the will to freedom. The former paralyse action and give rise to all sorts of illusions and wishful thinking. The latter, on the contrary, encourages initiative for action, in the midst of which we come nearer to freedom. Given that initiative on the part of a sufficiently large number of Indians, a People's Army may come into being in no time.

An appeal must be made to the instinct of self-preservation. Self-defence is the active expression of that basic instinct. Instead of creating the illusion that, as soon as there will be some reshuffling in the personnel of the Government or a declaration by the British

Prime Minister, India will be out of danger, and in a position to defend herself, it should be made clear to the people that their courage and collective action can alone protect them against the invader. It should be explained to them how concerted action by a whole people can beat back the most formidable aggressor. The basic point to be driven home is that, in case of an invasion, there will be no power to protect the country. Risking the displeasure of the complacent and short-sighted foreign rulers of the country, it must be told that their much vaunted military preparations have not turned out to be very dependable.

Should the Indians suffer their homes and hearths to be overrun by new invaders, simply because the present rulers will not be able to defend the country? To do so, would be the height of stupidity. To do so, simply for the cheap satisfaction of spiting the present rulers, would be poor patriotism. When our country is thus practically defenceless, and consequently may pass on to the hands of new masters, it is for the fighters for Indian freedom to assert themselves and shoulder the responsibility of defending the country as their own. It is not for them to remain passive, doing nothing more than asking for freedom or hoping for better treatment at the hands of new masters.

If there are enough determined fighters for Indian freedom, who are intelligent enough to appraise the actual relation of forces, it should not be at all difficult to quicken in the masses the will to resist, and thus lay down the foundation for a People's Army. To blame the British Government for having placed India in the present predicament may sound very moral and patriotic. But in reality, it is immoral and unpatriotic, because it prevents the growth of the popular will to resist, without which India will never come near to the goal of freedom. As that will alone can forge a powerful instrument in possession of the people, to promote it is the only patriotic duty of the moment. Let that duty be performed by a growing number of Indians, and India will have a People's Army to conquer freedom for the people and establish a Government of the people.

Independent India, Feb. 1, 1942.

GAMBLING

The three days' debate in the British Parliament has thrown a flood of light on the military situation in the Southern Pacific, and revealed a perspective which is not at all reassuring. India being most directly connected with that front of this world-wide war, those concerned with her defence should be warned by the alarm sounded by no less an authority than the British Prime Minister. It remains to be seen how the authorities in India will react to the gave crisis. For the moment, they seem to be gambling.

We have all along maintained that, unless India was developed into a self-sufficient military unit, her defence in case of a large scale attack by a first class Power would be a very difficult, if not an impossible proposition. In peace time, the far-flung British Empire appeared to be a very imposing structure. That was a delusive appearance. The war has revealed its weakness, which was previously noticeable to all except those blinded either by complacence or by fear.

Experience has shown that, during war time, it is impossible to maintain the connection with the distant parts of the Empire, and consequently those parts must rely on their own initiative and resources in order to defend themselves. To the extent that this initiative is restricted, and the resources remain undeveloped, to that extent the distant parts of the Empire become the Achilles' Heel in a gave crisis like the present. Already in the beginning of 1941, it became clear that the Mediterranean route to India and farther East could be cut off any moment, and consequently the problem of Indian defence would take on an entirely different nature. The defence of India could no longer remain conditional upon supply from outside, particularly, from such distant countries like England or the United States, of indispensable weapons of modern warfare like aeroplanes, tanks, heavy artillery etc. Neverthless, those responsible for Indian defence refused to take notice of the most obvious danger, and thanks to that complacency or shortsightedness India might have been invaded from the West. The extension of the war into the Soviet territory prevented that.

In his speech in the Parliament, Mr. Churchill

said: "The valour of the Russian Army has warded off dangers which we undoubtedly had run. It is only by the victory on the Russian front and the Black Sea coast that we have been spared the overrunning of all those lands from the Levante to the Caspian which, in turn, gives access to India, Iran, the Persian Gulf, the Nile Valley and the Suez Canal."

The most obvious thing to do should have been to do the needful for removing the weakness of Indian defence. Nothing of the kind was done. As a matter of fact, as soon as the danger of invasion from the West receded, owing to the Nazis having their hands full on the Soviet front, the Indian authorities relapsed into their traditional complacency.

The situation, however, continued to be as insecure as ever, and that was not quite unknown, at least to the Metropolitan authorities. Mr. Churchill said, "While facing Germany and Italy, here and in the Nilé Valley, we have never had any power to provide effectively for the defence of the Far East." It is incredible that the inablility of the Metropolitan authorities to provide for the defence of the Far East including India was not known to those responsible for the defence of the latter. They should have fallen back on local initiative and the development of local resources. Perhaps the statement that practically nothing of the kind was done would be challenged. But facts are more convincing than arguments. And the measure of the efforts to make India shortcomings as regards her defence must be judged by the recent military events in Malaya.

In the estimation of what has really been done, and what may be coming, we can again be benefitted by the bold frankness of the Prime Minister. He said: "We have had a great deal of bad news lately from the Far East, and I think it is highly probable that we shall have a great deal more. Wrapped up in this bad news will be many tales of blunder and shortcomings both in foresight and action. No one will pretend for a moment that disasters like these can occur without there having been faults and shortcomings." Having said that much about the past, Mr. Churchill predicted that Japanese naval supremacy would last long enough to inflict many more heavy and painful losses.

These shortcomings resulted from the limiting factor of transport. The Prime Minister informed that there was no lack of troops or even equipment. Presumably, he meant that troops could be recruited in India endlessly, and that there were equipments in Britian which could be spared for India. But the latter could not be transported. In the first place, there was shortage of shipping, most of which had to be employed in the vital supply route across the Atlantic. Secondly, the Mediterranean route was full of perils. Thirdly, whatever quantity of aeroplanes, tanks and anti-aircraft and anti-tank guns could be transported, subject to the limiting factor of transport, went to the Nile Valley, and Singapore had to be satisfied only with 60,000 poorly equipped men.

The operation of the limiting factor of transport should have been anticipated long before it created such a dangerous position. It should have been upset by making India independent of the supply from distant England, which was bound to be seriously interrupted, if not completely stopped, in case of a war.

One reason of that stupid negligence is well known. In the absense of a highly developed metallurgical and chemical industry, the basic weapons of modern warfare cannot be manufactured. India laboured under that handicap; and instead of making a supreme effort for removing it, all sorts of plausible pretexts were discovered for justifying it. But there was another reason which has now been disclosed by the Prime Minister. He said: "It seemed very unlikely that the Japanese would attempt a distant invasion of the Malaya, an assult on Singapore and an attack on the Dutch East Indies, while leaving in her flank and in the rear the great American fleet. We reinforced Singapore to a considerable extent, and Hongkong to an extent which, we were advised, would be sufficient to hold the island for a long time."

It is incredible—the extent to which fatal complacency went! It should have disappeared at least after the Japanese occupation of Indo-China. The Japanese plan to seize the narrow neck of the Malay Peninsula is much older. And it is an elementary matter of strategy that, in order to carry through the plan, the invader must attack Singapore and establish himself on the surrounding islands. It was equally evident that the American naval bases in the West Pacific could not possibly be held against an attack, and that their lines of communication with the main bases, thousands of miles away across the Ocean, could by very easily cut off. Exactly that happened in the very first days after the outbreak of hostilities. The naval strategists, who did not anticipate this move, do not deserve the name. The American Navy, on other hand, does not seem to have been very conscious of its responsibility regarding checking Japanese advance towards the Dutch East Indies and Malaya. It was taken completely unawares in Pearl Harbour. Mr. Churchill informed: "On December 7, the Japanese by a sudden and treacherous attack crippled for the time being the American Pacific Fleet, and in a few days inflicted a heavy naval loss on us. For the time being, therefore, naval superiority in the Pacific and the Malayan Archipelago passed from the hands of the two leading naval Powers into those of Japan."

Evidently, the defenders of the Empire were lulled by a sense of false security. The problem of transport was no longer a theoretical proposition. It has operated as a seriously limiting factor in actual experience. But nothing was learned. If the defence of India and the more outlying parts of the Empire could not be helped from the Metropolitan Olympos, then they should be left to the problematical protection of the American Navy, which also proved to be a broken reed at the very first moment.

But the situation was known to be much too insecure to be treated with such incredible complacency. Mr. Attlee, winding up the debate, depicted it as follows: "Our position in the Pacific depended on our command of the sea, and we have not got that. The coast of Malaya is a very long one. The defence of Malaya depended on sea power, and we were weak there." Having disclosed the perilous position, he argued that it could not be improved by declaring that the position was insecure, because that would have been only inviting an attack. That is playing the ostrich game. It was not necessary to advertise weakness. But it was necessary to remove it. Mr. Attlee himself admitted that that was not done, and explained why: "There is a great deal to be said for making India a great arsenal of the British Empire in the East. It is a long term policy, on which more ought to have been done in the past years. But in the actual circumstances of the time, there is restriction of machinery and lack of trained personnel. We were restricted by the fact that, though India had great potential economic power, she had not actual power."

The explanation is hardly satisfactory. It only calls for the obvious question : why? This question was not answered. Mr. Hore-Belisha, a former Secretary of State for War, said : "The scheme of defence evidently did not anticipate the kind of attack that was launched. Perhaps it was thought that the monsoon would intervene or that the jungle was impregnable. But all these considerations fell into insignificance compared with the real and fundamental cause of the reverse." The fundamental cause was a sence of false security, and the belief that nothing adverse could ever happen to those who knew how to delude themselves. Mr. Shinwell pronounced an pronounced truth when he said that "the outstanding feature of the Ministers appears to be a capa city for deluding themselves." The rebuke may not be applicable to the members of the Metropolitan Government. But the cap certainly fits admirably the heads of the men on the spot. The former simply could not help. It was the obvious duty of the latter to help themselves. But they are helpless in their bureaucratic isolation, and consequently ran the risk of gambling with the fate of a whole nation. Mr. Haden-Guest asked: "Why the system of defending the Far East by a small garrison was persisted in when it was clear that the war was to be expected?" He charged the Government with the non-use of the man power available in Malaya, Burma and India.

Even this criticism of the policy, which has left India practically undefended against a serious invasion, does not go to the root of the problem. It is not a question of man power. The Malay Peninsula has been lost, and more may follow, because of the shortage, amounting to a practical absence, of aeroplanes, tanks and anti-aircraft guns. Even a precious warship like the "Prince of Wales" could not have the assistance of an aircraft carrier. Therefore, the fullest use of Indian man power will not improve the situation. The decisive question is of armaments. They cannot be supplied in sufficiently large quantities from England and America, because other, more important, fronts must have the preference. Besides, even if they were available, from distant countries, they could not be transported, firstly owing to the shortage of shipping, and secondly because of the perilous condition of the lines of communication. The situation has not arisen overnight. It should have been anticipated. But the foresight was lacking. No serious effort was made to build up a modern armament industry in India.

From the very beginning of the war, we demanded the industrialisation of the country as the basic condition for its militarisation. We pointed out that before long all war fronts to the east of Suez would have to be supplied from India. Although the usual arguments advanced against the possibility of a rapid industrialisation of India were mostly frivolous, there were some serious difficulties. They arose from the belief that the economic *status quo* was sacrosanct ; it should be disturbed on no account. On the one hand, all blame is laid at the door of the Government, which is expected to do everything, leaving the Indian capitalists to gather in all the profits. The Government, on the other hand, would not interfere in the least with the right of private property, which right is supposed to include the right to mismanage, to the extent of seriously prejudicing public welfare. Rapid industrialisation, so very essential for defence, could easily take place if vested interest was subordinated to public safety, at least as a measure of emergency.

That was not done, and even now there does not seem to be the least desire to do so. Consequently, the position of India is as perilous as it has been described by the Prime Minister.

Only the spirit of a reckless gambler can remain unperturbed in the midst of such a situation. The sentiment of the present rulers of the country seems to be that, if India will be lost, what does it matter to whom she is lost. One can thus gamble with something which was reckless fortuitously, so to say. But there must be Englishmen who are beginning to realise that the old-fashioned Empire is bound to disintegrate owing to its own weakness. They, bound is with the Indians who, in their turn, are not blinded by a suicidal nationalism, should take an entirely different view of the situation and apply themselves courageously to the task of doing the needful for defending India against the danger of becoming a powerful base of world reaction.

"Independent India", Feb. 8, 1942

CIVIL DEFENCE

It is reported that in its last session the National Defence Council was given information about Fifth Column activities in India. It is hoped that the ominous information will public in the members the sense of public responsibility, and that they will advise the Government to take effective measure for combating the danger. They will have to do more; they should take the field themselves for exposing the falseness of the brand of partriotism or nationalism or anti-imperialism, which serves as the smokescreen for the nefarious activities of the Fascist Fifth Column. Failure on the part of the members of the National Defence Council to act courageously in these critical days will prove the uselessness of that body.

In any case, now that the authorities have recognised the supreme importance of guarding the home front, it can be expected that the idea of civil defence will assume more concrete and practical forms. We have all along maintained that the fundamental problem of Indian defence is political and psychological; that, in case of an invasion, decisive events would occur on the home front; and that the home front is the most vulnerable sector of Indian defence. Therefore, we are glad that our persistent efforts have at last succeeded in making the authorities take notice of the danger.

Now the question is about the ways and means of combating the danger. The present civil defence activities do not serve the purpose. Because, the yignore the fundamental problem of the defence of the home front.

The very idea of a home front may not yet be properly grasped by those who are responsible for the defence of the country. It grows out of unprecedented nature of this war, which is a world war in the sense that all the nations are involved in it. It was a world war even when only a few States participated in it. Its world-wide character was determined by the relation of forces underlying the international events during the two decades which constituted its background. In other words, the present conflict was bound to be a world war. It is a world war, because it is an international civil war. As such, it cannot possibly leave any nation unaffected. Battles of this gigantic epoch-making war are bound to be joined even inside the countries which may not be formally belligerent. Unless this war is regarded in this light, it cannot be correctly characterised as a world-wide conflict between the forces of progress and reaction.

In a war like this, nations are not arrayed against nations, not even States against States. Every single nation is divided into warring camps. Parrallel to, or rather, cutting across, the lines along which the armies of belligerent States are fighting, there run inside all the countries deep chasms separating the forces of progress from those of reaction. In a number of countries, decisive events have taken place on this latter front. In others, the process of differentiation is going on as preparatory to the coming clash. There, the home front still appears to be intact. There, the very idea of a home front may not be yet grasped. That was unfortunately the case in India until very recently, although nowhere was the danger greater.

Because of her political position, the situation in India was more complicated from the very beginning. In that position, the idea of a united nation, with a common interest, appeared to be almost unchallengeable. Therefore, it was difficult for India to be divided on the issues involved in this war. Nationalist preoccupation overwhelmed all other considerations, and the progressive forces appeared to be stampeded against their better judgment. The entire Indian nation thus appeared to be swayed by the noble ideals of patriotism. In that atmosphere, any suspicion of treachery would be entirely out of place, and therefore it would be ridiculous to talk of the defence of the home front. Since there was no danger of the nation being betrayed, the question of guarding the home front did not arise.

That picture of national homogeneity remained undisturbed so long as the content of the concept of Indian freedom was not subjected to a critical analysis. Everybody would accept the idea of freedom as an abstract principle. But there would be much divergence of opiniom regarding the definition of the principle, and particularly about its practice. Practically every Indian wants national freedom, meaning thereby. some change in the present political status of the country. But there is no unity about the form and shape of the freedom to come. As soon as that question is raised, the superficial national homogeneity breaks down, and India, like any other country, is divided, the forces of progress and those of reaction aligning themselves respectively with the parties to the international civil war.

Those, who want Indian freedom as the means for the economic prosperity, social emancipation and cultural progress of the masses, cannot believe that their aspiration will be satisfied by the transfer of political power to the hands of Indians no matter whatever may be the ideas and ideals cherished by these latter. In our time national freedom by itself has ceased to be an ideal worth fighting for. A nation can be politically free and very powerful, and yet the majority composing it may be deprived of the most elementary forms of liberty. That has been the case in Japan, Fascist Italy, Nazi Germany and their satellites. Nevertheless, exactly those countries command the sympathy and admiration of the average Indian nationalist.

That fact determines the division of India into sections respectively allied with the parties to the international civil war. That fact creates a home front in India, which is so very vulnerable because the process of differentiation between the forces of progress and reaction has been retarded by the nationalist preoccupation. Unless that process is expedited, by a correct approach to the problems of civil defence, the most unfortunate thing may happen in this country: objectively progressive forces may be stampeded over to the wrong side of the international civil war.

Only a very small section of the Indian people will be benefitted by a forcible maintainance of the present worn-out social relations and their threadbare moral and cultural sanctions. All those ugly relics of a dead past must be swept away, if the masses of the Indian people are really to be free, so as to enjoy economic prosperity, social emancipation and make cultural progress. Therefore, the place of the Indian masses in this world-wide struggle against Fascism is predetermined. Unfortunately, they have been misled in the name of nationalism. They should be taught to take up their place. That is the only way to guard the home front. Only when the Indian masses will be mobilised on the right side of the international civil war, will the Fascist Fifth Column be isolated, and then it will not be a difficult task to condemn them as traitors, even if they masquerade as patriots and stamp them out.

While the Indian masses constituting the overwhelming majority of the nation, together with the consciously progressive minority, are thus bound to be a force in the world-wide struggle against Fascism, nationalism has not been very discriminating. The prevailing nationalist opinion is that it is immaterial for India whichever side wins this war. Indeed, the less thoughtful nationalists wish the victory of the Fascist Powers. It may be argued that the wish does not necessarily imply any sympathy for Fascism, but is a simple outcome of nationalist preoccupation. That may be the case with the more politically backward. But as a rule, it is clearly a matter of choice. The illusion, which spares the average nationalist the shame of being indifferent to a change of master, is that none of the Axis Powers will be able to establish its domination in India, and therefore will come to terms with the Indians. In other words, the average nationalist expects that it would be easier to come to terms with Fascism than with

British Imperialism. Now, one would be incredibly stupid to believe that any Indian National Government, established after the British Power has been overthrown by an invader, and in agreement with the latter, would not be compelled to bear his mark. In other words, thus "freed", India would have to be either a part of Japan's "Prosperity Sphere" or a member of Hitler's "New Order". An indiscriminate idea of national freedom thus logically prefers an alliance with Fascism, assuming that an outright Fascist domination can really be avoided.

With such an indiscriminate ideal of freedom, nationalism becomes the smokescreen for the Fascist Fifth Column in this country. The popularity of nationalism provides the Fascist Fifth Column almost an unlimited scope of activity.

Nor is the preference for some sort of relation with one or the other Axis Power limited to the average nationalist, who is swayed rather by emotion than guided by intelligence. It is to be deduced from the policy of the Congress, and some individual Congress leaders have spoken quite clearly to that effect. Gandhist pacifism preaches appeasement with all and sundry, including the Fascist Powers. The preachers of that doctrine claim to have a very definite idea about good and evil. Therefore, they could not possibly advocate amicable relations with the Fascist Powers, if they regarded Facism as an evil. Of course, they say that they believe in overcoming the evil by non-resistance. But the practice of that doubtful ethical doctrine in the given situation will amount to undermining the all-important home front. The latter has become so very vulnerable in India because of the close association of short-sighted reactionary nationalism with the dogmatic pacifism of Gandhi. Having exposed the practical implication of the Gandhist doctrine of non-violence, one need not, however, doubt that the prophet himself is actuated with the best of motives. But that is not the case the with apostles. With them, the strict adherence to non-violence has become a convenient pretext for sitting on the fence when the forces of progress and reaction are in death-grips, not wishing to spoil the chance of coming to terms with the latter, whose victory is taken for granted more by wishful thinking than on the score of events.

That being the case, it is mistaken to believe

that some gopalachariar between the Government and the Congress will solve the problem of Indian defence. Notwithstanding the high hopes raised by the pronouncements of Mr. Rajagopalachariar and some other Congress leaders after their release, it is now clear that the Congress is playing for a high stake. The attitude taken up by Pandit Nehru supported by the Congress President, that India must have all or nothing, is not quite the insanity that it appears to be. The Government is in a tight cornor. Before long, India may be actually invaded. Therefore, it is hoped that, if the Congress can hold out long enough, the Government may be compelled to accept its terms, that is to say, declare India free.

It would seem that there should be nothing objectionable to this attitude unless one raises the all-important question what the freedom will look like. But apart from other considerations, one could not altogether forget the ground on which the Congress originally launched upon its policy of non-co-operating with the war. It was that India had been declared a belligerent country without being consulted. If the Congress leaders accepted the idea that the fight against Fascism was justifiable, them, it was not necessary to quarrel about details. Presumably, it was not taken for granted that India would join the fight against Fascism. Hence the insistance upon her having the opportunity to make the choice freely. If the freedom was given she might have chosen differently. Having borne that implication of the Congress policy in mind, one cannot believe that everything will be all right as soon as real power would be transferred to the Congress leaders, as the accredited spokesmen of the nation. They may use that power for coming to terms with the invader.

That is not an idle speculation. The Mahatma is an unrepentent advocate of the policy of appeasement. When Hitler threatened England with invasion, he advised the English people not to resist. He would not advise the Indians differently, if India were invaded by the Japanese. As a matter of fact, the advice has already been given indirectly. A former president of the Gandhi Seva Sangh, Mr. K. G. Mashruwala, in a recent article, recommends non-violence as a politically sound proposition, and expresses the opinion that India should follow "a policy of appaesement, whatever it may cost". He further declares that "there has been no cause of war as between India and any foyeign country." Therefore, "politically, India should counsel peace and not clamour for war or share in the war effort." That is clear enough. India has no reason to wage a war against Japan. That being the opinion of the spiritual mentors of Congress publicly it is only logical to deduce that, given the power, the Congress would not allow the continuation of such a war. The political opportunism of other Gandhist leaders has been even more outspoken. It has been maintained publicly that, when the future hangs in the balance, it would not be wise for the Indians to annoy other Powers. This idea must be very prevalent in the higher circles of the Congress; otherwise, Mr. Rajagopalachariar would not have been compelled to deprecate it publicly.

All these facts create an atmosphere very favourable for Fifth Column activities in this country. The atmosphere is favourable politically as well as psychologically. Therefore, the danger cannot be combated in the simple manner in which treason is combatted under normal circumstances. Fifth Column activites, or activities, which amount to them, have a moral sanction in this country, so to say. Because, they can sail under the false colour of patriotism. The organisation of civil defence, therefore, should be such as to be able to solve the fundamental problem of the situation. Its primary object will be to carry on propaganda which will hasten the process of differentiation between the forces of progress and of reaction. It must base itself exclusively on the former, even if they may not appear to be sufficiently strong at the moment. It should be borne in mind that only through the instrumentality of the progressive forces crystallising inside the Indian society, can the masses be mobilised in the fight against Fascism, and that the fight has to take place primarily on the home front.

Fascism being the bulwark of a broken down *status quo*, it can be successfully fought only by those who have no stake in it. The fall of France placed before Europe the choice between revolution and a relapse into maediaval barbarism. The choice was not easily made. But it was made eventually under the pressure of circumstances, though not consciously, but certainly in fact. The fateful choice must be made in India, if she is to be saved from the misfortune of being the stronghold of reaction even after it has been defeated in the rest of the world. The danger of Fascist Fifth Column forebodes that misfortune for India. Therefore, the authorities will not be able to cope with that danger unless they realise the fact that the forces involved in this international civil war must be in operation in India, so that, having secured her home front she may be able to present a blod front to the Fascist invader. Civil defence should mean mobilisation of the Indian masses to resist reaction, internally as well as coming from outside in the shape of a Japanese invasion. That can take place only on the initiative and under the leadership of the progressive elements in the public life of the country. Will the Government have the courage and foresight to help the growth of an Anti-Fascist People's Front in India ? Because, only then the home front will be secured, and all the nefarious plans of the Fifth Column will be frustrated.

"Independent India," February 15, 1942.

THE ATMOSPHERE CLEARS

Our doubts about the usefulness of the Cripps Mission have been borne out. We warned that the hope of the mission succeeding was a forlorn hope. Even more time has been wasted than originally feared. The danger involved in this delay, therefore, may be proportionately greater, unless bold steps and drastic measures are taken to cope with the situation.

It would be hypocritical liberalism to say that there is no use apportioning blame. Because, it is evident that a settlement has been prevented only by the intransigence of the Congress leaders Had they taken up a positive attitude, the Muslim League would have followed suit. The revised formula regarding the control of the Defence Department should have satisfied all who are really anxious to mobilise the Indian people to resist invasion. Clarifying what was implicit in the original proposal, the revised formula pointed out that the Government of India would have all the powers to raise a People's Militia and organise Home Guards. With that power, any Government would be the dominating and decisive factor in the defence of the country, even it the control of the regular army remained with the Commander-in-Chief, not formally resiponsible to it. But the Congress leaders did not want a settlement unless it would serve their purpose, which evidently is something different from the defence of the country.

Their record and recent pronouncements left little room for doubt what they would do if placed in power. They wanted power not to wage the war, but to choose between war and peace. It is evidently a very perilous venture to place at the helm of affairs men who even now have not made their choice. Had the choice been made, no serious reason could be found to reject the proposal for an interim arrangement, after three weeks of protracted negotiations.

The British War Cabinet seems to have been fully alive to the danger involved in the attempted appeasement. Otherwise, there would be no occasion for a breakdown of the negotiations. Some concession regarding the control of Defence would have crowned the Cripps Mission with success. The refusal to go that far shows that even the peace-makers entertained doubts and misgivings about what the Congress leaders might do, if in possession of unrestricted power. What, then, was the sense of all this coaxing and cajoling, which only bloated up the political bargainers sitting on the fence.

If it was felt that co-operation of the Congress leaders was essential for the defence of India, any price should have been paid for it. On the other hand, if it was felt that it would be unwise to place everything in their hands, then there should have been no attempt at appeasement. The Congress leaders never made any secret of their wish to make peace with the invaders, and actually hoped that that could be done on honourable terms.

There was no question of distrust. It was a matter of precaution warranted by the publicly expressed views of the Congress leaders. There would be no restriction of the power to develop the defensive and striking potentialities of India to the highest pitch. The Congress refusal to accept even the revised British offer, therefore, proves that power is demanded for a different purpose. We hope that this ill-fated negotiation may have some positive result, in the form of curing illusions in high quarters. This lesson, assuming that at last it will be learned, should definitely preclude any resumption of appeasement efforts as already suggested in the Congress press. One paper has actually proposed that an assurance by the Viceroy, as given after the breakdown of the provinces, for the Congress accepting office in the provinces, may still pave the way to the formation of a National Government.

We also want the Viceroy to make a declaration to the effect that a .National Government, vested with the power and resumption:y as outlined in the Cripps' proposals, is going to be formed immediately. The party leaders having refused to be helpful, the National Government should now be formed with more responsible and realistic independent public men, chosen on their individual merit.

Patriotism is not the monopoly of any particular party. Therefore, a Government composed of independent public men, with a record of service to the cause of the country, will be a National Government, in addition to being a strong War Cabinet which, being free of party preoccupation and wire-pulling, will with a single-minded purpose apply itself to the supreme task of contributing to the joint efforts of demanded the Axis Powers. If there are party leaders willing to put their shoulders to the wheel, they will be welcome, but as individuals. The nature of the "National Government" demanded by the Congress has been very correctly characterised by Sir Stafford Cripps. In his letter to the Congress President, he wrote that it "would in fact constitute an absolute dictatorship of the majority, and subject all of them (minorities) to a permanent and autocratic majority in the Cabinet." Such a Government evidently would not be a democratic government. Therefore, the demand for the establishment of such an autocratic party regime cannot be put forward as the will of the people.

Thus, the breakdown of the useless and harmful negotiations does not in any way prejudice the plan of handing over to Indians the responsibility and power of defending the country against invasion, and transforming it into a sector of the World War Front against Fascism. Clear the debris of these ridiculous statements and counter-proposals, formulas and re-formulas, visits and return-visits, so that the people's mind may turn from the war of words, waged in an atmosphere of unreality, to the grim war of rude realities, which is ruthlessly coming nearer and nearer. Let men ready to act according to the need of the moment step forward to occupy posts which they alone can fill creditably and to the benefit of the common cause of civilised humanity.

The crux of the problem of Indian defence is how to make the popular masses take active and intelligent interest in the war efforts. The decisive factor is not personnel, but the policy of the Government. Indians living in the seven lakhs of villages and toiling in the towns and cities are not at all concerned with all this political bargianing and communal bickerings. An entirely different kind of appeal has to be made to them, and it is after all their enthusiastic co-operation which is needed for winning the war. At present, the Government has no policy. Its war efforts are planless, and its war propaganda has no appeal for the common man. The machinery of the Government moves as ponderously as in peace time. Even if some men at the top have some good ideas, they cannot be put into practice because the bureaucratic machinery cannot be adjusted to new ideas. Consequently, measures urgently needed to create the atmosphere, in which war propaganda can be carried on effectively and war efforts can have enthusiastic popular support, are either delayed indefinitely or not taken at all. Large amounts of money are spent on propaganda; but it is not realised that propaganda cannot be carried on in a vacuum. The success of any propaganda is conditional upon its psychological appeal, and the mentality of the masses is very largely determined by the experiences of their daily life.

A policy based upon these elementary considerations regarding the crux of the problem alone can lead to its solution. Such a policy is sure to enlist popular support to war efforts, thereby increasing the defensive and striking power of India. Let there be a Government armed with such a policy: it will be able to function very effectively, disregarding the unhelpful or even obstructive attitude of parties and politicians, who are more concerned with prestige and other petty interests than with the defence of the country.

The fundamental principle of the urgently needed policy should be to subordinate all sectional interests and other considerations to the purpose of enlisting popular support to war efforts. And there must be a centralised direction setting aside the departmentalism of the normal time administration, for the execution of the policy. No government, however execution, even if it included the popular party leaders, will be able to tackle the situation, unless armed with such a policy and determinded to put it into practice at all cost.

The vast bulk of the Indian people are not at all concerned with the issues which agitate the mind of the politicians. The so-called politically minded constitute a relatively tiny fraction of the entire population. Nevertheless, they can sway the masses so long as these are dissatisfied owing to other reasons. Remove those reasons, give the masses intensified, relieve the hardships and privations of their daily life, and the entire atmosphere will become favourable for intensified and successful war efforts.

Industrial labour is a vital factor in the scheme of defence—perhaps the most vital factor. The process of industrial production must go on uninterrupted, if the armed forces are to be properly equipped and fully supplied. But workers are running away from the threatened industrial areas, and all efforts to check the exodus have until now very largely failed. Nearly half the industrial workers of Calcutta and the neighbourhood have fled. Similarly alarming reports come also from less threatened areas. The exodus of labour cannot be checked unless measures are taken to make the workers feel that it is worthwhile for them to take risks. Far from doing that, even the most moderate demands of labour go unheeded. The result is the spread of dissatisfaction, which causes labour to run away in panic. This unfortunate situation is due to the absence of a centralised labour policy of the Government. The Labour Department of the Government of India cannot operate directly, because of the autonomy of the provincial governments to deal with industrial disputes. On the other hand, production is directly under the Central Government and is administered as an integral part of war efforts. It is evident that the process of production cannot be efficiently administrated without the co-operation of labour. Therefore, provincial governments cannot be allowed to have autonomous labour policies or deal with the labour situation in their own way. A central policy and a central control is absolutely necessary. So long that is not there, war production cannot be guaranted against occasional disturbance, either by industrial disputes or owing to labour running away in panic.

The delay or even refusal to redress the legitimate grievances of labour is still justified by fallacious economic arguments, which might be plausible in peace-time, but have lost all force in the present emergency. There should be no lag in the process of production, which must be speeded up to the highest limit. That is the supreme consideration of the moment. No argument is valid which interferes with it. Dissatisfied labour is bound to retard the process of production. Therefore, the grievances of labour should be sympathetically considered, expediously redressed, not out of humanitarianism, but as a matter of war-time necessity. That is not done, firstly because the employers generally seem to be more concerned with amassing private fortunes than with the defence of the country; and secondly, because the Government is unwilling to exercise its authority and emergency powers to make the exigencies of defence prevail upon sectional selfishness. Then, there is bureaucratic red tape, which also contributes to the complete chaos in handling labour.

The cost of living has gone up; but wages are not increased. As a matter of fact, real wages are falling. Yet, no definite policy has been adopted regarding the general demand for an adequate dearness allowance. Moreover, there is a clear case for a sufficient increase of wages, and payment of a war bonus, as well as for overtime work, are indispensable for increasing production. There is absolutely no valid economic argument in favour of the employers who would not contribute their quota to the common war effort. They are piling profits. If they would not voluntarily forego a part of it for the sake of creating an atmosphere necessary for the defence of the country, it is the clear duty of the Government to compel them to do so. Unless that was done, no amount of propaganda could persuade labour to take risks and participate in the war efforts enthusiastically, which is essential for maintaining the level of, and increasing, production.

A similiar pulicy is urgently needed as regards the peasant masses as well as the lower strata of the urban middle-class, which are subjected to all sorts of privations, thanks to war profiteering. The policy of controlling prices is practically invalidated by the slowness of the administrative machinery and many other more reprehensible causes. As a matter of fact, profiteering in foodstuffs and other articles of primary necessity is running rampant. In the absence of a Government policy, no effective control is possible.

The fundamental principle of the urgently needed policy in respect of all these particular aspects of public life as well as the whole problem of defence should be that property must be sacrificed if necessary, for the defence of liberty. Any Government, which will have the courage and foresight to adopt such a policy, will be a truly national as well as democratic government, and only such a government can undertake the difficult task of enlisting enthusiastic support of the people for the war efforts. Therefore, it was useless to spend all this time in negotiations for persuading the party leaders to form a Government. The first thing to do is to define the task of the moment and to realise what must be done in order to accomplish that task. Whoever is prepared to shoulder the task, setting aside all other considerations, and are able to realise what is to be done for its accomplishment, are the men of the hour. The intransigence and irresponsibility of the party leaders are no reason why others should not be vested with the power and authority with which they can apply themselves to the moment.

The breakdown of the negotiations over the Cripps' proposals should now clear the political atmosphere, so that those who realiset he supreme importance of the task of the moment may now have the opportunity of shouldering the responsibility which they alone can discharge.

"Independent India", April 19. 1942.

IMPRACTICAL AND DANGEROUS

Congress leaders like Pandit Nehru and C. Rajagopalachari are appealing to the people to prepare for resisting Japanese invasion. They are also saying that that should be done, whatever may be the attitude of the Government and whether the Government is reconstituted according to the needs of the situation or not. They are saying this just after the Congress demand for the establishment of a National Government has been once again rejected. We welcome the changed attitude, because it vindicates us.

We have all along maintained that the responsibility for defending India, not for Imperialism but for the sake of her own future, belonged primarily to the Indians, and that that responsibility must be discharged, and can be discharged, irrespective of the attitude or composition of the Government. With a Government under popular control, it would be easier to discharge the responsibility. But the absence of such a Government does not absolve Indians of the responsibility. On the countrary, in view of the fact that without popular resistance the country cannot be defended, and the present Government may not be able to organise such a resistance, it is all the more incumbent upon the fignters for Indian freedom to shoulder the responsibility, by all means.

For holding this view, and acting accordingly, we have been criticised, castigated and maligned by those who consider patriotism to be their monopoly. We Radicals were driven out of the Congress for saying exactly what leaders like Pandit Nehru and C. Rajagopalachari are saying to-day. On the first anniversary of the war, we celebrated the Anti-Fascist Day, when we warned the Indian people against the danger of Fascism, and appealed to them to join the world fight against the common foe, disregarding the attitude of the Government.

For that action, we were accused of having gone against the principle and policy of the Congress. We contended that, the Congress having previously condemned Fascist aggression and disapproved of Fascism itself, to advocate co-operation in the fight against it could not be a violation of the Congress principles and programme. Nevertheless, disciplinary action was taken against a large number of tried fighters for freedom, who had suffered and sacrificed for the cause no less than anyone else. In protest against that dictatorial behaviour of the leadership, many others severed their connection with the Congress. Moreover, they felt that the logical conclusion must be drawn from the pronouncement that Anti-Fascist propaganda and participation in the fight against Fascism were contrary to the principle and policy of the Congress. The conclusion was obvious. It was that fight against Fascism was precluded by the Congress principle and policy. If that was true, no fighter for democratic freedom could be a member of that organisation.

The policy pursued by the Congress since then has been neither wise nor fortunate. It encouraged Fascist sympathy, and consequently prejudiced the possibility of a popular resistance to the coming aggression by one or another Fascist Power. This suicidal policy could be pursued only on the assumption that the war could never touch India. We always fought against that complacency, and called upon the fighters for democratic freedom to prepare the ground for a popular resistance to the invasion which was sure to come. But, for two years and more, ours remained a cry in the wilderness.

At last, the danger has overtaken India. None but the slavish minded who, out of spitefulness, would welcome a change of masters, could any longer remain indifferent. Consequently, there is a general consternation. The danger has taken the nationalist leaders completely unawares. They have changed their tone, but they do not know what to do. That regrettable helplessness is the most remarkable on the part of Pandit Nehru. He talks about organising popular resistance to invasion more passionately than others, but admits tragically that he has no concrete plan of action.

In a press conference at Delhi, immediately after the failure of the Cripps Mission, Pandit Nehru toyed with the idea of the Indian people taking to guerilla warfare to resist the invader. The idea was promptly deprecated by the more powerful, though less popular, members of the Congress Working Committee. A few days later, at a reception given by the Journalists Association in Calcutta, Pandit Nehru, presumably therefore, sounded a different note. He said:

"'Some misapprehension has been caused in the public mind by my use of the expression 'guerilla warfare' in my speech at the press conference in Delhi. We cannot think loosely of guerilla warfare. To think in terms of guerilla warfare in India under the present circumstances was to think in terms of unreality. Therefore, in the present circumstances, it is not a practical proposition."

But on the same occassion, Pandit Nehru expressed views which should guide his action, and of his colleagues, if they really meant to do what they have been saying recently. He said: "Unless the State and the people's organisations merge together, the people by themselves cannot do much. In fact, the State organisation could intervene if we attempted to organise defence by ourselves. It is the Government which organises guerilla warfare. Having no common ground with the State, I do not seehow guerilla warfare can be organised by us."

Holding such views, one could not non-co-operate with the Government and yet seriously consider the idea of organising popular resistance to invasion. But Pandit Nehru prefers to draw a wrong conclusion from a right view of the situation, and its possibilties. He declared that "in the present circumstances, it is not a practical proposition to organise defence by ourselves". Why not? The circumstances can be changed immediately, by the Congress joining the Central Government and returning to office in the provinces. Other parties non-co-operating now will follow suit. Even then the State may not be ideally democratic. But Government composed of Congressmen and other Indians will have all the power necessary to do what Pandit Nehru apparently wishes to do. Those in supreme command of the regular army may not be under the complete control of the civil Government. But certainly they would not be so insane as to hinder the organisation of auxiliary forces, indispensable for the defence of the country in a war like the present; and even if they were insane, they would not have the power to prevent the civil Government doing what is essential for the defence of the country.

Therefore, the blame for not creating conditions favourable for the oganisation of popular defence does not belong to the Government, whatever may be its other faults of omission and commission. The Congress leaders are shirking the responsibility, and others are aping them. It is idle for them to complain bitterly, and it is make-belief to talk of doing what is admittedly impractical,

Instead of doing what he shoul do, so that popu-lar resistance to invasion could be organised, namely, abandon the sterile policy of non-co-operation, Pandit Nehru throws out the baby with the bath water, and declares: "To think in terms of guerilla warfare in India under the present circumstances, is to think in terms of unreality". And to justify this surrender to the wishes of more powerful colleagues, he reverts to the old position: "It is absurd to call this war a people's war." Of course, he could not now revive the old bogey of the 'imperialist war'. But thegolden mean discovered by him goes against himself. "It is a war ultimately for each country that is invoved in it for survival." So, after all, it is a war of the Indian people. But logic is not Panditji's strong point.

However, what does he propose to do? That is highly interesting. Waiving off the idea of organising popular resistance as impractical, Pandit Nehru plumps for the even more impractical programme of "Self-sufficiency and self-protection." He need not be told that units working with such a humanitarian and mutual help purpose would be absolutely of no use in resisting invasion. Yet, he would do nothing more than that. Why? Because the official Congress idea of "resistance", which he does not dare discard, does not admit any warlike preparations. The Congress policy, as stated by himself, does not visualise anything more than "non-co-operation, aggressive or passive." That is how the invader will be resisted ! And it is not yet certain whether non-co-operation will be aggressive or passive. Then, aggressive non-co-operation being a contradiction in terms, the resistance which the Congress would offer to the invader, will be "passive non-co-operation." The aggressor is hardly likely to be scared away by that broken sward. As a matter of fact, he may regard that as a welcome, knowing fully well how to deal with such a symbolic resistance.

If the idea of organising active popular resistance is impractical, the "practical" policy of the Congress is positively dangerous. And we do not believe that the alternative policy of organising active popular resistance is impractical. The Congress does not *want* to adopt it. It has made a deliberate choice. All those tall talks, to-day in one strain, to-morrow in another are no thing but a smoke-screen.

"Independent India", May 1, 1942

CARDS ON THE TABLE

The Cripps mission has ended exactly as we apprehended. Instead of improving the situation in any way, appeasement diplomacy has caused a considerable deterioration. The resolution of the A. I. C. C. meeting at Allahabad declares that in consequence of the Cripps negotiations "the spirit of non-co-operation with Britain has grown." Having declared that, the A. I. C. C. resolution lays down a policy which has been correctly characterised by Mr. Rajagopalachari as "neutrality", and which in practice may amount to worse. Thus, the delay caused by appeasement diplomacy has been dangerous. The Congress attitude is naturally pleasing the Axis Powers, and encouraging the Japs to invade India with the confidence that there will be no popular resistance. Such an attitude is positively prejudical for the defence of the country.

The negative result of the ill-conceived and ill-fated Cripps mission, however, is not an unmixed evil. It has cleared the political atmosphere. Illusions have been urgently, and the clay-feet of gods have been exposed. The rude realities of the Indian situation to-day stand out in the clearest relief. Unfortunately, those in power would still play the ostrich game not only at their risk, but risking the future of the Indian people. Therefore, plain speaking is urgently needed.

The Congress leaders have laid their cards on the table. That is the positive result of the Cripps mission. There is no room for hopes and speculation. Misinformed and misguided friends of India may no longer talk lyrically about the anti-Fascist and democratic ideals of the Congress. We all along knew what cards the Congress leaders held, and how they wished to play them. Now it is no longer necessary for us to point out the implication of the policy which the Congress has pursued ever since the war broke out. The A. I. C. C. resolution is a clear statement of it. There is little ambiguity. It nullifies all the fulminant pronouncements of Pandit Nehru which have been misleading world opinion and raising false hopes.

The following is the most significant passage

of the resolution: "India's participation in the war was a purely British act imposed upon the Indian people without the consent of their representatives. While India has no quarrel with the people of any country, she has repeatedly declared her antipathy to Nazism and Fascism as to repeatedly If India were free, she would have determined her own policy, and might have kept out of the war."

The Congress leaders are not of the opinion that India should join the world struggle against the Axis Powers as a matter of principle. If they were at the helm of affairs, India might not be involved in the war, or even might have been in the other camp. Otherwise, this insistence on the right of deciding has no point. This attitude, unworthy for whoever pretends to be fighting for freedom and democracy, is justified with the banal declaration that India has no quarrel with the people of any country. That is all beside the point. None of the countries engaged in the war against the Fascist Powers has any such quarrel. It is not a matter of quarrel at all. It is a conflict of ideas and ideals. The war is not against Germany, Italy or Japan. It has been precipitated by a socio-political system which, having overwhelmed the forces of freedom and progress in those countries, and having seized others in its bloody tentacles, threatens to overrun the rest of the world. To maintain that the freedom or general welfare of any progress nation could be promoted or protected by neutrality in this world struggle, is simply absurd. It is worse; because, for all progress purposes, it amounts to saying that the destruction of Fascism is not a condition for thefreedom and progress of the whole world. Or that, in a world dominated by the Axis Powers, particular countries can be nationally free.

That is the opoinion of all orthodox full-blooded nationalists who identify nationalism with the aspirations of certain sections of the people. They do not believe in democracy, and do not favour any progress except in the retrograde direction. As a matter of fact, Fascism is the expression of antiquated Nationalism, and Nationalism historically has become an antiquated cult. Therefore, Fascist sympathy has been an outstanding feature of Indian Nationalism all along.

The average Indian nationalist worship sat the shrine of supermen like Hitler and Mussolini. Ashamed of the sense of his weakness, he pines for a strong man to appear on the scene to take

Mother India by the throat and treat her children like dumb-driven cattle. National freedom may be anything but democratic freedom. It should be freedom to sacrifice for the greatness of the nation, and power for the strong man to make the nation great at the cost of the people. Those are typically Fascist ideas. Therefore, nationalist India could never be in the anti-Fascist camp.

For these two and a half years, we have been trying to drive this point home. It was not an easy task. It was swimming against a powerful current of prejudice at home and ignorance abroad. But history is a stern teacher, and the logic of events is irreistibly convincing. If language is meant to express ideas, then the A. I. C. C. resolution vindicates us, and none should have any doubt about what is to be done to transform India into an active asset in the world struggle against Fascism.

The methed of non-violent non-co-operation, reaffirmed as the only form of resistance to the invader, will be capitulation for all practical purposes. Such method may be to an extent effective against a civil government. But how is it to be practised against an invading army? Particularly when scorched earth policy is ruled out?

Indeed, the master strategist of non-violent warfare has already disapproved of measures which would have to be adopted if the method was to be practised at all. In the current issue of the 'Harijan' the Mahatma condemns measures being taken in Bengal with the object of depriving the invader of the advantage of the certain easily available means of transport, such as country boats, bicycles etc. Evidently, the "resistance" through non-co-operation would not include even such measures as to deprive the invader of easily available facilities. Everything will be there for him to seize and use for his purpose. That means that there will be absolutely no resistance.

The actual wording of the resolution is remarkable. "We may not bend the knee to the aggressor, nor obey any of his orders. We may not look to him for favour or fall to his bribes." So, whatever resistance is visualised will be entirely discretionary. One may or may not. If this is not a thinly veiled advice to capitulate, then words have no meaning. Then again: "In places wherein the British and the invading forces are fighting, our non-co-operation will be fruitless and unnecessary." The meaning of this passage is positively mischievous:

Wherever there will be any active resistance to the invader, even "non-violent non-co-operation" should not be practised. That is to say, invaders should not be embarrassed.

Moreover, the whole resolution is dishonest. On the face of it, the only resolution is practice of non-violence. But it is not at all the issue involved. In another place, the resolution complains against inviting foreign armies to defend India, and declares: "The vast man power of India herself is not utilised for the purpose. It is significant and extraordinary that India's inexhaustible man power should remain untapped." Evidently, the guiding principle of the resolution is not pacifism. It is refusal to defend the country until and unless the Congress leaders have the power to decide whether India should take part in the war against the Axis Powers or not. And given their neutrality or indifference as regards the issues involved in the war, they would be more likely to make peace with the invader than resist, if they had the power to decide.

If this is kept in mind, the sinister significance of the following pivotal passage of the resolution becomes crystal clear: "The present crisis makes it impossible for the Congress to consider any scheme or proposals which retain, even in a partial measure, British control and authority in India". Suppose that the demand of the Congress leaders was conceded; what would then happen ? If we are to believe that the Congress policy is determined by the principle of non-violence, the only resistance even then will be non-violent non-co-operation, that is to say, capitulation, for all practical purposes. Or, after a token resistance by an improvised army, peace will be concluded with the invader. In view of the expressed desire to prefer Iadia's staying out of the war, this inference is irresistible.

Seconding the resolution, Babu Rajendra Prasad made that very clear: Referring to the fact that Russia is still not at war with Japan, he said: "Russia has taken this course in accordance with her own interests; why can we not do the same?" There cannot be any doubt about the purpose for which the Congress leaders want the complete disappearance of all power and authority except theirs.

The perporation of the mover of the resolution was even more meaningful. "Our freedom is coming. It is a matter of a few months. Let us not be found wanting at this moment."

When such a declaration is made simultaneously with the resolution not to resist invasion, which is coming first, it is quite legitimate to wonder what is the freedom heralded so confifiently. It would not be at all far-fetched to infer from this significant declaration that the heralded freedom is expected to come in the wake of the imminent invasion. And only that expectation could possibly allow the policy which the Congress has all along pursued and which the A. I. C. C. has reaffirmed on this very eve of the Japancse invasion.

Members of the Forward Bloc parade the streets of Bengal towns and villages with the slogan: "Let us go forward to hail the rising sun of freedom." The slogan found its echo in the A. I. C. C. meeting, and it was voiced by the mover of the Working Committee resolution.

Nationalism has vindicated Subhas Bose. To-day he is the hero of Indian Nationalism. Those who hounded him out of the Congress are to-day toeing his line, and he has entered into an alliance with the Axis Powers. That explains why, in spite of Pandit Nehru's fulmination, and "fascination for the idea of guerilla warfare" the A. I. C. C. placed all the cards on the table, and adopted a resolution to the effect that there could be no resistance to the imminent invasion, and that the Congress leaders should have power only to keep India out of the war.

"*Independent India, May 10, 1942*

SAVE INDIA FOR FREEDOM

By Basudha Chakraverty

The tide of Fascism which has submerged a numeer of countries has reached the Indian Ocean and is convulsing the Bay of Bengal; nor are the rivers streaming out of them unruffled. It is roaring against the Indian points. A fall of gloom descends over the coastal provinces largely due to the fearful uncertainty as to what may happen. Nobody is in a position to feel the strength of assurance of a united stand. Few feel even the necessity of making a stand, for what may happen is not regarded as an unmixed evil. The triumphant progress of Japan has the appearance of an Asiatic renaissance; and our minds being still cast in the feudal mould, it strikes a responsive chord ever in our hearts. So, not quite consciously though expectations are being aroused of a feudal resurgence particularly as people are going back to the villages and feel themselves sheltered in the semi-feudal scheme of things obtaining there. So the tortoise prepares to go back into its shell. Already there are hopes of re-vitalization of the old village-centred culture which broods on the dead past and is content.

So, it seems oncoming Fascism is already achieving its object. There is before us today no perspective of freedom and progress and the danger with which it is threatened. Our outlook being in prevailing historical conditions individualistic, each is thinking only of his or her personal safety and security and in the process returning to the religion that is the vaunted Indian characteristic. Our back-ground is the long-exploded eternity. At the moment we would have no objection even to return to the old landlord—ridden economy. If it has exhausted itself its principles will nevertheless be valid in other relations of production. That is feudalism in industry—the terror that is Fascism. We are not alive to the danger because we are subjectively at the feudal stage. We are historically too undeveloped to realize the implications of the danger that comes with the "dawn breaking in the East". We are reconciled to the idea of being again held in trust by somebody foreign or native, that is our superior. There, unknowingly, we are in for an indefinite period of blood-sucking exploitation not to speak of nullification of abiding values of life such as arts and culture.

This is counter-revolution with a vengeance. We might profitably contrast it with the facts in China for whom we profess age-old friendship. There the people are not on the way of return to feudalism; there they will not return to religion and icons are being broken up for use as war material. The contract vivifies the context of this war between expanding progress and closed door reaction. Unless we do something about it promptly, we shall have to stew in our own juice of communal religion. The steam-roller of Fascism will grind all of us down and there will be no more for us leisurely politics, interested communalism or romantic communism. All this is already a mockery.

An India, it has been said, died at Plassey. But the world has marched along since then and we cannot go back to Plassey. Yet it seems, the intervening period has been nothing but an episode and there is a real effort to go back to the old India. It is not the natural and legitimate desire to end foreign rule; had it been that, there would have been a stand to prevent another and far more oppressive phase of foreign domination. It is just the inclination to shed off all that contact with the West has given us; even the fruits of political ideology, literature and science. In nothing is this so manifest as in the total failure of even the western educated intellectuals, to give a lead, to take a stand for uninterrupted and increasing contact with modern civilization. These ladies and gentlemen supposed to be repositories of India's best of the hour are not now seen anywhere in the picture. They are unable to rise above the existing level of mass consciousness.

There is still a faint hope, one that is dim today but may, under the impact of circumstances, grow into an upsurge. The present crisis has driven the upper classes into retreat; the exodus from endangered areas is symbolic thereof. This retreat can and should be made a rout by an elemental call to the lower middle class, workers and peasants to take for a moment a full measure of the situation and do their duty to themselves. That energy, once set into motion, is capable of taking care of both Fascists from abroad and cowards at home. The international civil war that this anti-Fascist war is, must be realized here too in the stern, clear economic context. Thus alone can the Fascist tide that has touched the shores of India be yet beaten back by surging anti-Fascism. Else, there is no hope of saving India's chances of freedom. A time like this calls for and often secures action. We are no longer at the stage of discussion but of action and propaganda. We must tell our fellow-men and women that this is the hour for them to come to their own, to realize the political and social freedom that will set them on the path of progress and end the slavery that asks them to dote on pseudo-ethical nonsense. The need is there to keep pace with the modern world, to use achievements of science to further economic and cultural happiness. To them rather than to the emigrants to Plassey we must turn. We must bring to them news of Rangoon in flames, Mandalay in ruins. We must share with them the bleak prospect that is before us. The propertied classes are at most afraid of the unsettlement to be caused by foreign invasion; the peril of Fascism as such does not etner into their reckoning but is nonetheless real for the masses whom then, in terms of that peril, we must mobilize. Can that mobilization yet be done? Can the fifth-column be isolated, exposed and destroyed? If it is impossible, there is no hope for us. We must get dead serious about it and must, for that purpose, break through the hedonism such as is as a reaction against apprehended disaster, rampant in Calcutta today. Shall we rise up to the hour or betray our lack of seriousness—perhaps secret readiness to fall in with Fascism—by presisting in party quarrels? We must go out to the towns and villages. We must announce the necessity of freedom. We shall have to do that not for the sake of old Russian immortality but to save our own chances of survival. It is the last hour.

May 1, 1942.

WIN THE PEOPLE TO WIN THE WAR

By Ellen Roy

In an editorial on "Racial Relations", the "Stateman" (May 8), taking stock of the situation, wrote that "the Congress has preferred to continue its quarrel with the British rather than to take up a quarrel with the Japanese. It is idle to apportion blame, but there are lessons to be drawn from an analysis of the situation. The most obvious fact about the hatred of the British in India is that it comes chiefly from the "intelligentsia"....and that it is first preached in English." And in another place: "The fact that English education produces this anti-English reaction.... seems to point to some definite failure either in the English system of education or in the British attitude towards India and Indians." The failure is explained to consist in the "gap between British history (full of enthusiasm for freedom etc.) and the history of the British in India."

One is inclined to agree. But the lessons hinted at in the "Statesman" article are not followed up to the conclusions to be drawn from them for action.

It strikes the "Statesman" that this race hatred proceeds from the intelligentsia, the England returned or English educated, and from the large towns. For, "in the villages there is fortunately no such race prejudice." That may be so for the simple reason that Englishmen seldom live in the villages, while in the cities they are very much in evidence, and always have the best of everything, in a way that hundreds of millions in this country can never dream of, and therefore not feel the jealousy which arises from comparison. The few Indians, however, who are rich enough, and sufficiently close, financially and socially, to the British ruling circles, not only dream of, but aspire for, the additional privileges and advantages that the British in India have made it tacitly understood to be their due. And because they can never quite reach the same status, they are the first to get conscious of the barrier thus erected. Race prejudice is after all not a one-sided affair. While recognising and deprecating it on the part of Indians, one must remember that, with them, it is only a reflection of the earlier guilt on the part of the British in India.

It is not because they are English educated or England returned that a certain section of the people is foremost in their hatred of the British; it is because only the privileged few *can* be English educated or England returned, and because only the rich and those higher up run their heads against the barrier between Europeans and Indians, originally erected by the former, that race hatred comes primarily from the "intelligentsia" (leaving the question open whether the English speaking politicians and employees really constitute *the* intelligentsia of the country.) It is not a contradiction that the better off are the more dissatisfied. In modern European countries, it has always been found that the highest paid and most advanced sections of the workers, for example, press workers, mechanics, etc., who ofter earn more than the "white-collar proletariat" in the offices, are the most dissatisfied and rebellious, obviously because they are near enough the higher rung in the social ladder to feel the restriction of not being able to break out of their class, in the ordinary course.

Thus it is that from the privileged few in India came and comes the vocal anti-British sentiment, and it is easy for them to arouse the millions through depicting the much more glaring contrast between their conditions of life and those of the British ruling class, while comparison with the Indian ruling class is carefully evaded on the plea of "nationed unity". The "Statesman" observes correctly that "by this means it is possible to paint into a composite anti-British picture the grievances of peasants against their own Indian landlords, of workers against their Indian employers, and a long series of abuses which are part of the indigenous system of the country, and which the British have never had the courage or the power to alter."

This is true. The campaign against the British super-rulers has always come very handy to the Indian ruling class for diverting the Indian peasants and workers from their more direct grievances against their own landlords and employers and home-made forms of caste and other oppression. That does not mean that there were no grievances against the British, who acted much the same in similar position, and very much different from how they would act in similar positions in England. But the main grievance, as far as progressive Indians are concerned, was that the "civilising mission", for which the "Statesman" even now expects Indians to have a "consciousness of debt", and which, in a historic sense, ought not to be altogether denied, never gave the British in India "the courage to alter" those very reactionary and retrogressive features in Indian social and public life which they now openly condemn. The true curse of Imperialism is that it was profitable for the British in India to rely on, and foster, in India those very forces which have always stood in the way of Indian progress due to their socially reactionary nature and function, and which are now turning against the master who fed them and kept them artificially alive, for his own benefit. In this world conflict, which has placed Britain on the side of the forces of progress as against the Fascist form of retrogression of human society, their own creatures in India, those anachronisms galvanised by themseluvs into a festering existence, are dragging them down to-day, jeopardising victory in the war.

But victory in this war is not an affiair of the British in India. Others are keenly interested in it, and are therefore closely following the thinking processes of their allies, the British in India, some of whom have beeg shocked out of the ruts of a complacent belief in their own godlikeness in terms of power, invincibility and righteousness, by catastrophic events and a sense of impending disaster. No race through on their side should stand in the way of achieving that victory. No patronising attitude of conferring help should enter into the new relation. We shall perish together unless we can pull through together. The one without the other has no power to resist the imminent danger. Let all concerned draw the lessons.

The first lesson should be to realise the alignment of forces In India. Who will unreservedly fight this war as their own? The prejudiced ones must be left out of account. Prejudice dies hard; and let no one underestimate the the depth of the existing prejudice, nurtured over decades on a fertile ground of objectionable facts. And among the most prejudiced are those "Frankensteins" of British Imperialism, the feudal-patriarchal and feudal-capatalist upper strata of Indian society, who are to-day biting the hand that did wrong in feeding them; among them is also the semi-and pseudo-intelligentsia which was taught western language and western habits without being imbibed with the spriit of western culture and the essence of western civilisation; and who hate the latter because they do not master it, while it has torn their roots out of the soil of another civilisation, which, if antiquated, was at least their own, but is no longer theirs, and left them uprooted, frustrated and without a perspective of growth.

But all of them together constitute only a tiny fraction of the Indian people. The whole nationalist movement, except in its vaguely emotional repercussions, has never touched more than the fringe of the vast bulk of the population. This hollowness was exposed in all the recent movements, particularly in the anti-war Satyagraha. The masses were not touched at all by it; therefore it was a failure; a desultory affair which fizzled out without anybody really noticing the difference between the campaign and its end.

That proves that the masses of the people, who are in compulsory contact with reality due to their daily toil, are unaffected by the virus of race hatred and negation. They are sound. But they are dumb. And if there is to be any fighting by the people against invaders, it will be they who will do it, or there will be none. For that, they must be made articulate, transformed from an conscious dumb-driven mass into an ordered aggregate of men conscious of their human dignity. They have to be aroused to the consciousness of the danger that threatens them. They may be made to realise that danger. But if it is to inspire them with anything more than fear and terror, they must be made to feel that the alternative to that danger is something else than the *status quo*, their present condition.

And here, a civilising mission of the British in India may indeed come into play. It can be no reason of pride for them to present to their democratic allies, after 200 years of rule in this country, a semi-feudal backward India, not indeed the brightest jewel, but a dark spot in the British Crown, where ninety per cent. or more of the people are illiterate and underfed, where peasants cannot keep enough of their produce to feed themselves, where industrial workers are labouring ten hours and more a day for 18 rupees and less a month. Nobody can say that the British in India had not the power to change it. They did not have the courage. They did not have the will. The power they had was used for more profitable pursuits than a civilising mission. It mattered only to the extent that it guaranteed cheap labour, and kept it cheap. And labour can be kept cheap only if it is kept backward and ignorant and half of it unemployed, while the other half work too much, impairing both labour and production, and compelling the rest to over-crowd the land which cannot nourish even those living on the badly irrigated, hardly ever manured and wooden-ploughed fields.

With such, the war cannot be won. And that is not a state of things for whose preservation a man would fight enthusiastically, even against something worse. If the fight against Fascism is one for freedom and progress, the latter must be given a concrete content. The, peasant and the Indian workers cannot think in abstractions. It has become an axiom that freedom means free dom from want, and progress stands for the elevation of human being out of the animal state, where all activity serves only sheer physical maintainance, to a state of dignity where every human being can think higher ideas and pursue nobler ideals. And that cannot be done on an empty stomach. The pursuit of freedom and progress in this sense must be declared a policy, and elaborated in a concrete programme in terms of politics and economics, which the people will understand and appreciate, and for the realisation of which they will fight any obstacle on the way. They will fight Fascist aggression as—but only as—an obstacle on the way to something they want to achive.

The British in India complain that the grievances of peasants and workers against their own landlords and employers are diverted against them through the channels of race hatred. These grievances are thereby conceded as legitimate. What have the British in India done to remove them? They have had the power. And they still have it. To use it for the right purpose before it is too late even if that will be a departure from the traditional policy, may be the only way to avoid losing it to the Japanese Fascists—which would be bad for the British in India, but much worse for the Indians in India. They have never faltered to put in jail opponents from among the aggrieved when they "made a nuisance of themselves"; it will be a much easier job to do the same to the much small number of aggrievers, when the latter will jeopardies the chances of victory by opposing the adoption of a policy as outlined above. But there must be a policy.

Such a policy and programme must be thought out, worked out, openly proclaimed and boldly put in action. The British in India cannot eliminate race hatred against them by trying to please all. "Indians" are not a species by themselves. They are a complex society with conflicting elements, as human society everywhere, and rather a little more complex. You can never please all of them. You cannot build up war industries in a very short time, and leave the national wealth locked up in feudal estates; you cannot have war necessities produced at controlled rates, and allow the private owners of industries unbridled liberty to produce whatever they like if it pays better; you cannot make the workers stick to their jobs in danger zones, and at the same time allow their employers to deny them a human existence; you cannot expect the peasants to form guerilla bands to fight the common enemy, while they must think of the landlord, who would rather shoot tigers than Fascists, and who will secure his profit from the harvest by taking on another tenant, and the partisan fighter will find the plot of land gone that he has tilled all his life and gone out to defend—because it is not his own.

The British in India also have to choose sides. And they must choose those who want to win the war, or do all that is necessary to make them want to do so. It can be done. But this war cannot be won against the people, nor even without the people. Therefore, first win the people; then they will win the war.

May 20, 1942.

UNITED NATIONS DAY

United Nations Day was to be a world-wide demonstration of the determined will to victory on the part of all the forces fighting the Fascist Axis. Therefore, Radical Democrats in this country took prominent part in the celebrations in many places.

The platform on which the United Nations stand united is, so far, to win the war, and nothing else. That is a big proposition, but not enough. All those arrayed against the Axis Powers in this war agree that the war must be won. But many must be asking: What then? The United Nations have no programme as yet. The Atlantic Charter does not embrace all of them. Nor is the relation, future or present, between those standing on the United Nations' platform as yet defined. The deficiency is apparently felt and discussions like those of the London Chamber of Commerce are designed to make up for it.

Perhaps, the designation of United *Nations* is not very happy. It raises all the problems of nationalism with its unfortunate implications. Is this a war of nations? Is there any nation undividedly, enthusiastically and consciously fighting the Axis as the exponent of Fascism, and Fascism as the spearhead of reaction and retrogression? And are those fighting on the side of the Axis nations united in upholding Fascism? Are we fighting the German, Italians, French, etc., as nations?

We have called this war an international civil war. The fronts do not coincide with national frontiers. They go right through every country. The "United Nations" have been said to possess one hundred million allies on the Continent dominated by the Axis. Nor is the Axis without subtle agents behind our own front. Even when celebrating United Nations Day, we should not forget that this is not a national war, but a war against Fascism, which means, a war for democracy, the rule of the people—everywhere. Such a war can only be fought, and such a victory only be won, on the broadest, international Peoples Front. Such a platform will contain its programme in the name, and the unity of those rallying on it will be much broader and deeper.

But whether unity be of nations, or of peoples, to enumerate 28 of them will not do. If we claim that this is India's war too—and this is the main plank of India's "National War Front"—then India must have her recognised place among the other nations or peoples. Constitutionally, it may be correct to say that she is included among the United Nations as part of the British Empire or Commonwealth. But then, if equal effort and enthusiasm—in face of even greater danger—are demanded of India as of Canada or Australia, and others, then India's name should not be missing. The deficiency of a flag and a recognised National Anthem should not stand in the way. They are only symbols, and not essential factors in the making of a nation.

Constitutional relations are subject to change. In the relation between Britain and India, such changes are under consideration at present. The writing down of the new terms of relationship has presented difficulties. This theoretical approach of creating new relations on paper is bound to be an artificial and difficult process. Historically, new constitutional relations have almost always evolved in practice, and Constitutions been made to give legal and written shape to already established conventions.

New conventions are developing in the relation between Britian and India. India is gainiug a new diplomatic status. She has representatives on all the Commonwealth bodies created for the conduct of the war. She has an Agent-General in China. She will, we trust, have direct diplomatic relations with all the Allied countries soon, including the U.S.S.R. particularly, now after the signing of the Anglo-Soviet Treaty of Alliance. She is going to have something very near a War Cabinet, if only her leaders can make it that.

India's freedom is thus evolving in practice. It is in the procees of making. If she can throw up the leadership to shape this process, the legal and constitutional recognition of India's freedom will be only a formal step, the recognition of a fact which will be already a reality.

Daily "Independent India", June 17, 1942

INTERNATIONAL SOLIDARITY AGAINST FASCISM

By K. K. Sinha

It is as if the titanic world struggle through all its horrors and brutality is asking the idealists the ominous question: Is there any basis of unity between nations, between peoples, between man and man? And nobody can avoid the question except by refusing to believe that he is a part of this world.

"Unity" has become a hackneyed term, so much so that it has come to be an end by itself. It being contrary to the laws of social development, it has remained impractical and its pursuit today not merely betrays an innocent confusion of thought but acts as the greatest hindrance to purposive action in pursuit of the common human ideals of progress and the removal of obstacles from the path of humanity on its onward march. Unity of nations must therefore be based on a common immediate objective to avoid frustration like the fate of the League of Nations

What can that objective be? Events have made the choice for us all. The war against Fascism is the concern of all the peoples of the world, not because some Fascist countries have adopted a policy of aggression towards weaker nations, but because of the nature of Fascism as a social phenomenon and its danger to human society as a whole. It is this fundamental objective appreciation of Fascism that has made nations united together in resisting it, in spite of the predilictions of kings, presidents and governments of many countries. Thus unity of nations has as its object the destruction of Fascism as a social disease. It is a purposive unity driving them to action. The recognition of this fact facilitates and speeds up the realisation of the goal.

While we talk of 'unity' and 'nations', the traditional meaning of these terms are undergoing continual changes in the impact of the war. As a corrollary, the concept of 'internationalism' is also passing through a transformation. Today there are two "internationals." Germany, Italy, Japan, Hungary, Finland, France, and a host of others represent an international Fascist unity. Britain, Soviet Union, China, United States and others represent international anti-Fascist unity.

So, mere internationalism is an ambiguous and confusing slogan. A country or a people has to declare to which international camp it belongs. Then there is another aspect, and a more far-reaching one, of internationalism. Within each of these international camps, in each country—whether Germany or Britain—there exist simultaneously Fascist and anti-Fascist camps. Thus one cannot separate one nation from another (except Russia) characterising it as Fascist or anti-Fascist. It is proof of the fact that Fascism is a deep-rooted social disease in the whole human organism and not merely the power politics of a few nations or groups. This war is veritably an international civil war. It has thus broken up the traditional territorial and mechanical concepts of unity and nationalism. United Nations against Fascism must therefore convey a new conception of thought: Unity of the different peoples representing one organic indivisible human society striving to destroy the forces of the past which have outlived its utility in the promotion of social growth.

What is the place of Nationalism in the context of this all-embracing social conflict? Abstract nationalism, representing 'independence of the nation' without a social and economic content, without guaranteeing the progress of the bulk of the people, on the basis of unity of all-native exploiters and exploited, is not an ideal worth fighting for. No nation, no people can remain isolated and unaffected from the two international camps, simply because it is part of the indivisible human organism. An attempt at isolation by a people will be like cutting a limb away from a living body—it harms both, more the limb as it dies away. Therefore, a neutralist attitude in the name of nationalism puts it in the camp of those who want to retard the progress of human development, which is only another name of the Fascist Axis. Thus nationalism as a historical phenomenon promotes the cause of Fascism in this epoch. Let us fight for our ideals in terms of its concrete social contents and not in terms of abstract and spiritualist conception of nationalism.

The international Fascist Axis is the spearhead of international Fascism as a social organism rooted in every country. It is active, living and aggressive. One cannot arrest its growth, confine it, temporise its onrush, compromise with it. Either it overwhelms human society or it is overwhelmed. If its destruction is the object of progressive human society then the anti-Fascist forces have to be equally active and aggressive. The profession of "unity of nations" must therefore have to be practised in a realistic manner. The international anti-Fascist Peoples' Front must represent a military, political, economic and philosophical leadership. The role of the Soviet Union as a spearhead in this task becomes more manifest day by day. But it will perform this historically necessary function not as a 'nation' but as representing the culmination of the next phase of human development in one sixth of the globe. An international fraternity has to be built on a broader and surer foundations than on an internationalism constructed on the corner-stones of nationalism. The slogan "workers of the world unite" resounding throughout the world ever since the nineteenth century throws up a perspective of the new principle of internationalism on the foundations of which can be built the superstructure of the new social order. But this is not a wishful imagination of a period after the war. The Anglo-Soviet Pact of 1941 is evidence of the tendency towards a fundamental unity of the peoples of two countries and more, for the primary purpose of defeating Fascism.

The historic Anglo-Soviet Treaty of 1942 has not only inter-related War with Peace but also built up the anti-Fascist Axis as the decisive spearhead of the world anti-Fascist forces, organising the much needed political, military and moral leadership of the people. This seals the fate of the Axis powers. Thus the new internationalism heralded by the Anglo-Soviet relation has merged the struggle for freedom of the different peoples into this world anti-Fascist struggle. Let the Indian Peoples striving for national freedom shake hands with the people of the United Nations and thus contribute to the realisation of our goal as well as that of the peoples of the world.

June 28, 1942.

ON THE CROSSROADS : BACK-WARD OR FORWARD?

BY VIMAL PRASAD JAIN

[Presidential Address at the United Provinces Conference of the Radical Democratic Party, Saharanpur onJune 29, 1942.]

History is forgotten very soon. We often do not remember even the events that took place during the last four or five years. Before this war broke out, innumerable resolutions were passed from various platforms in the country calling upon the progressive elements everywhere to compel their governments to crush the Fascist movement before it grew too strong. Equally numerous resolutions were passed to sympathise with the victims of Fascist aggression. " China Day", " Spain Day", " Abyssinia Day" were celebrated to demonstrate the solidarity against the common enemy. The Indian National Congress was the loudest of all in denouncing that menace. Our Socialist Pandit was so much elated with internationalism and hatred of Fascism that no speech of his was complete without a brilliant exposition of his internationalism and burning hatred for Fascism.

Were all those speeches for the gallery only? Were all those resolutions insincere or meaningless? Were they but meant to deceive the progressive forces of the world, or were they passed mechanically, without understanding their significance? Otherwise, how it is that as soon as the progressive elements throughout the world made up their mind to fight the menace of Fascism, our Socialist Pandit and the whole Congress organisation ceased talking about resistance to Fascism and sympathy for the aggrieved countries—and ended with resistance to war efforts, thereby helping the victory of Fascism?

It is not we who have gone over to the Imperialist Government to fight this war. We had been fighting the menace of Fascism all the time, long before. The line we are following today is not a new line to us. We have been following it ever since the advent of Fascism in Italy and Germany. Our attitude was made clear in this country as early as 1934, when our guide and comrade M. N. Roy wrote a book on Fascism while he was in jail, in which he laid down our policy and programme for the defeat of Fascism. Anybody can refer to it who cares to. Thus, I put it to you: Is it we who have changed sides and are betraying our policy and the interest of the people, or those other nationalist leaders? We were anti-Fascists then and we are anti-Fascists today, and we are not going to rest till we have redeemed humanity of this dark chapter of its history.

We are fighting Fascism not because we have any soft corner for Imperialism or capitalist governments in general, but because we want the freedom of the Indian people. Nobody who knows the real nature of Fascism will pause for a moment to decide what course he has to adopt when threatened with a Fascist victory. He will at once rally with all those other forces throughout the world who stand to fight Fascism, conscious that under Fascism even those conditions are absent in which we have been carrying on our fight for freedom so long. What is Fascism after all? Take out all the progressive elements and liberal tendencies of Imperialism, put the clock of history back to two or three hundred years, fall back on the methods of barbarism known from the middle-ages, and add the implements of coercion of the twentieth century—and you are face to face with Fascism.

Lenin once wrote that to know the character of any war, it is essential to go into the history of the preceding decade; because war is the climax of the historical and social currents during that period. If you examine the history of the period after the last war, you will find two things going on side by side: revolution and counter-revolution. Counter-revolution is as much an international force as revolution. Both have allies and protagonists in every country throughout the world. All the progressive elements stand in the camp of revolution, and the others in the opposite camp. A veritable civil war has been going on ever since the Russian Revolution in every country of the world. International counter-revolution tried to destroy the cathedral of revolution built up by the toiling masses of Russia on one-sixth of the world's surface. When military intervention did not succeed in crushing it, the political front against revolution was formed and extended through all the countries of the world. In no other country did revolution succeed, and the result of its defeat in Italy and Germany was the rise of Fascism which developed more and more consciously into a weapon to strike at the bulwark of revolution. For that it had to suppress, in the countries where it ruled, first of all the forces sympathising with revolution, that is, with progress. Under Fascism, no strike is tolerated, no trade-union activities allowed, no class and political organisations can exist. This regime eliminates even the limited liberties which are created by the enlightend and liberal opinion characterising the most moderate forms of democracy. The Fascist Government, based on decaying capitalism, fighting desperately for survival, does not even put up the show or sham democracy and is responsible to none.

Before this war broke out, the British Government, like most others was were conniving with the attempts to put out the burning light of revolution. They chose Hitler to do the dirty job of suppressing the popular forces rising all over Europe. The agression on one European country after another was connived at. The people were hoodwinked by those Governments. The Abyssinian representative cried in vain for support in the League of Nations. The criminal neutrality of the so-called democracies in face of active Fascist intervention in Spain was not the lat act of that treachery. The strangling of Czechoslovakia followed; Austria had already gone, and Poland's turn was to come.

But there was a progressive element in those capatalist countries which was not prepared to yield any further- The fruits of cultural progress and modern civilisation, which they had built up in the course of centuries, were at stake, and they were not prepared for the plunge into medieval barbarism. They decided to stop the Fascist onslaught and forced their governments to wage war against Fascism. They made up their mind, though hesitatingly, to face even the logical consequences of the defeat of Fascism in a war. There is today an element in England which has begun to think that there is something fundamentally wrong in the present system of their social and political life. The striking success of the system prevailing in the U. S. S. R., exhibited in this war, aroused every thinking man and woman to shake off old prejudices and face boldly new ways and new ideas.

Now you may ask the very legitimate question: Perhaps you are right, but what about India's freedom? My answer is that our fight for freedom has merged in this war which is being waged on an international front to save progress and liberty. In the very beginning I told you that every country is divided in two camps. The victory of the progressive forces of the world includes the victory of the progressive forces of India. Imperialism stands on the cross-roads today. There are only two ways for its choice: either it must choose the road which will lead ultimately to a better though different world; or it shall have to take up the road back to medieval barbarism and give in to the Fascist Axis.

But consciously or unconsciously, it has already chosen side. It is standing with its face towards the road of Fascist defeat, that is, the road of progress and freedom. Because it may not be very happy nor very conscious about it, the help of the progressive forces was never needed more than today. It is time to summon every ounce of progressive energy to push forward on that road, and to see that it really leads towards its logical end. England has a tradition of adaptability. You remember that England fought the French Revolution for two decades, fiercer and longer than any other country. But it could not escape its effects. And I shall not be surprised if, in the same way, England will emerge a Socialist country out of this war. But to guarantee such a development, it is all the more essential that the progressive forces in this country also should be there to push it onwards on that road.

OUR PARTY & ITS TASK

Summary of Speech at The U. P. Conference of The Radical Democratic Party, Saharanpur on June 29, 1942.

Yesterday's demonstration proves that the influence of our party is growing—more rapidly than we dared expect. Recently, in co-operation with the Indian Federation of Labour, we succeeded in organising equally powerful mass demonstrations against the danger of Fascism and in support of ruthless struggle against it.

The Radical Democratic Party was founded less than two years ago. In this short time, we have succeeded in building up a country-wide organisation, not of politically backward blind followers, but of trained political workers. Our party alone shows the way out of the confusion and hollowness which characterise the public life of the country. The way we indicate is the only way to freedom. The larger the number of people travelling that way, the sooner will India reach the cherished goal of freedom.

But we do not believe that the entire Indian nation can and ever will travel that way. A homogeneous nation was always a fiction. Even that fiction no longer fascinates. The world of our time is not broken up into a number of nations which live independently, with occasional wars. The world today is divided into two camps. The line of demarcation runs through each and every country, splitting up each nation into two warring camps. Everywhere they may not be actually facing each other on the battlefield. But everywhere they are moved by conflicting ideas and are actuated by antagonistic ideals. Both may talk of freedom; but in reality, one stands for freedom, and the other for enslaving and exploiting the rest. That is the case also in India.

India will not move a single step towards freedom until her public life is liberated from the influence of the people who, on the pretext of fighting for national freedom, would keep her away from the path of freedom on which she must travel with others including those who might have been our enemies until yesterday. Our Party has been trying to clarify the line of demarcation between Indians and Indians. It is the spearhead of the popular forces, who must have real freedom—freedom from miseries and privations which mar the daily life of the masses, not simply replacement of Englishmen by Indian politicans. Therefore, it alone can marshal Indian democracy on the world front against Fascism.

There can be no national front in the fight against Fascism. Every Indian is not an anti-Fascist. Unfortunately, there are far too many who are pro-Fascists and Fascists themselves. Curiously enough, the Government refuses to take notice of this rude reality. It is deceiving itself. If it does not see things in their proper perspective, and act courageously, allying itself definitely with those Indians who can never belong to the camp of Fascism; there will be serious trouble. The Congress leaders are preparing for it.

The same policy of the Government will be to strengthen the hands of the Anti-Fascists, and in order to be a genuine anti-Fascist, one must outgrow the nationalist outlook. One cannot be an effective fighter against Fascism, and yet clamour for the establishment of a National Government which would claim the right and power to get out of the fight against Fascism, irrespective of others engaged in that fight. What India needs, for her own freedom, as well as for helping the defence of the freedom of others, is not a National Government composed of, or controlled by, Indian Petains, but a Government composed of men who want to defend India as a sector of the International War Front against Fascism—a Government which will defend the country against Axis invasion, and destroy the forces of Fascism inside the country as essential for that defence. Such a Government will be a really Democratic Government as well as a National Government if democratic freedom is meant by national freedom. As a really democratic government, acting as such, it will command popularc onfidence, now captured by demagogy, and consequently be a strong government which would sternly suppress the forces of reaction masquerading as advocates of national freedom. Any further delay in the advent of such a government increases the danger of India's position. The threatened Japanese invasion of India will most probably synchronise with the flare in the Middle East. So, there should be no complacency. It would be foolish to expect the monsoon to do our job. The situation is critical. It demands quick action, determined action, and clear-sighted action. The Radical Democratic Party will stand at the post, with the confidence that the day is not far when it will be called upon to shoulder great responsibilities. It is preparing itself for playing the role which history has allotted to it.

THE LAST STEP

The die is thus cast. The Congress has declared its position; it has made its choice. It has decided to organise a movement of mass civil disobedience amounting to an 'open rebellion' just when the country is threatened by foreign invasion and on the safety and security of India depends the freedom not only of India herself but of the United Nations and more particularly of China and Russia. Gandihji and the Congress may not be able to get the necessary support from the country, their grandiose plans may fail, their open rebellion may after all turn out to be nothing worse than a petty nuisance. But these are different matters; their intentions are clear, their sympathies undisguised. Whatever their professions, the action proposed to be taken by them marks them out as the enemies of the war efforts of the United Nations.

In view of the action proposed to be taken—the launching of a mass civil disobedience movement with the demand for the withdrawal of the

British power—the long preamble to the resolution mouthing noble sentiments about resisting aggression and expressing deep sympathy with the Allied cause is meaningless and hypocritical. It is just a playing to the galtery, an attempt to hoodwink ill-informed liberal elements in England and America. The Mahatma has been very generous in this respect to the Socialist Pandit. As a concession to him the Mahatma has allowed the Working Committee to adopt the long winded preamble which can be paraded before the world as evidence of the anti-Fascist sympathies of the Congress. But the preamble is cancelled by the operative part which decides upon the course of action and entrusts its direction of Mahatma Gandhi.

The Working Committee admits the 'rapid and widespread increase of ill-will against Britain and a growing satisfaction at the success of Japanese arms.' It is also aware that this development 'unless checked will inevitably lead to a passive acceptance of aggression.' And what is the Working Committee's remedy to check this development? A mass civil disobedience movement with the slogan 'quit India.' Will this movement increase or decrease the ill-will against

Britain add the satisfaction at the success of Japanese arms? The movement if it succeeds will increase those feelings a thousand-fold and will thus lead to 'a passive acceptance of aggression.' While thus talking about resisting aggression the Working Committee is paving a smooth way for its easy success.

In the conditions of today foreign aggression can be successfully resisted in our country only by the united efforst of the Government and the people. Instead of bringing the two together and developing a united effort the Congress has decided to develop a conflict between the two. There are always a thousand and one points of difference between the Government and the people. Where a foreign Government exists they can be counted by many thousands. It is not difficult to seize upon any one of them and thus inflame the people against the Government. In normal times it may be a legitimate method for effecting changes in the personnel and policy of the Government. In critical times like the present it assumes an entirely different character. If the two Working Committee resolutions are read together it is clear that it is the intention of the Congress leaders to seize upon every small or big grievance of the people not so much to secure its redress but to utilise it for alienating the people from the Government and the war efforts. The direct result of this policy will be greater hostility between the Government and the people, a greater indifference towards war efforts, and a keener desire for the success of the Japanese arms. With these as the direct results of their policy how can the Congress leaders prepare the people for resisting aggression?

It is not likely that Gandhiji's civil disobedience movement will receive any large measure of support in the country. In spite of what he may say it is very likely that it will end in sending to jails a few thousand Congressmen and possibly in a spectacular fast by the Mahatma. It is not likely materially to affect either production to war funds or loans. It may be barren of these results, but it is bound to have other and more dangerous consequences. It will seriously affect the morale of the people, it will make them more and more anti-British and pro-Fascist, it will sap their will to resist, it will make them indifferent to foreign aggression. The all important home front will thus be seriously weakened. With an insecure home front success on the other front, in this total war, is extremely problematical. Gandhiji and the Congress will be rendering this great service to the Axis cause by starting a civil disobedience movement at this hour of great peril to the cause of human freedom.

The preamble to the resolution has expressed a lot of sympathy for the cause of human freedom and has disavowed any intention to cause embarrassment to the United Nations. But the sympathy is mere lip sympathy. It does not lead to any action. On the other hand what is contemplated to be done is contrary to professed sentiments. Men and organisations are judged not by their intentions and professions but by their actions. Judged by that test the Congress stands today in the camp of Fascism and counter-revolution. The private intentions of a few of its leaders or public professions meant for the gallery will not alter this verdict based on concrete actions.

Frustrated and spiteful nationalism has thus reached its destined goal. In Germany and Italy it gave rise to Nazism and Fascism. In India it is culminating in a movement calculated to help them materially. That movement is not yet strong, it is still required to wear the trappings of anti-Fascist phraseology, it is still required to profess sympathy for the cause of the United Nations. But its character is unmistakable. Being born of frustrated nationalism it could not be otherwise. It is going the way that similar movements in other countries did. And if it is allowed to grow it will in our country result in the establishment of similar conditions, namely, the triumph of Fascism and the destruction of the forces of progress and freedom.

The inner logic of the ideology that has been governing the Congress for the last twenty years has inexorably led it to the stage that it has reached today. It cannot travel any other way unless it throws overboard the heavy ballast of reactionary nationalism that it has been carrying all these years. Various efforts were made during the last twenty years to persuade it to take that fateful step. Unfortunately for the Congress those efforts did not succeed and it became a more and more pronounced and aggressive exponent and bulwark of reactionary nationalism. It is now taking the last step in that direction and openly allying itself with Fascism, which is but another name for reactionary and aggressive nationalism.

The proposed action of the Congress will be sought to be justified on the grounds of nationalism. As a nation, it is contended, we are primarily concerned with our nation's freedom. And as it is denied to us by the British Government the latter is our primary enemy. Whatever therefore our sympathies for China or Russia we cannot forget our quarrel with our primary enemy and cannot help taking advantage of his difficulties for winning our nation's freedom. This is an honest nationalist position leading straight to the camp of Fascism. There are some nationalists in our country who courageously take up that position. Subhaschandra Bose represents them. The Congress lacks the courage and the straightforwardness of those nationalists. While attempting to do something, which is not far diffierent from what they would do it is still trying to hide its real character under a cloak of beautiful phrases and lip homage to noble ideals.

This bluff must no longer deceive people here and abroad. Now at least they must recognise the real character of the Congress and its actions. If there had been even a little substance in its anti-Fascist professions no amount of crimes and mistakes of the British Government would have persuaded it to stand aloof from the momentous struggle for human freedom and progress and to embark on a movement calculated to seriously weaken and disorganise it. Absence of anti-Fascist convictions and presence of pro-Fascist sympathies are alone responsible for the attitude that the Congress has adopted towards the war. They have grown during the last two years and have now resulted in the Congress deciding to abandon its policy of non-embarrassment. The Congress will no longer be a non-belligerent or a neutral. It will be on the other side of the barricade. Cowardice or impotence may prevent it from making too big a trouble. But even if the Congress is able to render indifferent or passive a large section of the people of our country it will be of immense aid and comfort to the Axis Powers. The Congress is out to render that aid and comfort to the Fascist. That determines the character of the Congress and should determine the attitude towards it of every progressive and freedom-loving person and organisation.

"Independent India" July 19, 1942

AFTER ME-DELUGE

The resolution of the Congress Working Committee has caused consternation everywhere. As the London 'Times' puts it, "The resolution will be received with satisfaction in Tokyo, Berlin and Rome, and with apprehension and incredulity in Chunking, Moscow and Washington." The strong opposition in the British press will be of course dismissed as prejudiced opinion of the interested party. But as against that treatment of the unfavourable British press opinion, it might be recollected that until recently public opinion as a whole in Britain was crystallising in favour of some understanding with the Congress. Therefore, it will not be fair to dismiss the present reaction in the British press as simply the prejudice of an interested party.

The resolution has not been favourably received by the American press either. There also it has been not only severely criticised, but condemned as unhelpful and even mischievous. There are many Indians who would dismiss the unfavourable reaction in the American press as the expression of imperialist solidarity. But the Congress counts on American sympathy and support for its demand for the withdrawal of the British. The Working Committee resolution, as a matter of fact, was primarily meant for America. It was a manifesto to the American public. That being the case, its unfavourable reception in America proves that the Congress leaders have overplayed their hand.

Nevertheless, there are not many among Indian nationalists, of any shade of opinion, who doubt the justification of the resolution. They all admire its boldness, although some may be afraid of their own courage. The more sober elements appreciate the apparent moderation of the resolution as its strong point. But practically none of them see the danger and difficulties involved, and even those who do see them are indifferent about the consequences.

For the average nationalist, it is a simple proposition. India wants freedom. She should have it. No opposition to her being free, here and now, is valid. The British should get out. They need not worry about what will happen to India afterwards. That is India's concern. If she is prepared to take the risk, others should not worry.

This is a thoughtless attitude. On principle, nobody would dispute India's right to freedom. But even those who have dedicated their lives to the cause of Indian freedom may not all agree that withdrawal of the British by itself will mean freedom for India. Sooner or later, that withdrawal must take place. But it is not possible to disregard the very practical question : What will replace the present regime ? Transfer of power presupposes the existence of a party to which power is transferred. There is no united opinion about the party to which power will be transferred upon the withdrawal of the British. Therefore, it is apprehended that immediate withdrawal will be followed by chaos and confusion which, under the given circumstances, will most probably help the prospective invade. Even among the nationalists, who would not consider anything but India's right to be free, there are some who can imagine possible dangers and difficulties, which are likely to overtake India if the Congress demand can be enforced immediately. But they also seem to feel that it would be worthwhile to take the plunge. That feeling is reflected in the following passage of the Congress Working Committee resolution :

"The Congress realises that there may be risks involved in such a course. Such risks, however, have to be faced by any country in order to achieve freedom, and more specially at the present critical juncture." Ordinarily, this spirit may be appreciated as bravery. No radical change can be always and entirely free from a temporary confusion and dislocation of normal relations. But the present position is peculiar. The peculiarity is that there is a third factor waiting for a change to intervene. Therefore, if the desirable change in the relation between India and Britain is marked with chaos and confusion in India, it may be no better than a change of master. The apparently bold decision to take risks for the sake of winning freedom, will be a mere bravado, in the absence of a practicable plan for avoiding the desirable change to be so degenerated. So far, there is no such plan. There is nothing more than wishful thinking and speculation.

The magnitude of the risk is not minimised. It is very clearly visualised in the resolution itself. "This frustration has resulted in a rapid and widespread increase of ill-will against Britain and a growing satisfaction at the success of Japanese arms. The Working Committee view this development with grave apprehension as this, unless checked, will inevitably lead to a passive acceptance of aggression. The Congress is anxious to avoid the experience of Malaya, Singapore and Burma." But how is this process of deterioration to be checked? It is very difficult to share the belief that the whole psychological atmosphere of racial animosity and bitterness and spitefulness will disappear with the withdrawal of the British.

The nature of the problem is not clearly grasped, and there is so much confusion about the proper approach to it, because feelings are running high: frustration and bitterness preclude sober judgment; animosity and spitefulness make for short-sightedness and even induce the nationalist to court disaster deliberately. India's fate, indeed, hangs in the balance today. Never was an appeal to reason so very necessary. If India is to be saved, riotous sentiments should be tempered with reason. If that happens, then the problem of Indian freedom will appear in an entirely different light, and the relation between

Britain and India will no longer appear to be an insuperable obstacle. The readjustment of that relation, then, can be a process so as to avoid the danger of chaos and confusion which, in its turn, involves a change of masters.

While appealing to reason, it should be borne in mind that no discussion can be fruitful, unless there is a minimum agreement. There must be an agreement at least about standards. If the two parties start from contradictory premises, no agreement is possible. Without an agreement about standards or promises, any discussion is bound to be a talk at cross-purposes.

In order to convince the nationalists that the Congress is pursuing a wrong policy, wrong from the nationalist point of view, it is necessary to prove that the policy will not lead to freedom. The proposition that India is entitled to be free does provide the basis for a general pursuing But that is not enough. To begin with, freedom must be defined. Otherwise, we may be pursuing different ideas while believing that we are working for a common object. Practically speaking, unless we know exactly where we want to go, it is not possible to judge whether any particular road is the right one or not.

The Working Committee resolution is of great importance, because it compels all history, ful fascinating to examine the basis of a common agreement as regards the kind of freedom they want. The resolution opens up a very fascinating perspective—fascinating for the uncritical. "For the first time in India's history, the realisation will come home that the Princes, Jagirdars, Zemindars and the propertied and monied classes derive their wealth and property from the workers in the fields and factories and elsewhere, to whom essentially power and authority must belong. On the withdrawal of British rule in India, responsible men and women of the country will come together to form a provisional Government representative of all important sections of the people of India, which will later evolve a scheme by which a Constituent Assembly can be convened in order to prepare a Constitution for the Government of India acceptable to all sections of the people."

While the later part of the plan is rather wishful thinking, the former part is simply amazing. The inclusion of the fantastic idea that only upon the withdrawal of the British power, *for the first time*, it will be realised that workers in the fields and factories are the creators of all wealth which has until now been appropriated by a small minority, makes the above conception of Indian freedom—fascinating only for the uncritical. Why was the realisation of the most obvious absent among those who have been leading the struggle for Indian freedom? bastic social fact, which primarily deprives of the people of all freedom, a creation of the British rule? Did not Princes, Jagirdars, Zemindars, proported and moneyed classes exist in India before the British came?

The picture is apparently fascinating, because it hides a negation of freedom. The implication is that, upon the disappearance of the British, all antagonism between classes and communities will disappear, and consequently the process of setting up an Indian National Government will smoothly follow. It cannot be assumed except by the most incorrigible utopian that, upon the withdrawal of the British Power, the Princes, Jagirdars, Zemindars etc. will also forego their property and privileges, and power and authority will automatically belong to the workers in the fields and factories. Since no such thing is likely to happen, the withdrawal of the British will most probably be followed by a Government controlled by the Princes, Jagirdars, Zemindars, etc. and that sort of a Government will be celebrated as the National Government ushering in freedom for India. A dictatorship of the propertied classes economicз the economic life of the country and deriving power from that control, can alone secure the process of compelling all sections of the people to accept a National Government, as visulised in the Working Committee resolution. That is the only practical way for replacing the British power by an Indian Government. But evidently that will not be freedom in the democratic and progressive sense. If such a dictatorship is not visualised, then the process outlined in the Congress resolution is simple wishful thinking. Nothing like that is likely to happen.

A realistic apprciation of the conflicting factors of the situation, as it is, precludes such an optimistic view. A dreamer in other respects, the Mahatma is very realistic in politics. Therefore, he does not share the glib optimism of the Working Committee resolution. Only the previous week he wrote in 'Harijan': "What the happen after the all-powerful British hand is withdrawn, will depend on how we act at that stage, if we ever reach that stage. We may quarrel among ourselves, or we may adjust our quarrels and agree to set up an ordered *rule on behalf of the people.* It may be a democratic constitution or unadulterated autocracy or oligarchy".

That is a very frank statement. The chances in favour of a democratic constitution are only thirty per cent, and even then the Mahatmic concept of democracy can hardly be acceptable to any modern democrat. He wishes to set up an *ordered rule* on behalf of the people. The people themselves shall not have anything to do with it. They are to be ruled in an orderly manner. That is a familiar doctrine in defence of autocracy. If that is not the meaning why should the Mahatma choose the expression "on benalf of the people"? Words have meaning. A Democratic Government was defined as "government of the people,by the people, for the people." In course of time it became clear that the implication of "for the people" practically negativated the rest of the definition, because it deprived the people of the right of actually weilding power. It is now generally admitted that this fundamental defect of democratic practice must be removed, if really democratic freedom is to be established. The supreme leader of Indian nationalism wants only a *government for the people* which naturally will not be a democratic government.

So, the question for all thoughtful nationalists is: will they welcome or tolerate "unadulterated autocracy or oligarchy" as freedom? Their leaders would. Their idea of freedom is replacement of the British power by any sort of an Indian government. That is made sufficiently clear by the Mahatma, and his word is law. Even if, perchance, it will be a democratic constitution, it will be a rule on behalf of the people; in other words, paternalism or benevolent despotism. Assuming that even that should be deferable to the present regime, one cannot expect that to happen. The chances are not fifty-fifty. On the computation of the Mahatma, they are 30 to 70 even against nominal democracy. Therefore, it is sheer wishful thinking to assume that once the British power is out of the way, India will attain freedom somehow, even if she may have to pass through a period of chaos and confusion. In fact, the inevitable period of chaos and confusion will be very favourable either for the invader or for the establishment of a native autocracy.

The Mahatma is admittedly of the opinion that freedom for India need not be anything more than the satisfaction of his wish, and he would be equally satisfied whether the British rule is replaced by a nominally democratic government or an unadulterated autocracy or oligarchy. In a press interview given to explain the Working Committee resolution he demanded "unconditional withdrawal of British power without reference to the wishes of parties or the people as a whole" and then exclaimed with a passion "leave India to anarchy or God" Is there no other choice? For the Mahatma, there is none. His thought process, his vision, is circumscribed by his egocentrism.

In that interview, he sounded a new note which is ominous, The fate of the Indian people should be thrown into a chaos or in the lap of the god of Wardha without any reference to them. That is not democracy. That is not a demand of people fighting for freedom. That represents the ambition of the autocrate. The newnote was in the Mahatma's repeated reference to parties. He demanded that no parties should be consulted. But he speaks on behalf of a party. So, the demand is that power should be handed over to that party. He further hinted that after the withdrawal of the British power, parties will disappear. So, "free" India will have her Fuehrer and his lieutenants. She will ex- further: "withdrawal" Fascism.

Should one man's vanity be allowed to gamble with the fate of honest and incidentally jeopardise the future of the world ? The fate of others may not disturb even an honest nationalist; but he should be concerned with India's fate, unless his nationalism was nothing nobler than the slave's spitefulness.

If the present Congress policy succeeds (assuming that the Japs or any other Axis power will leave India alone) she will have a kind of freedom which offers no attraction for the modern progressive man. If it fails, as it most probably will, nothing better than chaos, confusion and possibly Japanese conquest are in store for India.

But the Mahatma wills that it shall be so. Like the ill-fated King Louis who gambled with the fate of France, the Mahatma is guided by the motto "After me, Deluge." The egocentrism of a man is about to push India over the precipice. She is not coming anywhere near freedom. The vision of real freedom must be opened before her so that she can get over the fascination for the false and misleading ideal of nationalism.

"Independent India", July 26, 1942

LOST OPPORTUNITY

By Ellen Roy

Many things, Pandit Jawaharlal said in his press conference on Thursday, sound unexceptionable. It is true that the main concern of all feedomloving Indians must be "how to win this war, how to avert the disastrous consequences which might overtake the country we went on as we are going on; how to function in an effective way to stop aggression; how to develop a spirit of resistance in the people to fight aggression; and to think in terms not so much of independence directly as of meeting the present situation." Why has Pandit Nehru discovered that only now, and why has the Congress never done anything to promote these objects, but only to frustrate them?

It is also true that the conception of the war as it has been carried on by the Allied Powers is all wrong, being "a conception of trying to maintain the status quo, maintain the balance as it was before the war." But what has the Congress done to promote the realisation of the right conception, which could only emerge as an exigency in the prosecution of the war? Has the Congress not done everything to stultify the process by opposing the war as a whole, and pretending to have nothing to do with it?

All these things were clear from the beginning of the war, and the Radical Democratic Party was the first and alone in this country to point them out. But it was natural that things were so, and „actually could not be otherwise. It is infantile romanticism to expect the British Government to beat its chest and declare that they have always been wrong and now they would throw themselves headlong into the revolutionary implications of this war, (which Pandit Nehru has at long last discovered.) Such things do not happen. The most revolutonary act that could be expected from the British Government was to go on fighting Hitler. That is an objectively revolutionary act. It would have been quite in keeping with imperialist tradition to have made peace with Hitler when thing did not look any too bright (and he was engaged on the Soviet front.) That is what all the reactionaries, including Hitler, expected when Hess went to England.

The fact that the war went on proves that its revolutionary implications, its verbally professed but otherwise ignored character of a war for freedom, (which Pandit Jawaharlal has now discovered) are objectively working themselves out, bit by bit and very slowly, and against all the odds of history and tradition (and the love of a ruling class for powers and privileges.) What is needed is more subjective consciousness of the process ond acceptance of the methods necessary to win the war. That can be done only by demanding more of this war, more of war efforts, never by opposing the one or the other, on whatever grounds.

Pandit Nehru obviously agrees with these observations which we have spoken out since the beginning of this war. But we do not agree with his methods of promoting the historical process and meeting the situation. For more than two years he has done everything to make the situation as bad as he complains it is today. He says that for 3 or 4 months Congress has been fighting a growing pro-Japaness feeling. But he does not say that for more than two years everything he did and said, and every other Congress leader did and said, created the pro-Japanese feeling. He deplores the passivity of the people, but for more than two years he told them that this war was not their war and they need not care and had noththing to do with it It is quite natural for him to be doubtful if his word would carry weight should he now go and preach the contrary, without saying that the Congress was all wrong for all this time. As be would never do that, he can only increase the confusion and add the chaos and complications.

Looking at the mess the Congress has made, it is worthwhile to recapitulate what might have been if the Congress had adopted the policy proposed by the Radicals from within the Congress, when the war broke out, a proposal for which they were expelled from that organisation. How different had it been if Pandit Nehru had said what he says today in the beginning of the war! If the Congress Ministries had not resigned, or after resigning had returned to office fortified by the inclusion of representatives of other popular parties! The people were not anti-war then; they were beginning; they wanted lead and guidance. And the Congress failed them utterly. Had they not abandoned their posts of responsibility, army recruitment, taking place under an Indian Government, would have determined the nature and spirit of the army as a people's army; the Civic Guard might be a People's Militia instead of what it is today; a Home Guard, millions strong, would be in existence today The people, instead of being sullen and sulky, resentful and spiteful, would have echoed the slogans of freedom raised from thousands of popular platforms. The whole propaganda machinery of a dozen provincial government, and by now of the Central Government, would have been at the disposal of the slogans of freedom. And freedom would have taken on a wider and higher meaning; it would have come to mean not only national independence; but, under the impact of progressive social ideas gaining strengh throughout the world from the very exigencies of winning the war, it would have come to mean freedom for all, to all the constituents of society (to the down-trodden, to the minorities). It would have been recognised that the Muslims were right in preferring to be good neighbours than quarreling brothers, and Pakistan would have ceased to be a stick to beat all and sundry.

In the general exultation over the release of the forces of freedom in this war, which might have taken place in this country also, a unity which has never existed in history, and never less than today, might have evolved, and the foreign rule would have been like a hat too small for the head on which it sat, (and if pressed, it would have been blown up like the cover a kettle full of boiling water.) None could have stopped the process which was predetermined if the forces of freedom had put their shoulders to the war efforts from the beginning. Any government trying to interfere from the top, would have appeared as a saboteur, a Fifth Column element, while now it appears the other way round. The howl that is raised in the world press today against Indians, would have been raised against those who stood in the way to India's industrialisation or to anything happening in India which, while serving India's liberation, was meant to strengthen the Indian sector of the world war front.

A great npportunity was missed by the Himalayan blunders of the Congress and its vain overestimation of its own strength and cleverness. The Congress has served India badly. Whatever they say today is weak sophistry, half-truth and hypocrisy, attempt to hide their mistakes which they are unable to rectify for a false sense of prestige. They cannot undo the mischief they have done, even if they recognise it today. They are not even one in the desire to do so. They have never known to fight for freedom from the Britisn Government ; they have never been prepared to rouse the people to fight, because they fear and hate the masses except in the shape of religious listeners and blind worshippers. Therefore also they are today afraid of rousing the people to fight aggression, and as it cannot be done without the masses of the people, they won't fight it at all. They are a reactionary and bankrupt leadership. Their spell over the people - or what remains of it—is a morbid and religio-superstitious spell. Unless it is broken, India's teeming millions will never appear as so many human beings and upright men, but remain the bedrugged and sleeping giant who cannot stand up and fight, but only suffer and serve as bugbear in the eternal Congress game of bargaining for power with this or that foreign ruler.

Pandit Nehru konws it in his clear and calm moments. He should have more of them. He should for a while shun the charmed circle of Wardha with its monotonous hypnotism shrouding a scene where nothing but a profane game of party power-politics is going on, in an atmosphere utterly out of tune with contemporary history and the objective strivings of the Indian people. If he cannot free himself, he can never free others. And those who had hopes in him will have to deplore another "Man Overboard".

August 2, 1942.

THIS WAY TO FREEDOM

Manifesto of the Radical Democratic Party.

There can be hardly any doubt about the decision of the A. I. C. C. meeting in Bombay. It is practically certain that the Working Committee resolution will be endorsed, and the Mahatma will be requested to resume formally the supreme leadership of the Congress to launch a mass movement for enforcing the demand that the British should immediately withdraw from India.

It is not yet known what form the movement will take. But the Mahatma has declared that it will be an open rebellion, and that it will be short and swift. Presumably, the Mahatma is on the point of making a miracle which he so often promised, but never declared

Closely acquainted with the situation in the country and the mood of the masses, the Radical Democratic Party does not share the general nervousness caused by the Congress threat. We believe that the Congress leaders are bluffing, and that their bluff can be called. They should know that not many Congressmen are prepared to go to jail, and that mass jail going is not likely to frighten the British out of the country.

Something more serious must have to be undertaken. There is enough discontent in the country, to be exploited by unscrupulous demagogues. But any serious mass movement, resisting emergency measures or causing dislocation of war production, will be suppressed by the authorities. The only result will be greater sufferings and perhaps even sacrifice of innocent lives for saving the prestige and satisfying the vanity of bankrupt politicians. That is certainly not the way for India to come nearer to freedom.

Talking always about national freedom, the Congress leaders have been deceiving and misleading the country. Assuming that they are really concerned with the freedom of the Indian people, it cannot be said that they have proved themselves equal to the task of leading the people towards freedom. Freedom can never be had for asking. One must know how to attain it. Ever since the war broke out, the Congress leaders have committed one blunder after another, which not only made them politically bankrupt, but prevented India from availing of the great freedom, presented by the war.

Again with the name of freedom, the Congress leaders are politically to plunge the country into chaos and country In which would certainly result if they had their way. In this fateful moment, all fighters for Indian freedom must examine the record of the Congress leaders before following them in a new adventure, which is bound to be either futile or dangerous,

The Congress leaders say that they are full conscious of the risks involved in the step they are asking the country to take. But they argue, there is no other alternative. Because, unless India is free, she cannot defend herself against the imminent invasion. That sounds very plausible, and therefore the guileless may again be stampeded into a catastrophe.

But was it not possible for the Congress to avoid being driven into the present position? While still inside the Congress, we suggested an alternative line of positive action, which, if pursued, would have by now brought freedom practically within our reach. We advised against the resignation of the Congress Ministries. Even after that mistaken step was taken, we agitated for Congressmen returning to office and form coalition ministries together with the Muslim League. Today, every Congressman realises, although few may have the courage to speak out their mind, that had the policy recommended by us been adoptad, the conditions in the country would be entirely different. Constitutional limitations could not possibly prevent Provincial Ministries, backed up by the two major parties, from acting freely in order to do everything necessary to enthuse, mobilise, equip and otherwise prepare the people to face the coming danger of invasion.

Then came the August Offer to increase the number of the non-official Indian members of the Viceroy's Executive Council. That was an opportunity to rectify the previous mistake. We recommended acceptance of the offer with all its palpable inadequacies. A non-official Indian majority should be able to influence the policy of the Government, if the Indian members of the Government knew what they wanted and how to get at it. The proposed reconstitution of the Central Government could have been followed up by the restoration of constitutional regime in the composed on the basis of Congres-League coalition ministries.

Finally, Sir Stafford Cripps came with the Draft Declaration of the British War Cabinet. India's right of self-determination was fully recognised in that declaration. The interim arrangement indeed did not provide for a complete transfer of power. But that inadequacy was rather a matter of formal constitutional procedure. An Executive Council, composed of Indian leaders, of vision and ability, could have functioned as a War Cabinet, for all practical purposes.

Until the last moment of the Cripps negotiations, the Working Committee seems to have taken that view. Nevertheless, finally, yet another grave blunder was committed.

Does this record inspire confidence ? During these three fateful years, the Congress leaders have time and again failed to act as practical politicians. They talked of freedom, but they squandered away opportunities for the Indian people to win it. Having been thus frustrated by their own ineptitude, they now propose to plunge the country in chaos and confusion.

Blundering politicians should no longer be

allowed to gamble with the fate of the Indian people. Intelligent fighters for Indian freedom must raise their voice against the gamble. Can any sensible man imagine how the policy of the Congress will bring India anywhere near freedom ?

The Radical Democratic Party has all along indicated the road to freedom. The Congress leaders would not travel that road. They chose the blind-alley of negation. They may now commit political suicide Their desperate policy is not likely to achieve anything more spectacular.

But the Indian people must live, and therefore must take to the path of realism, far-sightedness and practical politics, opened up before them by the Radical Democratic Party.

The Cripps Offer has been reaffirmed on behalf of the British Government. All intelligent fighters for Indian freedom should demand immediate implementing of the offer, and help the establishment of a Government backed up by all the progressive and democratic elements in the public life of the country. In the given situation, nothing can prevent such a Government from functioning as a War Cabinet, provided that the right men will be chosen.

Practically all the political parties and other parties catastrophe. except the Congress, can be expected to join hands in this effort to save India from a possible catastrophe. But the initiative must come from the Government. Let the Viceroy immediately get in touch whith the leaders of politicalparties and other organisations which are opposed to the Congress policv, and secure their co-operation for implementing the Cripps Offer.

That will take the wind out of the Congress sail, The Congress leaders, Congress amuck, stung by the poignant feeling of frustration, will be isolated. And the country will be given a new leadership, capable of steering out of the present difficulties towards the goal of freedom which has been placed within its reach.

August 4, 1942

PROGRAMME FOR VICTORY

By Rajani Mukerjee

The war against the people declared by the Congress has not only interfered seriously with peace and order in the country, but has brought an amount of dislocation which has been most dangerously undermining the defensive strength of the country against imminent Fascist aggression. If the disastrous movement cannot be arrested, then nothing can prevent a Fascist occupation of the country. It is in the interest of Indian freedom that the suicidal movement must be resisted and suppressed. A determined and farsighted policy alone can achieve that.

But a determined and farsighted policy is conditional upon a correct understanding of the character of the movement launched by the Congress. This movement is not simply a protest against the arrest of the leaders. Nor is it the doing of unorganised hooligans. It can be properly appreciated if it is examined in the context of world events. Wherever the Axis

Powers have won, there they have had their agents to pave the way for them. The task of their Fifth Column is to undermine the power of resistance of the attacked country. The present movement launched by the Congress is a happened of what happened in Europe. It has very effectively and dangerously threatened the development of India's defensive power at a time when the war may extend into the very heart of India. The anti-Fascist professions of the Congress must not be taken seriously. The resolution drafted by Gandhi Ji, seized and released to the press by the Government, shows the inner working of the Congress mind.

The Congress leadership is clever enough to exploit and foment the discontent due to economic hardships. To make the Congress movement abortive, the wind must be taken out of its sail. Some immediate popular measures must be taken by the Government to inspire confidence. The necessary repression should be only part of a total policy of the Government. A democratic Government should be formed with Anti-Fascists without the least delay. It must proclaim a programme for extending substantial relief of the hard-pressed and poverty-stricken masses, and win their sympathy and support. Having thus won over the people, the Government will easily resist the growth and continuation of the Congress movement.

We suggest the following plan of action. (1) Governments at the centre and in the provinces should be formed only with avowed Anti-Fascists pledged to a comprehensive plan for mobilising the country's resources for winning the war. People with divided allegiance, with covert or overt sympathy for the Congress movement must be removed from positions. whatever these positions may be—a seat in the Treasury Bench or a Sub-Inspector of Police in a village thana. (2) There must be a stricter control of the press. Proprietors of papers which have suspended publication in protest against the arrest of the Congress leaders should be compelled to resume publication, with the liberty of preaching disaffection curtailed. The absurd position of newspapers indulging in anti-war propaganda and enjoying ministerial patronage should be ended by planning their publication. The Government is to carry on vigorous pro-war propaganda through its own press organs, radio and periodical literature in co-operation with anti-Fascist

popular Committee A committee to be appointed by the Central Government for every powers with powers to control the propaganda carried on through radio, press, National War Front, etc. The members of the Committee should be selected from anti-Fascist organisations, having no sympathy with the Congress movement (3) The Congress movement is to be nipped in the bud by the removal of such persons from their field of political activity who may otherwise spread the movement. (4) The economic crisis must be dealt with by the
of a plan for increasing the increasing power of the people and guaranteed, them a better standard of living. The plan is to include (a) extensive industrialisation, increasing output of war meterials and providing employment for the unemployed; (b) increase in the real wages of the increase; class through the grant of war bonus, dearness allowances etc. so that not only will the pre-war standard of living be guaranteed, but the prospect of better living be materialised; (c) in cases of factory and mill-owners themselves closing down their plants in sympathy with the Congress movement, strong action should be taken and the enterprises confiscated

and run by the Government; (d) relief should be immediately extended to the peasantry not merely by stopping the payment of old rents and debts, but by remission of current rents and debts and interests thereon. Such other measures should be introduced in the tenancy law as may enthuse peasants to defend the country against foreign invaders; (e) where the peasantry has been ruined by natural causes. monetary help should be immediately extended and cultivation of substitute crops should be encouraged (f) the sale of those crops to be organised so as not to allow the real growers to be deprived of a large part of income by the unscrupulous middlemen; (g) facilities for cheap credit and introduction of scientific methods of agriculture to be provided

5. Attention to be paid by the Government to the most pressing problem of the moment, the continuous supply of food, which can be guaranteed with success only if (a) the Government with the help of popular anti-Fascist organisations, immediately open stores in local markets for retail sale of commodities at controlled prices under strict vigilance of officials and non-officials; (b) the management and control of the stores will be taken over by a joint committee with

equal representation of the Government and the consumers; (c) supply of commodities should be regulated and controlled by a hierarchy of similar committees with a Provincial Committee at the top; (d) in all matters regarding the change of controlled prices, control committees should have a decisive voice; (e) rationing of the commodities which run short must be introduced.

These popular measures will bring great relief to the people who will thus be won over by the Government and will naturally become more sympathetic towards it and its activities. This psychological change will enthuse the masses of the country, and they will, and of their own necessity for preserving the newly Russia:: privileges, resist foreign aggression. The history of Europe lying prostrate at the feet of triumphant Fascism, and the history of the successful reistance to Fascim by England, Russia and China should bid good-bye to the illusion that a regular army alone can stem the tidal wave of Fascist aggression. A People's Army alone can put up that successful resistance to the organised death and destruction of Fascism. A dissatisfied and discontended people, smarting under all kinds of grievances, deprived of all happiness in life, and therefore seeking an opportunity to overthrow the existing order of things, is a standing menace to the security of the country. This standing menace has to be removed, if India should have a powerful People's Army which can, in co-operation with the regular army, defeat Fascist aggression and help saving world freedom and democracy.

TOWARDS SOCIALIST COMMONWEALTH

Now that the end of the war is in sight, and there is no room for any serious doubt but how it will end, the future of India has to be visualised in the perspective of the inter-relation of her internal forces. Who is going to settle the fate of India? Most nationalists, whose politics is determined by no more noble ideal than the spitefulness of the slave and racial animosity, expected the Axis Powers to deliver India from the yoke of British Imperialism. All of them may or may not have been organisationally associated with the Fifth Column of the Axis Powers. Many of them would not consciously work for a change of masters. Some of them may have entertained the romantic belief that out of the chaos resulting from an Axis invasion a free India would arise. Whatever may be the difference, they all hoped that victory of the Axis Powers would present India with the chance to be free. That hope is now dashed. Therefore, interesting developments may be expected in the nationalist politics of India. And the reaction of the British Government to those developments most probably will be equally interesting.

The perverse hope of the imbecile that the deliverance of India will result from the victory of the forces whose avowed purpose is to enslave the whole world, is dashed. But this war has brought India much nearer to freedom than can be imagined by narrow-minded nationalism. Self-reliant fighters for real freedom never believed that it can come as a gift. Great changes take place, defying the wishes of men who may appear to be ruling the destiny of the world. This war heralded a period of great changes. It was bound to remake the world. India, being a part of the world, could not possibly be left out of that imperious process.

Freedom, of course, never comes as a gift. But the opportunity may be missed by those to whom it is presented. Therefore, if after this war India cannot be free, that will be mostly because of her own fault. As soon as the war is over, India will have to exercise the right of self-determination which has already been pledged to her not by the generosity of anybody, but under the terrific impact of the epoch-making changes which are being experienced by the whole world. Therefore, it is time to raise the question, to whom does the right of self-determination belong? In other words, who are going to settle the fate of India?

The Axis Powers are out of the run. British Imperialism as an agency of subjugation will not survive the war. But that will very largely depend on what will happen ni India. Isolationist nationalism must also go if India is to celebrate the disappearance of British Imperialism. Because, the economic relation between two countries, so closely associated for such a long time, cannot be sundered without harming both. The disappearance of Imperialism will be beneficial for both the countries if that relation is raised on a higher leval of voluntary co-operation. That perspective of a closer association and mutual dependance of the various members of the human community is repugnant to isolationist nationalism. The aspiration of the latter, which may not mean economic liberation of the bulk of the Indian people, is bound to have a reaction in Britain, and may delay the disappearance of Imperialism.

The isolationist nationalist opposition to a continuation of the relation between the two countries even on the higher level of voluntary association and mutual co-operation will have more than a sentimental reason. The impact of the war has not been felt uniformly in all the countries. It has been left much less in India than in Britain. Consequently, while the latter has already progressed far enough on the path of epoch-making changes precipitated by this war, the social and economic structure of India has remained practically unaffected. The danger of invasion now being out of the realm of practical possibilities, the internal life of India is not likely to experience any change during the remaining period of the war.

It is quite conceivable that victory will bring Britain quite near to Socialism The silent revolution going on in that country under the impact of the war cannot possibly be scotched by victory. The association with such a post-war Britain will unavoidably have in India repercussions which cannot be welcomed to the orthodox nationalism wedded to primitive capitalist, if not actually feudal, social and economic ideas. The reactionary core of isolationist nationalism will then stand retaining Relation with a Britain in the throes of socialist reconstruction, although possibly still retaining the present political institutions, including the "Impire", will be positively dangerous for the reactionary forces which constitute the social background of isolationist Indian nationalism. That relation will be liberating foı the Indian people, but it will be disruptive for those who wish to become the rulers of the country in the place of the British Imperialists.

The possible development on the above lines is not altogether without an analogy. The history of the Asiatic peoples subjugated by the Tzarist Imperialism is the case in point. Of Course, the analogy will not be complete unless Britain experiences a full-fledged revolution. But in different periods of history, revolution may not have identical forms or travel a uniform path. In any case, the point is that all the reactionary elements (landlords, priests and pre-capitalist traders) opposed the incorporation of their countries in the Soviet Union theirs was a cry for national freedom. They would not be subordinated to "Red Imperialism" after the disappearance of the Tzar's Empire. Fortunately for the peoples who had experienced the misfortune of Tzarist domination, and also for the world as a whole, the reactionaries masquerading as national liberators did not succeed. The result of their failure was the liberation of the peoples of those countries.

The post-war relation between Britain and India may not immediately be raised to such a high level. But the far-reaching changes in the social and economic structure of the Metropolitan country will necessarily influence its relation with other parts of the "Empire". In other words, the structure of the "Empire" as a whole will be undergoing a change. Consequently, the epoch-making liberating changes which did not come to India during the war, will eventually be experienced by her also. The nationalist ideal of an autarchic capitalist economy on the basis of galvanised feudal relations will become a dream never to be realised. But the disruption of that dream will bring real liberation for the Indian people. The process may be slow. Forces pulling in the contrary direction will still remain in operation. But on the whole, the perspective is one of masses. The decisive factor, however, either to retard or accelerate it, will be the relation of forces in India.

A free play of those forces, therefore, alone can create conditions for a depends reconstruction which will be beneficial for the British people and liberating for the Indian masses. That will, of course, be determined by the dynamics of the inter-relation of forces in India. But the British Government happens to be one of those forces and until now is the decisive force. In other words, it primarily depends on the British Government whether the liberating forces in the political life of India will be allowed to assert themselves on the situation. Until now, the British Government has operated as an obstructive agency. In the near future it may become the instrument of a dying Imperialism. As such, it will stand on the way to the elevation of the relation between two countries on the higher level of mutual benefit. As a matter of fact, the standard-bearer of dying Imperialism may be the patron of isolationist nationalism. The dubious policy of the British Government, practised on the specious plea of democracy ever since the beginning of this war, has been tending to this direction. Its consummation will deprive India of the benefit of victory over the Axis Powers. On the other hand, it will be a reaction to the influencing changes experienced in England.

British Imperialism, as far as India is concerned, expresses itself through British industrialists having a stake in the economic life of this country. They are as much interested in maintaining the semi-feudal Indian status quo as the Indian traders and industrialists who are the power behind the nationalist movement. That is a new relation of forces—rather an identify of interests, which may settle the fate of India. How far that relation has been influencing the policy of the present Government of this country is a question of far-reaching interest. Indeed, it is the crucial question which must be raised and asked by those who are moved by the ideal of real freedom, a freedom which is not to be attained at the cost of others.

British industrialists in this country may not be any more enamoured with the relation with a socialist Britain than their Indian blood-brothers. They may be sentimental about "home". But if the home will be on fire, it would be equally natural for them to be anxious about the security of their new home. The world thus may witness a re-cnactment of the American revolution, the actual possessors of the colonies revolting against the mother country.

This is not a more fantasy. All these may be remote possibilities. But when the period of post-war reconstruction is drawing near, it is necessary to visualise all the problems that it may contain.

This highly interesting possibility of Englishmen having stakes in the economic life of this country, championing the cause of India becoming completely independent of a socialist or semi-socialist Britain, is only touched here in order to make the point that the present Government still remains the decisive factor of the situation. If it realises even now to which dangerous direction its policy of drift, justified by a concern for democracy, has been heading, it will be able to contribute not only to the establishment of freedom, which has accrued to India as a result of this war, but will also make a substantial contribution to the transformation of the Empire into a real commonwealth of free peoples. The chance for rendering such great service to the cause of human liberation and progress is seldom given to any Government. Will those who hold the destinies of India in their hands in this critical movement be able to rise up to the occasion?

The task is not at all so complicated as it is made out to be. The approach to the problem is clearly indicated by the very concept of democracy. If it is to be a rule of the people, let it be a rule of the people. Don't allow a vocal minority, vocal because it is powerful, to usurp the rights and prerogatives of the people. The right of self-determination belongs to the peoples. They should be given the opportunity to assert that right. That is democracy. Anything else, even though done on the pretext of democracy, is betrayal of democracy.

The change in the tide of the war will before long cause interesting developments in the political life of the country. The strategy and tactics of nationalist politics were determined by the assumption that the Axis Powers were going to win. As soon as that assumption will no longer be tanable, the strategy and tactics of nationalism will necessarily change. It will become practical politics. Petainism having suffered a shipwreck also in India, Darlans will appear before long on the power scene of this country. The door to the place of power has been graciously left open for those prodigals to walk in as soon as they would repent. Is power, then, going to be transferred to the Indian Darlans? What will be the graciously . for such a betrayal of Indian democracy and abject surrender on the part of the Government against which the Darlans of tomorrow were in open rebellion until yesterday, The obvious retort to this question will be: Who also is there to take over the responsibility? The democratic reply to this obviously prajudiced question is: Let the Indian people decide.

The democracic procedure is an election. The Indian people should be given the chance to elect the Government of the country. The result of that election will be government by the fact of those who will be actually in power before and at the time of the election. Who are to compose the interim government? That is the crucial question.

Given the experience of these dangerous years of war there should be no mistake on the part of the present rulers of the country in answering the question. But let them be guided by the conventional democratic procedure. None of the existing major political parties can even claim to represent the Indian people. All of them together cannot make that claim. Because they only represent the present electorate which constitutes only a small minority. Therefore, an interim:government which can guarantee that a general election, in which the entir people will participate, will have the desired result, should be composed on the basis of other standards. The obvious standard is proved adhesion to democratic principles. Scrutinise the programme of all the existing major parties, and you will find that democratic freedom for the people at large is not visualised in any of them. Among progressively-minded people, for whom freedom is not only a slogan, there cannot be much disagreement about the measures to be taken to promote the welfare of the bulk of the Indian people. A government composed of people who are categorically committed to those measures will be the only democratic government possible under the given circumstances.

That will be an interim arrangement. The main function of the provisional government will be to educate the people about their rights, and give them the opportunity as soon as possible to record their verdict standard the future of the country. Those who have proved their competence standard: by their behaviour during these fateful years of war may not measure up to the conventional standard of responsibility. But the experience of this war has shown that saviours can come from the most unexpected quarters. Russian Communists are today respected as allies. But until hardly two years ago, even the present rulers of England and America did not believe that anything good could even come from the Bolsheviks. Even their competence was doubted. Not a few military bigwigs in England and America believed that Hitler's war machine would go through the Soviet Union like a knife through a lump of butter. Experience has destroyed all that prejudice. Why allow prejudice to linger still in this country, and thus betray Indian democracy the name or democracy?

The Red Army, a creation of revolution, has done many miracles. It is the object of general admiration today. But it is not realised by many that it has won the war for India. If Hitler's war machine could break' through the Caucasus, today India would be caught in a gigantic Axis pince. Thus, Indian freedom has been guaranteed by revolution. Will it then not be an irony if the benefit of the Red Army winning the battle for India will go to Indian Fascism? And that exactly will happen if the present rulers of this country will not get over their prejudices and free themselves from other evil influences, so that the Indian people can have the opportunity of shaping their own destiny, so that right of self-determination may be actually available to them.

PART THREE

RESOLUTIONS

ON INTERNATIONAL SITUATION

The All-India Conference of the League of Radical Congressmen, held at Dehradun on June 2 and 3, 1940, endorses as correct the analysis of the international situation made by the Central Executive Committee of the League in its meeting held in October 1939, and published by the League in the form of a thesis under the title "India and War." On the basis of a review of events occurring in the meantime, this Conference affirms that the international situation has developed generally as anticipated in the Thesis of the C. E. C., though the development has taken place in the direction which appeared to be less likely at the time of the meeting of the C. E. C. The League of Radical Congressmen is still of the opinion that a triumph of Fascism and the establishment of its domination, directly or indirectly, all over Europe will mean a serious setback for the forces of revolution throughout the world, and will constitute a great menace for the Union of Socialist Soviet Republics. Therefore, without desiring the victory of the Imperialist Powers, to-day engaged in an armed conflict with Nazi Germany it is not permissible for the fighters for freedom, democracy and progress to act in such a way as may contribute to the imminent victory of Fascism. The activity of Radical Congressmen will be determined by this consideration. On the other hand, this Conference declares that the masses of the Indian people must be mobilised for freedom to be undertaken by availing of an opportunity which may be presented before long by the possible development of the international situation.

As regards the conflict in Europe, this Conference is of the opinion that the imminent danger of the Fascisation of entire Europe can be prevented only by the intervention of the U. S. S. R. It is due to the British policy of isolating the U. S. S. R. that Europe has been present into the present disastrous conflict. An Anglo-Franco-Soviet anti-aggression pact would have prevented the German invasion of Poland and Europe might have been spared the present ordeal. This Conference is of the opinion that that fatal blunder can still be rectified, and the willing cooperation of the U. S. S. R. enlisted for a genuinely anti-fascist campaign. The Soviet Government has already condemned the Nazi invasion of Holland and Belgium. If England and France really wish to check the victorious march of Fascism, they should abandon the anti-Soviet policy and immediately resume the negotiations, the breakdown of which encouraged Germany to invade Poland.

This Conference unconditionally supports the foreign policy of the Soviet Government, and believe that the policy was warranted not only for the defence of the Soviet Union, but to check the advance of Fascism eastwards, and also to guarantee the future of the forces of revolution.

This Conference deprecates that alarmist propaganda about a foreign invasion of India, and condemns it as a pretext for arousing an anti-Soviet sentiment. It is deplorable that such a tendencious propaganda is being carried on by Congressmen and in the Congress press organs. To talk of defending India, while she still remains a British possession, is shameful, because it betrays the preverse desire to defend the slavery of the Indian masses.

Since the conflict in Europe continued even after Nazi aggression eastwards was checked by the clever Soviet foreign policy, and consequently the present fierce clash has been precipitated, those concerned with the freedom of India cannot but be indifferent to the fate of the parties invoved in the ruinous conflict. The situation has developed in such a way as makes an early peace no longer desirable. Because an early peace now will be a peace dictated by Nazi Germany or a peace sought by Nazified England and France.

That is the danger which threatens the world today. Since an indefinite continuation of the war will be suspen- ruinous for both the parties, suspension of hostilities on the background of a Nazified Europe fighters for the moment to be the more likely perspective. A far-sighted, well-calculated, realistic plan of action on the part of the fighters for Indian freedom may change that gloomy perspective. By striking the decisive blow for India's freedom in the opportune moment, we shall prevent the reorganisation of the forces of international counter-revolution under the domination of Nazi Germany.

Resolution of the Conference of the League of Radical Congressmen, Dehradun, June 2 and 3, 1940.

INDIA AND WAR

The recent developments in the international situation can no longer permit an attitude of neutrality towards the war on the part of progressive and freedom-loving elements in the world. The international part of Fascism, which is taking place with the active attitude or passive connivance of the ruling classes of many a country, can be arrested only by a mobilization of all democratic masses in a genuine anti-Fascist struggle. It is, therefore, the considered opinion of this Conference that the Indian people should actively participate in the anti-Fascist struggle.

This participation cannot be made conditional upon any declaration of Indian Independence to be made by the British Government. In the first place, such a declaration cannot be made by the British Government. And, secondly, even if any declaration is made, it can be only of a formal charactern which, cannot confer any rights on the Indian people Independence is not a thing which can be granted by one nation to another by a declaration. It has to be fought for and won as a result of revolutionary mass action.

The fight for Indian Freedom cannot be isolated from the larger fight for human freedom. It is only by actively participating in the latter fight that the Indian people can take effective steps towards the securing of their own freedom from the shackles of British Imperialism. India could have made a large contribution towards the growth of human freedom and the destruction of the dark forces of Fascism, which today are seeking to destroy it, by striking a decisive blow for the destruction of Imperialism. The given situation in the country does not allow that to be done immediately with any hope of success. The task, therefore, is to preserve the popular forces and prepare them for decisive action on a more favourable opportunity which may ensue before long.

The conditions for this cannot be created by the present policy of non-cooperation which has resulted in a complete stalemate and demoralization and degeneration of the political life in the country. They can be neither created by following a policy of war resistance, which is neither possible nor desirable. War resistance on the contrary will prove definitely harmful, to the interest of the world struggle against Fascism, and therefore to the Indian struggle for freedom. Nor can they be created by a tham "struggle" of the Satyacraha type which always ends in a demoralization and destruction of the forces of struggle. Under the given circumstances, active participation in war is the only course open to the Indian people. They will not be thereby helping British Imperialism, but will on the contrary be weakening it by developing and strengthening the anti-Fascist forces in England and Europe. They will be also thereby working for their own freedom, for the opportunities created by the active participation, in the anti-Fascist struggle, can be utilized for carrying to a successful end the anti-Imperialist struggle. This conference therefore appeals to the Congress to straightforwardly and honestly adopt this course, which under the given circumstances is the only course that can be adopted with advantage to the interest of the national struggle. This Conference also calls upon the Congress to address an appeal to all the anti-Fascist forces in the world, more particularly the Soviet Union, in order that a world anti-Fascist Bloc may be built up for the complete destruction of Fascism.

Resolution of the Bombay Provincial Conference of the League of Radical Congressmen, July 29, 1940.

ON WAR

Reaffirming generally the original thesis on "India and War" and the resolution of the All-India Conference held in the beginning of June, this meeting of the Central Executive Committee of the Radical League declares that, in view of subsequent developments, the present war must now be characterised as anti-Fascist war.

This conclusion about the character of the war is determined *inter alia* by two outstanding events in the process of the realignment of international forces, and also of the social forces with national boundaries.

One of those events is the conclusion of the Triple Alliance of the Fascist Powers, which represents a revival of the Fascist Anti-Comintern International, disrupted for a time by the clever stroke of Soviet diplomacy, namely, the Soviet-German non-aggression pact. The Triple Alliance is primarily directed against the Soviet Union, which consequently can be expected to join the war before long. Another repercussion of the Fascist Pact has been to stimulate the efforts for Anglo-Soviet and Soviet-American rapprochement, which may eventually result in the formation of an anti-Fascist alliance.

The second event which decisively influences the influences the war is the political eclipse of Chamberlain and the prospect of the Conservative Party disintegrating under the impact of the democratic forces on the political life of Britain.

Chamberlain's policy of appeasement represented the interests of British Imperialism. The very outbreak of the war, therefore, was contrary to those interests. Therefore, from the very beginning, the war was not an imperialist war. But so long as Chamberlain continued to be a member of the British Government, and under his leadership the Conservative Party constituted the majority of the Parliament, the possibility of a revival of the Imperialist policy of appeasement remained. In the presence of that possibility, the war could not be called an anti-Fascist war in the fullest sense.

The retirement of Chamberlain, and Churchill's assumption of the leadership of the Conservative

Party indicate the disappearance of that dangerous possibility. The formal Conservative majority in the Parliament still remains but for all practical purposes, it has become inoperative. That proves that genuinely anti-Fascist, democratic forces, have come to dominate the situation. The change in the relation of social forces is bound to determine not only the purpose with which the war is waged, but also how it shall be waged. It is bound to become a people's war, waged with the purpose of destroying the menace to popular freedom and popular welfare everywhere.

In the period of transition, no possibility is altogether excluded. The development of the present conflict and its eventual outcome will, therefore, be ultimately determined by the operation of the democratic and progressive forces throughout the world. We in India must shoulder our share of the responsibility.

If, thanks to the supreme effort on the part of the democratic and progressive forces everywhere, the war ends in a crushing defeat of the Fascist Powers, the world as a whole will enter a new period of social reconstruction. Enlightened and far-sighted members even of the British ruling class are beginning to realise that the way cannot be expected to be followed by the restoration of the *status quo ante bellum*. The totalitarian war waged by the Fascists is bound to compel far-reaching democratisation of war efforts in the other camp. In Britain, the process has already gone far enough. The same thing is bound to happen also in India, provided that the democratic and progressive forces in this country will be able to assert themselves on the situation. Radical changes in the relation of forces, compelled by the exigencies of war, can be expected to remain in operation even afterwards. In course of the international struggle against Fascism, the forces of popular freedom will gain upper hand in their respective countries, and, having defeated Fascism, will not certainly abandon the position of vantage.

Finally, India's relation to the war is becoming even closer, owing to the rapid development of events in the Balkans and in the Mediterranean. Having failed to reduce Britain to sue for peace on the basis of the recognition of the Nazification of Europe, the Fascist Powers are succeed· a large-scale attack upon the outposts of the British Empire. The perspective of the British Empire disappearing need not disturb us; but, if victorious, the Fascist Powers cannot be expected to stop at that. If they succeed in penetrating the Near Eastern countries, there will be nothing to prevent their invading India and they will not conquer India to set her free.

In view of this immediate danger, as well as for the considerations regarding the character of this war as a whole, the C. E. C. of the Radical League once again declares that the progressive and democratic forces in India cannot be indifferent to the outcome of the war, and therefore must participate in it actively for promoting the cause of Indian freedom and also to contribute to the victory of the progressive and democratic forces throughout the world.

Resolution adopted by the Central Executive Committee of the L. R. C. at its meeting held at Meerut on 26th and 27th October, 1940.

ON RELATION WITH THE CONGRESS.

Having regard for the character and the most probable outcome of the present war, from the very beginning, the Radical League was in favour of India participating in it, voluntarily and purposefully. For a whole year, the League tried its best to persuade the Congress leadership to abandon its futile and harmful politics of negation in favour of a realistic and far-sighted policy. The Congress leaders have never been opposed to progressive in war on principle. Indeed, they even went to the extent of rejecting Gandhist pacifism, which they had professed previously for years. But actuated with the spirit of bargaining for nominal concessions, they Resolution,! larger issues, and acted in the most narrow-minded and short-sighted manner. The failure to secure some nominal concessions for the offered co-operation placed their prestige at stake. For the sake of group prestige, they made a fetish of non-violence in which they do not believe. Restored as the dictator of the Congress, the Mahatma compelled the A. I. C. C. to pass the Bombay Resolution, which offered indirect help to Fascism.

Being decidedly of the opinion that the victory of the Fascist Powers would seriously prejudice the cause of Indian Freedom, the Radical Congressmen could not possibly approve, even tacitly, the policy of the Congress leaders.

Radicals thought that energetic anti-Fascist propaganda would gradually enable the rank and file of the organisation to realise the harmfulness of the policy pursued by the leaders, and to force a change. But the authoritarian machinery of the Gandhist leadership would not allow us to exercise our democratic right. Radical Congressmen were expelled from the organisation or otherwise penalised for anti-Fascist activities and for criticising the pro-Fascist policy of the leadership Therefore, Congress membership has become incompatible with anti-Fascist conviction, if it is to be acted upon. Determined to act according to their conviction, Radicals can no longer carry on the struggle for freedom effectively, while remaining inside the Congress.

An organisation with any internal democracy, and virtually betraying the ideals of freedom, democracy and progress in the most critical moment, cannot possibly be an instrument for gaining democratic freedom.

On the other hand, the futility of Gandhist politics and the authoritarianism of a reactionary leadership have for some years been disrupting the mass basis of the Congress. The pronounced Hindu-religious prejudices of Gandhism have alienated the Muslim masses; other large sections of the population have also drifted away. Consequently, to-day, the Congress does not command the confidence of a majority of the nation. Whatever may be its profession, in practice, it has discarded nationalism in favour of Gandhism, which is the ideology of reaction in every walk of life.

Two-and-half years of ministerialism, followed by a year's political passivity, has destroyed the Congress as a mass organisation. It exists only on paper, and reaction exclusively as a bureaucratic machinery controlled by a numerous group of pseudo-Gandhists. The machinery does not allow the least initiative from below. Consequently, the primary membership of the Congress has been reduced to a political nonentity.

If the Congress still retains a measure of popularity, that is entirely due to its Mahatma Cult, which naturally appeals to the backward masses. That popularity may be utilised for reactionary purposes, but it is no asset for a progressive political movement, much less can it be the foundation of a party to lead tne Indian people's struggle for freedom.

In order to have the freedom to act according to their conviction, and with the object of providing a new rallying ground for the politically advanced elements gradually getting dissatisfied with the reactionary outlook and practical futility of Gandhist politics, Radical Congressmen should forthwith undertake the task of organising a new political party. For years, we worked with the purpose of building up a revolutionary party of the Indian people on the basis of the masses mobilised under the banner of the Congress. The deterioration of the internal life of the Congress, together with its present highly objectionable policy, compel us to strike out a new path.

Therefore, it is resolved that the Radical League shall henceforth function as an independent political party with the name "Radical Democratic People's Party." It is further resolved that a Special Conference be convened to announce formally the inauguration of the party and adopt its programme, formulated on the basis of the declaration of the object of the League of Radical Congressmen. Meanwhile, all Radicals shall resign from executive posts and elected committees of the Congress, because they cannot share the responsibility for executing the present Congress policy.

Resolution of the C. E. C. of the L. R. C., Meerut, October 26-27, 1940.

ON NATIONAL DEMOCRATIC UNION

One after another, leading Congressmen are finding their way to voluntary imprisonment. They may get a morbid satisfaction in the doubtful glory of cheap martyrdom. But the feeling among those who are not carried away by appearances is of keen disappointment. It is difficult to help feeling that, in these fateful days, the popular trust is being betrayed by those in whom it was placed. If the Congress leaders believe that their responsibility to the country is discharged by simply running away from it, they are mistaken.

The inconsistency and selfishness of the attitude are glaring. The world is wanted to understand India's case. While sympathy the world to come to their aid, the Congress leaders refuse to have the slightest concern for the troubles of the world. By a curious process of reasoning. they have come to the Conclusion that the refusal to raise a finger to save the world from going up in flames is the surest way of winning the sympathy of the world for the cause of Indian freedom.

But the problems facing the country cannot be forgotten even in the midst of this atmosphere created by whipping up artificial emotion. The problems still remain there, to be solved by those who can grasp them properly and find a correct approach to them. They will be solved, and our country will come out of the crisis with flying colours, as soon as others will have the courage to do what the Congress leaders failed to do.

The first thing that the Congress leaders failed to do was to realise that no country can stand aloof from a struggle, on the outcome of which depends the future of the entire world. Their second failure was the refusal to recognise that India was involved in that struggle, whether she wanted it or not. Their third mistake was to bargain for some verbal concessions, when it was within their power to make substantial advances by their own efforts towards the goal of freedom. Their fourth failure was to lay down the responsibility to the people for no purpose other than to make a protest, which they hoped would enable them to derive a hard bargain. Having taken up an untenable position by virtue of a series of failures, they were compelled to move willy-nilly towards the present position of political suicide. Leaving the bankrupt politicians to their fate, others must apply themselves to the task of rectifying those mistakes

The world crisis and its unavoidable repercussions in India have placed her in a position to work out her own destiny by participating in the common struggle for the future of humanity. It is silly to make a grievance of the natural reluctance of the British Government to part with power while failing to see that power is there for the Indian peeple to win it, if they only know how to do so. The British Government can get men and money for the purposes of the war. But powers waging a totalitarian war cannot be confronted, much less defeated, with men and money alone. The energy and determination, and the will to victory, of the entire people must be mobilised for the purpose. That cannot be done through the present war efforts of the Government. These efforts are utterly inadequate for combating the widespread Fascist sympathy and whispering pro-Fascist propaganda under the cover of nationalism or anti-imperialism. Complete democratisation of the war efforts is urgently needed for combating this grave danger, which will seriously undermine the striking as well as the defensive power of India. Systemtic anti-Fascist propaganda conducted non-officially is essential for the purpose of enlisting voluntary and purposeful support for the war.

Popular representatives can occupy positions of power immediately in the provinces where Congressmen have deserted the trust placed in them by the electorate. There is a Congress majority in the Legislatures of those provinces. That technical difficulty, however, can be easily overcome by an agreement between the executive authority and the popular responsibility willing to shoulder the responsibility of office. It is too late for such patchwork as interim ministries. The situation must radically change. There must be a complete realignment of forces. Emergency Ministries should be formed in the provinces without constitutional governments, firstly, for the task of democratising the war efforts, and secondly for preparing the country for a general election as soon as possible. Given popular ministries, which will act according to the interests of the people, and the activities of the Radical Democratic Party to mobilise the masses in the struggle against Fascism for their own freedom, the outcome of the general election will be pre-determined.

With these considerations, this Inaugural Conference of the Radical Democratic Party resolves to strive for the formation of a National Democratic Union composed of all the parties and groups opposed to the futile policy of the Congress. While making this resolution, the Conference appeals to the Muslim League, the Hindu Mahasabha, the Democratic Sawrajya Party, the Independent Labour Party, and all other democratic and popular bodies to join the proposed National Democratic Union. The constituents of the Union will retain tullest independence as regards all controversial issues, to be settled in due time. They are expected to act jointly only for the object for which the Union will be formed.

Realising the gravity of the danger of Fascism, the Radical Democratic Party is determined to fight it, irrespective of the attitude of others. But this Conference deplores the policy of drift pursued by the Government, warns against complacency and wishful thinking, and emphasises the urgency of active co-operation of all who, in the first place, wish the defeat of the Fascist Powers.

Resolution of the Inaugural Conference of the Radical Democratic Party, December 20/22, 1940.

PARTICIPATION IN WAR EFFORTS

It is resolved that, while striving for the formation of the National Democratic Union and association of popular representatives with pronounced anti-Fascist conviction with the Government in the Centre as well as in the provinces, the Radical Democratic Party shall find ways and means for mobilising Radical opinion in support of the war against Fascism.

The district units of the party organisation throughout the country are hereby directed:

1. To set up Anti-Fascist Propaganda Committees, with the co-operation of the democratic and progressive elements in the locality;

2. To co-operate with the war efforts of the Government by carrying on anti-Fascist organisation n every possible manner;

3. To join the War Committees and Civic Guards wherever and whenever local conditions will be found suitable for fruitful activities.

Resolution of the Inaugural Conference of the Radical Democratic Party, December 20-22, 1940.

MESSAGE TO BRITISH DEMOCRACY

The Radical Democratic Party concluded its Inaugural Conference by resolving to send the following message to British Democracy. The resolution to send the message was moved by M. N. Roy, and was adopted with acclamation.

Fellow-fighters against Fascism !

The outbreak of the war in Europe has created a severe crisis in the political life of India. Nationalist preoccupations and concern for group prestige prevent the major parties and outstanding leaders from seeing that the outcome of the war will make or mar the future of the entire world. Nevertneless, there are others who are fully conscious of the gravity of the situation, and do not therefore approve of the short-sighted policy pursued by the Congress. Whatever may be its motives or justification, in practice the policy is antagonistic to the striving of the Indian people for democratic freedom and social progress. Therefore, it must be combatted by the democratic and progressive forces in the public life of India.

The Radical Democratic Party has been formed with that purpose. The Inaugural Conference of the Party sends its heartiest greetings to British Democrary, and offers fullest co-operation in the fight against Fascism.

Let it be mentioned at the same time that the Government of India must change its policy, if the genuinely anti-Fastist elements in this country are to assert themselves on the situation effectively with the purpose of mobilising popular support for the war.

Much time has been wasted in wooing the narrow-minded nationalist and communalist leaders, whose behaviour in this crisis is determined very largely by Fascist sympathy. In this crisis, pacifism also operates as an indirect ally of the violent system of Fascism.

There should be no more delay in reinforcing the Government through the association of genuinely anti-Fascist popular elements. As soon as that is done, our Party will be able to marshal the Indian Democracy, to stand shoulder to shoulder with British Democracy, with the conviction, courage and determination necessary for winning the war against the deadliest enemy of human freedom, we fare and progress.

EMERGENCY MINISTRIES

The Bengal Provincial Conference of the Radical Democratic Party endorses the resolution adopted by the Inaugural Conference of the Party held in Bombay, and resolves to mobilise all the resources of the provincial party organisation for enlisting popular support for our line of action.

This Conference is of the opinion that a way

out of the present crisis has been indicated by the formation of the National Democratic Union as contemplated in the resolution of the Inaugural Conference of our Party. This Conference is of the opinion that the recommendations made in the statement issued by the conference of independent public men held in Calcutta recently are based on a practical and realistic appreciation of the situation. Therefore, this Conference resolves to help the building up of the National Democratic Union as a powerful popular factor, so that its recommendations could be acted upon without any further delay. Although the programme of the Democratic Union is receiving a growing volume of support, many people still seem to be paralysed by the obstructionist policy of the Congress and are still content with expressing the pious wish that there should be some understanding between the Congress and the Government. Assuming that the Satyagraha Campaign by the Congress is based upon a sincere belief in non-violence, one cannot see how the Congress can ever co-operate with war efforts. That being the case, it is a vain hope that the Congress will change its policy, unless it discards the creed of non-violence, which it cannot do so long as Gandhian principles determine its policy. Moreover, the attitude of the Congress, and particularly the Satyagraha Movement, has not for any practical purpose prevented India's participation in the war. Therefore, there is no reason why those who advocate India's voluntary participation in the war should not be regarded as the representatives of the Indian people, and as such should not shoulder the responsibility of conducting the present administration of the country and shaping the destiny of the Indian people. This Conference is decidedly of the opinion that the formation of Emergency Ministries, supported by all who take a practical and realistic view of the present situation and its potentialities, is the crying need of the day. Because the association of popular representatives with the government of the country, in the centre as well as in the provinces, will enable India to shoulder her responsibility with honour and credit, therefore, this Conference resolves to secure popular support for this demand.

Resolution of the Bengal Provincial Conference of the Radical Democratic Party, January 18 and 19, 1941.

WAR EFFORT IN INDIA

The success or failure of the war efforts in India will be determined by the attitude of the popular masses. To guarantee success, it is necessary to secure their voluntary support. The implications of this war and its relation with the interests of the Indian people should be clearly explained to them. No purpose can be served by the efforts to raise a little money and antagonize the people in consequence. It only helps the anti-war propaganda, and in the long run the Fascists. To counteract the potential Fascists in India, anti-Fascist propaganda must include the demand for the protection of the masses against war-profiteering. The money necessary for the prosecution of the war should be raised from those who are making profits out of the war industries.

In view of the fact that the operation of the war efforts machinery, together with other causes, has created suspicion and prejudices in the mind of the people, the War Committees and officials should step back and let popular organizations take their places. Eventually, the War Committees themselves should be reconstructed on a popular basis.

The Civic Guards cannot do anything if they are kept isolated from the people. In the first place, they should form the vanguard of the people's fight against native Fascism. They must be given some political education, as are the Home Guards in England; otherwise, they can do nothing against the insidious anti-war propaganda. They should be entrusted with the task of carrying on anti-Fascist propaganda, and the necessary literature must be supplied to them. They must be brought in touch with the people through day-to-day welfare activities.

Popular organizations and independent persons should be given all facilities for carrying on a systematic anti-Fascist campaign, and a substantial portion of the funds raised by the War Committees should be spent for that purpose.

The Conference recommends that funds for financing war efforts, particularly, for building up industries, should be raised through the floatation of loans. It was decided to forward a copy of the resolution to the Provincial War Board with the offer of all co-operation of the Radical Democratic Party for the democratization of war efforts on the above lines.

Resolution of the Bengal Provincial Conference of the Radical Democratic Party, January 18 and 19, 1941.

STRONG WAR CABINET

The immediate object of Sir Stafford's visit as declared by the Prime Minister is 'to promote concentration of all thoughts and energies upon the defence of the native soil.' That is the object of all who are anxious to defend the future of India against the danger of Fascist domination. If all the parties accepted this position, without any reservation, at least for the moment, there would be an end to all the 'fierce constitutional and communal disputes'. They have persistently refused to do so. The hope of securing their co-operation on the basis of a definite offer thus would seem to be rather a forlorn hope The Government seem to be terrorised by the vocal politicians, who have persistently refused to be influenced by any other considerations than narrow nationalist and communalist interests. That shows their failure to appreciate the gravity of the immediate issues, or indifference in that respect. It is a caricature of democracy or constitutionalism to regard them as the sole makers of India's destiny.

What is urgently needed to meet the sitution effectively is the formation of a strong War Cabinet composed of popular public men, chosen on their individual merits, such as are ready to promote the concentration of all thoughts and energies upon the defence of the native soil, and who would not wait for any promise, declaration or offer from the British Government. In these fateful days, the cause of Indian political progress and general welfare can be promoted only by far-sighted patriots who realise that the national interest of India cannot be separated from the fate of the rest of the world and that therefore the future of India is conditional upon the defeat of the forces of evil bent upon the destruction of the achievements of modern civilisation, which have laid down a solid foundation for a new order of greater freedom and equality. A government composed of men chosen from among such patriots will be a truly National Government as well as a strong government, which the country needs so very urgently in this crisis.

Practical promotion of the welfare of the people is the essence of democracy. Defeat of the Axis Power and destruction of the evil of Fascism, which has become an international phenomenon, not leaving India untouched, are the conditions for the future of mankind, which includes the Indian nation. Therefore, a government which will set aside all other considerations for concentrating all energy and resources on the crucial task of winning this war would be a truly democratic government A National Government is not worth having, it may even be a fraud, if it is not a democratic government. By applying itself to this task with a single minded purpose, it will be representing the will of the Indian masses, who would suffer untold miseries, if Fascism triumphed.

"It was open for the British Government to help the establishment of such a government in India immediately. That would obviously have been helpful in every respect. It is highly deplorable that, instead of taking that only sensible and practical step, the British Government has allowed itself to be misled in a policy which inevitably means a dangerous delay in taking the most urgently needed measures for the defence of India."

Resolution of the Central Executive Committee of the Radical Democratic Party, New Delhi, March 29. 1942.

DECLARATION OF THE BRITISH GOVERNMENT

His Majesty's Government having considered the anxieties expressed in this country and in India as to the fulfilment of promises made in regard to the future of India have decided to lay down in precise and clear terms the steps which they propose shall be taken for the earliest possible realisation of self-government in India. The object is the creation of a new Indian Union which shall constitute a Dominion associated with the United Kingdom and other Dominions by a common allegiance to the Crown but equal to them in every respect in no way subordinate in any aspect of its domestic or external affairs.

His Majesty's Government, therefore, make the following Declaration:—

(a) Immediately upon cessation of hostilities, steps shall be taken to set up in India in manner described hereafter an elected body charged with the task of framing a new Constitution for India.

(b) Provision shall be made, as set out below, for participation of Indian States in the Constitution-making body.

(c) His Majesty's Government undertake to accept and implement forthwith the Constitution so framed, subject only to:—

(i) The right of any Province of British India that is not prepared to accept the new Contitution to retain its present constitutional position, provision being made for its subsequent accession if it so decides.

With such non-acceding Provinces, should they so desire, His Majesty's Government will be prepared to agree upon a new Constitution giving them the same full status as the Indian Union and arrived at by a procedure analogous to that here laid down.

(ii) The signing of a Treaty which shall be negotiated between His Majesty's Government and the Constitution-making body. This Treaty will cover all necessary matters arising out of the complete transfer of responsibility from British to Indian hands; it will make provision, in accordance with undertakings given by His Majesty's Government, for the protection of racial and religious minorities; but will not impose any restriction on the power of the Indian Union to decide in future its relationship to other Member States of the British Commonwealth.

Whether or not an Indian State elects to adhere to the Constitution, it will be necessary to negotiate a revision of its Treaty arrangements so far as this may be required in the new situation.

(d) The Constitution-making body shall be composed as follows, unless the leaders of Indian opinion in the principal communities agree upon some other form before the end of hostilities:—

Immediately upon the result being known of Provincial Elections. which will be necessary at the end of hostilities, the entire membership of the Lower Houses of Provincial Legislatures shall, as a single electoral college, proceed to the election of the Constitution-making body by the system of proportional representation. This new body shall be in number about 1/10th of the number of the electoral college.

Indian States shall be invited to appoint representives in the same Provincial to their total population as in the case of representatives of British India as a whole and with the same powers as British Indian members.

(e) During the critical period which now faces

India and until the new Constitution can be framed, His Majesty's Government must inevitably bear the responsibility for and retain the control and direction of the defence of India as part of their world war effort, but the task of organising to the full the military, moral and material resources of India must be the responsibility of the Government of India with the co-operation of the peoples of India. His Majesty's Government desire and invite the immediate and effective participation of the leaders of the principal sections of the Indian people in the counsels of their country, of the commonwealth and of the united nations. Thus they will be enabled to give their active and constructive help in the discharge of a task which is vital and essential for the future freedom of India.

R. D. P. STATEMENT.

On the Declaration of the British Government.

The Radical Democratic Party has, from the beginning of the war, advocated unconditional support to it. It has done so out of the conviction that this war was the war of Indian democracy as well as of the democratic forces throughout the world. We did not believe that Indian independence could be achieved as a result of the bargain carried on by orthodox nationalist leaders. We were of the opinion that the defeat of Fascism in this war was the most essential precondition for Indian freedom. We, therefore, advocated concentration of all energies on winning this war.

We welcome the declaration of the British Government, because it once again admits India's right of self-determination—this time without any reservations. The British Government has even suggested a procedure. but the option is left to the Indians to prefer an alternative procedure. It is, however, premature to raise the question of the post-war procedure now, because the possibility of framing the Constitution of a free India is conditional upon the outcome ot this war. Therefore, to defend India against the imminent Japanese invasion and also against another possible invasion from the West, is the supreme task of the moment. And India can be defended only as a sector of the world Anti-Fascist Front.

If the Japanese invaders succeed in overrunning India, not only will this country lose the chance of becoming free; but the outcome of the whole war may be decisively influenced by that melancholy event. Therefore, the defence of India is not an isolated nationalist concern, and cannot be subordinated to any nationalist considerations.

Nevertheless, the offer may not be acceptable

to the Congress, because it evidently does not meet demands put forth from a purely nationalist point of view, and which may be justified as such. It does not make a gift of independence here and now; nor does it visualise immediate transfer of real power to a government composed only of Indians. While her future still remains in the lap of the War God, as an integral part of the world war front, for the present, politically also, India will have to labour under certain restrictions which may outrage the extravagant notions of nationalist prestige. Complete transfer of political power is not possible under conditions of military interdependence.

The Hindu Mahasabha, of course, cannot possibly accept the proposals which so very rudely disturb the dream of an "Akhand Hindusthan" which was believed to be shared also by the British Government.

The Radical Democratic Party has always maintained that a really democratic regime cannot be established in India unless the principle of self-determination is applied also to the inter-relations amongst the Indian peoples themselves. Therefore, we welcome the admission of India's right of self-determination going to that extent. The Muslim League will be well advised to accept the offer.

xxxvi

There is a new suggestion in the press statement made by Sir Stafford Cripps, while handing the document for publication, which must cause misgivings to those who are anxious to get down to the supreme task of the moment. He said that it was " only a declaration they would be prepared to make, if it met with a sufficiently general and favourable acceptance from the various sections of Indian opinion."

The implication evidently is that, in the absence of such an acceptance, the offer will be withdrawn. The Hindu Mahasabha has already rejected the offer. The Congress most probably will also take up a negative attitude. But the Radical Democratic Party is emphatically of the opinion that even then the scheme can be put into force with the help of a very large volume of truly representative popular opinion, and therefore it would be a great injustice to India and injury to the cause of progress and freedom if the offer was withdrawn. Continuation of the status quo will be most prejudicial for the object of mobilising India as an active force on the world anti-Fascist front.

The Radical Democratic Party always deprecated the efforts of placating leaders, who have failed to take a broad and realistic view of the situation, and who, if placated, could not be trusted with the destiny of the country in this critical period. The task of mobilising India on the international anti-Fascist front has to be accomplished by those who, from the very beginning, realised the gravity of the issues involved, and have been acting accordingly. The measure urgently needed for the defence of India's freedom and the promotion of the welfare of the Indian masses is the immediate formation of a War Cabinet on a non-party basis—a urgently on composed not of party representatives, but of individuals chosen on their merit. There are many far-sighted patriots who are capable of far-sighted the merit of the British Government's offer, as also the composed in the midst of which the problem of Indo-British relations is to be solved. The irrespective and the necessary power the mobilising India as a powerful sector in the world war front should be immediately handed over to them, irrespective of whatever may be the attitude of this or that party.

This war is going to change the world. India cannot remain unchanged, not only as regards political status; her economic life also is bound to receive a great impetus. Absolutely sovereign national States will be an necessary and economic inter-relations among nations will be closer. To progress politically towards the goal of a greater freedom, the Indian people will find it necessary and desirable to transcend the limits of a relatively isolated national existence. The potentialities of their economic life will be fully unfolded only in the context of a scheme of world reconstruction after the war.

The history of the relations between Britain and India is bound to culminate in a free, mutually beneficial association of two peoples as equal members of a commonwealth.

These considerations, which have always guided our policy, induce us to recommend to all the progressive and democratic elements of India to apply themselves to the supreme task of defeating the Fascist menace by making their greatest contribution through co-operation on the basis of the offer of the British Government. The supreme constitutional supreme'e for the formal establishment of the new relation, to be in force forthwith, for all establish- purposes, will be purposes, as soon as normal conditions are restored.

New Dehli, April 3, 1942.

RADICALS SHOW THE WAY OUT

Central Executive Committee's Statement

The breakdown of the negotiations for a settlement on the basis of the draft declaration of the British Cabinet, particularly in so far as a settlement was made conditional upon the attitude of the Congress, was a foregone conclusion. From the very beginning, Radical Democratic Partythe questioned the wisdom of the negotiations, and repeatedly expressed doubts and misgivings about what might happen should they end in erstwhile war-resisters gaining control of the Government of the country. Therefore, the Central Executive Committee of the Radical Democratic Party regards the appeasement efforts as a setback for the danger of Petainism. But the danger of invasion still remains to be faced, and the country must be prepared for it. The C. E. C. of the R. D. P. apprehends that the reaction to the rejection of the British offer by the major parties and older leaders, to whom it was made, may be a failure to do the needful for the rejection But India must be danger and the responsibility belongs primarily to the Indians. Everything should be done to enable them to responsi-: the responsibility. The establishment of a National Government has been delayed long enough by the obstructionist policy of the Congress and the unreasonable and unhelpful attitude of other parties and leaders. With the ruthless invader already inside our doors, no more precious time should be wasted in hoping against hope, and in recriminations.

xl

Reinforcement of the Government with the co-operation of popular Indian public men is the prime need of the day. Having felt this urgent need, and knowing that the co-operation of the leaders of the older parties, who have all along acted so com-irresponsibly and unhelpfully, could not be secured, for reasons which we also have exposed, the Central Executive Committee of the Radical Democratic Party suggested the formation of a War Cabinet on non-party basis—a government composed not of party representatives, but of individuals chosen on their merit. We repeat the suggestion, which should be acted upon, now that all chances of an alternative settlement have disappeared.

In these fateful days, the cause of India's political progress and general welfare can be promoted only by far-sighted patriots, who realise that the welfare of India cannot be separated from that of the rest of the world, and that therefore it is conditional upon the defeat of the forces of evil, bent upon the destruction of all the achievements of modern civilisation, which have laid down a solid foundation for a new world of greater freedom and equality. India is not wanting in such cannot A government, composed of men chosen from among them, will be a truly National Government, as well as a strong government, which the urgently needs so very urgently in this crisis.

Practical promotion of the welfare of the people is the essence of democracy. Defeat of the Axis Powers and destruction of the evil oi Fascism, which has become an international phenomenon, are the conditions for the future welfare of mankind, which includes the Indian nation. Therefore, a government, which will set aside all other considerations for concentrating all energy and resources on the crucial task of winning this war, will be a truly democratic government. By applying itself to this task with a single-minded purpose, it will be representing the interests of the Indian masses, who would suffer untold misery if Fascism triumphed. Anti-Fascism, not only in profession, but in practice, is to-day the only reliable token of democratic conviction, and the sole standard of popular representativeness.

Military defence is a purely professional matter. No useful purpose will be served by placing the Department formally in charge of a non-official, who may not possess the requisite knowledge and experience to administer it efficiently. No honourable man would care to be a mere figurehead. But what has come to be known as civil defence is of more importance. The unfortunate effect of the anti-war propaganda carried on for two and a half years, and done even now, must be removed, if India is to be successfully defended. Popular morale is the decisive weapon to win this war. With its scope widened and its functions clearly defined, the Department of Civil Defence can successfully accomplish the most vital task of creating the psychological conditions for popular resistance to invasion.

India's right of self-determination has been recognised. Now it is for the Indians to exercise that right. The National Government, composed as suggested above, will take concrete steps in that direction, and thus prove itself to be the most trustworthy and representative guardian of the welfare of the Indian people. The fundamental principles of a truly democratic Constitution, suitable for the outstanding peculiarities of the conditions of this country, shall be formulated, and the people shall be given the opportunity and all the facilities to express their considered opinion about them. Thus, a freely given, intelligent popular sanction will be available for the skeleton of a generally agreed Constitution, Such a Constitution, framed with the consent and active participation of the entire people, under the initiative and guidance of a truly democratic National Government, will establish in India the freedom for which the progressive forces throughout the world are fighting, and to the victory in which epoch-making fight India also should contribute.

Freedom is not an abstract ideal. For the masses of the people in India as well as in other countries, it has a definite connotation. It means freedom from all sorts of want, privations and disadvantages, which often render their daily lite an unbearable drudgery. No Government, even if it is composed entirely of Indians, will be a National Government, if it does not guarantee the establishment of such a freedom. What India needs is not a National Government, but a Democratic Government. A National Government is not necessarily a Democratic Government.

A National Government in the Centre alone will not be able to cope with the situation, unless the deadlock in a number of provinces is terminated. There also, emergency measures are needed to tide over the crisis. The Legislative Assemblies cannot function they have become out of date. The issue of the war, on which the deadlock occurred, was not before the electorate during the last election. Therefore, the present Legislative Assemblies may not be regarded as the only accredited spokesmen of the opinion of the electorate. In any case, having failed to function owing to the obstructionist policy of the majority party, Legislative Assemblies in those provinces may be formally dissolved. But under the ominous shadow of an invasion, a general election is out of the question. A general election of all the Provincial Assemblies as of the Central Assembly shall be held immediately after the war. Until then, provincial administrations may be carried on by Emergency Ministries, to be composed also according to the principles visualised for application in the establishment of a National Government in the Centre. Until the next election, under a new Constitution, the Ministers will regard themselves as responsible directly to the people, and discharge the responsibility by introducing measures which will protect popular interests and promote popular welfare, in addition to the supreme task of the moment, which is to intensify war efforts, no matter however great sacrifices that might involve.

New Delhi, April 12, 1942.

FIELD CLEAR FOR ACTION

Radicals Suggest an Alternative Course

As soon as it was announced that the British War Cabinet was sending a representative to India with the object of winning the co-operation of the major parties, particularly of the Congress, which had persistently opposed India's participation in the war, the Radical Democratic Party warned against the danger of the delay involved in that procedure. It also declared that the Cripps Mission was bound to fail. The failure was pre-determined by the well-known fact that the Congress leaders were guided by a narrow nationalist outlook, which was antagonistic to the cause of Indian freedom, and indifferent to the larger issues involved in the war.

Even after the failure of the Cripps Mission, there persisted the illusion that the Congress leaders could still be placated, if some more concessions were made to their demands. Consequently, the parliamentary debate on Sir Stafford Cripps' statement about his mission did not lead to any positive conclusion. The British offer was to be withdrawn, and presumably the *status quo ante* was to continue. That would be the most unwise course to take. The only result of the Cripps Mission has been to arm the Congress leaders with plausible arguments to whip up the anti-British sentiment. Something must be done to counteract that, if the result of the Cripps Mission was not to be entiry negative. The obvious thing to be done under the circumstances would be to go ahead with the plan outlined in the draft declaration of the British Government. That course was not taken, because the mistake of identifying the country with the Congress still persisted.

But now, the position has been made crystal clear by the resolution of the A. I. C. C. After this resolution there is absolutely no justification for the policy of carrying on somehow, with the hope that Congress leaders would come around sooner or later. The Radical Democratic Party has all along warned against the danger of encouraging Petainism inherent in the erroneous policy of appeasement. The A. I. C. C. resolution conclusively proves that ours was not a false alarm.

The resolution states once again that India (in so far as she is represented by the Congress) has no quarrel with any country, and that she is involved in this war against the Axis Powers not by choice, but under compulsion. The corollary to this statement is not left to be understood. It is explicitly declared that, if the Congress leaders were at the helm of affairs, India might have stayed out of the war. Here is the real reason for the breakdown of the Cripps negotiations. In course of it the peace-makers came to realise that, given unrestricted power, the Congress leaders thim do what they always wanted to do, namely, to keep India out of the war.

But this is not a statement of Congress policy. Times without number, similar declarations had been made by authoritative Congress leaders. Therefore, the very idea, that their co-operation could ever be enlisted for the purpose of this war, was altogether unwarranted. The Cripps Mission was the result of an entirely wrong understanding of the situation in this country. Therefore it failed.

Now the field is clear for action. In the past, complacency proved to be very costly; now it will spell disaster Procrastination will only aggravate the perils that beset the situation. The Radical Democratic Party is happy to know that British public opinion is beginning to realise that the Congress is not India; that it does not represent anything more than a vocal group of politicians, who have been dominating the situation because of the control of the press and the undue importance attached to them by the British Government. Welcoming this belated realisation of the truth of the Indian situation, the Radical Democratic Party urges that the necessary action should be taken without any further delay.

In an Open Letter to Sir Stafford Cripps, immediately on his arrival, and in a subsequent statement on the proposals of the British Government, the Radical Democratic Party indicated the alternative approach to the problem of enlisting popular support for war efforts.

We repeat that proposal, trusting that there should be no objection to acting upon it now. The Central Government should be immediately reconstucted along the lines of the Cripps offer. It would indeed be an irony to withhold from avowed anti-Fascists the authority and power offered to the leaders who would make peace with the invader. Power and authority should be entrusted to those Indians who have all along realised that the fate of India is inseparably tied up with the fate of the nations engaged in the war against the Axis Powers, those Indians, who have been acting according to that conviction, irrespective of the attitude of the Government.

This is no time to experiment with colourless liberalism. The dictum, that he who is not with us unreservedly is against us, was never so full of truth as it is to-day. The crying need of the moment is a strong Government, and a clearly defined policy. A Government, composed of men, with a record of public service and devotion to the cause of popular freedom, will be the most popular Government by virtue of adopting such a policy as alone can appeal to the imagination of the people, and such a Government will be a strong Government capable of coping with the situation.

There is no time to lose. The enemy is actually within the gates. Friends and allies of the enemy are operating throughout the country. Let the real leaders of the people have the power and authority so that they can tackle the task which they alone can accomplish."

Declaration of the C. E. C. of the R. D. P., New Delhi, May 5, 1942.

LET INDIAN DEMOCRACY ASSERT ITSELF.

Statement to the Press by M. N. Roy.

Sir Stafford Cripps' declaration in the House of Commons, that the offer of a substantial transfer of power to an Indian National Government, with which he came to India, is withdrawn, because the Congress leaders refuse to accept it, is an affront to democracy.

It is an open secret that the Muslim League was prepared to accept the offer. Its negative decision was made at the last moment knowing that the offer would be withdrawn because of the Congress refusal. There are other popular parties and organisations, which do not approve of the Congress policy. They are anxious to share the responsibility of defending the country. To-day, Hindu opinion is voiced more by the Mahasabha than by the Congress. With reservations about the future Constitution of India, the Mahasabha is prepared to join an Interim National Government. Finally,

Congressmen themselves are divided. Therefore, the Delhi resolution of the Congress Working Committee cannot be taken as the opinion of Indian democracy.

Sir Stafford Cripps came with the mission of winning the co-operation of the Congress leaders. Only that mission has failed. But the greater task of creating conditions favourable for India becoming an unshakable sector of the world war front still remains to be accomplished. For that purpose an interim arrangement as suggested in the Draft Declaration of the British War Cabinet must be made, irrespective of the negative attitude of the Congress. It is not democratic to allow a wilful group of politicians to prevent the Indian democracy from throwing its full weight on the side of world democracy.

The contention of the British Government presumably is that the democratic cause would be prejudiced if the Congress demand was conceded. Otherwise, the Cripps mission should not have failed. As far as India is concerned, a National Government as conceived by the Congress leaders would have been "dictatorship of the worst sort". That is the opinion of Sir Stafford Cripps. That being the case, the negative attitude of the Congress leaders cannot be a valid ground for with holding the offer of transferring power to Indian democracy.

Nevertheless, the authorities in this country as well as in Britain are reluctant to move in the right direction. They seem to be paralysed by the fear of an ill-informed public opinion. To end this deadlock, Indian democracy must assert itself vigorously.

The Bombay meeting of the A. I. C C. having resolved in favour of resisting India's participation in the war, I appealed to far-sighted and realistic patriots to come forward and give Indian democracy a new lead. The response to the appeal culminated in a well represented conference held in Calcutta on the 30th and 31st of December, 1940.

The conference resolved to recommend the formation of a National Democratic Union to organise public opinion in support of its objects. It was also resolved to hold an All-India Convention of delegates of all the parties, groups and other organisations, which favoured India's participation in the war.

As the General Secretary of the National Democratic Union, I made an extensive tour of the country, and enlisted the support of an increasingly large volume of public opinion in support of its programme. But there was no response from the side of the Government. Nevertheless, the National Democratic Union remained in existence, waiting for the opportunity to become a decisive factor in the situation. The opportunity has arrived. It is now more than ever necessary for Indian Democracy to stand on a common platform. The National Democratic Union provides that platform. Therefore, the plan of holding an All-India Convention may now be put into practice.

During the last year and a half, the danger to India has aggravated, and to-day the responsibility for organising the defence of the country is keenly felt by all Indian patriots, except those few who are blinded by an obsession, or stultified by having all this time pursued a negative policy. Therefore, the country stands in the urgent need of a new leadership which will do something more than quarrel with the British authorities and be resentful because impossible demands are not accepted.

On the other hand, the Government should also play its part. It should be made clear that the Cripps offer stands, and an interim arrangement on that basis will be made with the co-operation of those Indians who have a greater sense of realism and responsibility.

Dehradun, May 14, 1942.

LIII

UNITED ANTI-FASCIST FRONT

This Conference resolves to carry on a vigorous propaganda to the effect that a campaign demanding immediate withdrawal of the Anglo-American armed forces from India will be either futile or mischievous. In pursuance of this resolution, this conference directs all Party units in the province to remind the masses constantly that, according to the Mahatma himself as well as other Congress leaders, chaos and confusion will most probably follow the demanded withdrawal. That will be no freedom but the creation of conditions in which the masses will suffer most.

This Conference also resolves to warn the Government against the resumption of negotiations with the Indian Petains, who are holding out an olive branch hidden in bluff and bluster, and demands that the Government of the country be reinforced with the inclusion of proved anti-Fascists.

Having regard for the fact that some leftist organisations, which were previously opposed to India's participation in the war against Fascism, have now changed their attitude, this Conference resolves that the Radical Democratic Party, as the pioneer of the anti-Fascist struggle in this country, should take initiative for the formation of a United Anti-Fascist Front. In pursuance of this resolution, this Conference requests the Central Executive Committee of the Party to approach, through an open letter or any other means, the Kisan Sabha, Trade Union Congress, Students' Federation and the Communist Party, with the proposal that they should join hands with the Indian Federation of Labour, the Radical Students' Union and the Radical Democratic Party for mobilising the Indian masses on the International Anti-Fascist Front.

This Conference, at the same time, emphatically expresses the opinion that the primary duty of the Indian anti-Fascists is to fight Fascism on the home front, and advises the Central Executive Committee to make it explicit in any negotiations for joint action that the demand for the formation of a National Government which would claim the right to get out of the fight against Fascism, irrespective of the desire of other, engaged in that fight, is a Petainist demand, and therefore can under no circumstances be supported by anti-Fascists.

The menace of the impending invasion of our country demands that immediate steps be taken for speedy and intensified production of means and material of warfare. This Conference therefore demands that the Grady Report of the American Technical Mission should forthwith be implemented in all its entirety. But effective implementing of the Grady Report is not possible if intensification and speeding up of production is made entirely dependent on the incentive accruing from the profit motive. Indeed, experience in our country as well as elsewhere shows that unless war-time production is controlled there occurs unchecked profiteering on the one side and increasing burden on the poor on the other.

This Conference, therefore, demands that the Government should introduce a system of rigid and progressive taxation and levy on lines similar to those obtained in England and U. S. A., while providing effective measures for protecting the employees of the owners of the means of production as well as the public in general against the burden of taxation being transferred on to their shoulders by reducing working hours and improving living conditions or increasing the prices of articles of consumption.

Resolution of the U. P. Provincial Conference of the Radical Democratic Party, Provincialur, July 29, 1942.

LVI